CEHv13 - Countermeasures

1st Edition

https://ipspecialist.net/

Document Control

Proposal Name	:	CEHv13 - Countermeasures
Document Edition	:	1st Edition
Document Release Date	:	6th May 2025
Reference	:	CEH
Exam Code	:	312-50
IPS Product Code	:	20250204010601

Scan Me

Feedback:

If you have any comments regarding the quality of this book or otherwise alter it to suit your needs better, you can contact us through email at info@ipspecialist.net

Please include the book's title and ISBN in your message.

Understanding IPSpecialist Paperback vs. eBook Versions

At IPSpecialist, we strive to provide high-quality learning resources tailored to different learning preferences and needs. Whether you prefer a concise and focused study experience or a comprehensive deep dive into the subject matter, we offer two distinct formats:

1. Paperback Version – Concise & Structured Learning

Our paperback books are designed to be precise, structured, and exam-focused, ensuring that learners get all the essential information required according to the book's title and certification objectives. The concise format helps professionals, students, and exam candidates quickly grasp core concepts.

Key Features of the Paperback Version:

- Focused content with only the most relevant information necessary for the certification or subject.

- Optimized for quick reading and last-minute exam preparation.

- Covers core topics with clear explanations, key points, and essential study notes.

- Additional in-depth resources and expanded explanations are available through our GitHub repository.

Access More Detailed Content Online:

Since the paperback edition is concise, IPSpecialist provides exclusive access to supplementary materials, hands-on labs, and expanded concepts on our GitHub repository. This allows learners to delve deeper into topics as needed while keeping the book streamlined for efficient learning.

2. Kindle eBook Version – In-Depth & Extensive Coverage

For learners who prefer an extremely detailed and comprehensive approach, our Kindle eBook version provides **all**-inclusive coverage of the subject matter. This format is ideal for those who want to explore every aspect of the certification.

Key Features of the eBook Version:

- Extensive and detailed explanations covering all concepts in the domain.
- Rich with examples, case studies, and practical scenarios
- Includes online resources, additional references, and interactive links.
- Regular updates ensure you always have the latest information.

About IPSpecialist

<u>IPSPECIALIST</u> LTD. IS COMMITTED TO EXCELLENCE AND DEDICATED TO YOUR SUCCESS.

At IPSpecialist, we are passionate about empowering individuals to excel in the ever-evolving world of technology. As a leading provider of Cloud Computing, Cybersecurity, Networking, DevOps, Artificial Intelligence, and other emerging technologies, we strive to equip our students with the knowledge and skills they need to succeed in these dynamic fields.

Course Features:

- ❖ Self-Paced Learning
    - Learn at your own pace and in your own time
- ❖ Covers Complete Exam Blueprint
    - Prep-up for the exam with confidence
- ❖ Case Study Based Learning
    - Relate the content with real-life scenarios
- ❖ Subscriptions that Suits You
    - Get more and pay less with IPS subscriptions
- ❖ Practice Questions
    - Practice questions to measure your preparation standards
- ❖ On Request Digital Certification
    - On request digital certification from IPSpecialist LTD.

Free Resources:

For Free Resources: Please visit our website and register to access your desired Resources Or contact us at: helpdesk@ipspecialist.net

IPS Personalized Technical Support for Customers: Good customer service means helping customers efficiently and in a friendly manner. It is essential to be able to handle issues for customers and do your best to ensure they are satisfied. Providing good service is one of the most important things that can set our business apart from others of its kind.

Excellent customer service will attract more customers and attain maximum customer retention.

IPS offers personalized TECH support to its customers to provide better value for money. If you have any queries related to technology and labs, you can simply ask our technical team for assistance via Live Chat or Email.

About the Authors:

This book has been compiled with the help of multiple professional engineers. These engineers specialize in different fields, e.g., Networking, Security, Cloud, Big Data, IoT, etc. Each engineer develops content in their specialized field that is compiled to form a comprehensive certification guide.

About the Technical Reviewers:

Nouman Ahmed Khan

AWS/Azure/GCP-Architect, CCDE, CCIEx5 (R&S, SP, Security, DC, Wireless), CISSP, CISA, CISM, CRISC, ISO27K-LA is a Solution Architect working with a global telecommunication provider. He works with enterprises, mega-projects, and service providers to help them select the best-fit technology solutions. He also works as a consultant to understand customer business processes and helps select an appropriate technology strategy to support business goals. He has more than eighteen years of experience working with global clients. One of his notable experiences was his tenure with a large managed security services provider, where he was responsible for managing the complete MSSP product portfolio. With his extensive knowledge and expertise in various areas of technology, including cloud computing, network infrastructure, security, and risk management, Nouman has become a trusted advisor for his clients.

Abubakar Saeed

Having started from the grassroots level as an engineer and contributed to the Introduction of Internet in Pakistan and elsewhere, a professional journey of over twenty-nine years in various organizations, national and international. Experienced in leading businesses with a focus on Innovation and Transformation.

He is also experienced in Managing, Consulting, Designing, and implementing projects. Heading Operations, Solutions Design, and Integration. Emphasizing on adhering to Project timelines and delivering as per customer expectations, advocate for adopting technology to simplify operations and enhance efficiency.

Dr. Fahad Abdali

Dr. Fahad Abdali is a seasoned leader with extensive experience in managing diverse businesses. With an impressive twenty years track record, Dr. Abdali brings a wealth of expertise to the table. Holding a bachelor's degree from the NED University of Engineers & Technology and Ph.D. from the University of Karachi, he has consistently demonstrated a deep commitment to academic excellence and professional growth. Driven by a passion for innovation and a keen understanding of industry dynamics, he has successfully navigated complex challenges, driving growth and fostering organizational success.

Mehwish Jawed

Mehwish Jawed is a Senior Research Analyst with a strong background in Telecommunication Engineering and expertise in cybersecurity, artificial intelligence (AI), cloud computing, and databases. She holds a Master's and Bachelor's degree from NED University, with published research on TWDM Passive Optical Networks (PON). Her experience spans roles as a Project Engineer and Product Lead, and she has deep technical knowledge of AWS, GCP, Oracle Cloud, Microsoft Azure, and Microsoft technologies. Mehwish's skillset in AI and databases enhances her ability to deliver secure and efficient solutions across diverse platforms.

Mohammad Usman Khan

Muhammad Usman Khan is a Technical Content Developer. He holds a Bachelor's Degree in Telecommunication Engineering from Sir Syed University of Engineering & Technology. He holds the First Position in Telecommunication Engineering and received two Gold Medals, the first from Sir Syed University of Engineering & Technology and the second from the Institute of Engineers Pakistan (IEP). He worked on many Deep Learning projects. He is a Cisco Certified Network Associate (CCNA). He is also certified by the National Center of Artificial Intelligence (NCAI), which is a research institute of the Government of Pakistan in the field of Artificial Intelligence. He is also certified by the Nvidia Deep Learning Institute in Deep Learning with Computer Vision.

Tooba Nisar

Tooba Nisar is a cybersecurity professional with experience in network security, and penetration testing. She has extensive knowledge in domains including SSCP, GIAC GSEC, CompTIA Security+, CompTIA CYSA+, CEH, CCNA, and Linux for Penetration Testing. She holds a degree in Telecommunications Engineering from NED University of Engineering & Technology. She is currently pursuing post-graduation in Information Security from NED University. She also has experience with Fortinet solutions such as Fortinet FortiGate and FortiGate Operator. With more than 2+ years in reviewing and validating technical content, she ensures its accuracy and relevance. She translates complex cybersecurity concepts into clear, actionable insights for professionals and enthusiasts in the field.

Rafia Bilal

Rafia Bilal is a technical content creator specializing in cloud computing (AWS and Azure Cloud), networking, and cybersecurity. She has authored and contributed to multiple books, including AWS certification guides, cybersecurity, and networking resources. At IPSpecialist, her expertise extends to scripting, video creation, and voiceovers for technical training materials. Rafia holds a degree in Telecommunications Engineering from NED University of Engineering and Technology. Passionate about making complex tech concepts accessible, she helps professionals and learners navigate the evolving cloud and cybersecurity landscape.

Our Products

Study Guides

IPSpecialist Study Guides are the ideal guides to developing the hands-on skills necessary to pass the exam. Our workbooks cover the official exam blueprint and explain the technology with real-life case study-based labs. The content covered in each workbook consists of individually focused technology topics presented in an easy-to-follow, goal-oriented, step-by-step approach. Every scenario features detailed breakdowns and thorough verifications to help you completely understand the task and associated technology.

We extensively used mind maps in our workbooks to visually explain the technology. Our workbooks have become a widely used tool to learn and remember information effectively.

Practice Questions

IPSpecialists' Practice Questions are dedicatedly designed from a certification exam perspective. The collection of these questions from our Study Guides is prepared to keep the exam blueprint in mind, covering not only important but necessary topics. It is an ideal document to practice and revise your certification.

Exam Cram

Our Exam Cram notes are a concise bundling of condensed notes of the complete exam blueprint. It is an ideal and handy document to help you remember the most important technology concepts related to the certification exam.

Hands-on Labs

IPSpecialist Hands-on Labs are the fastest and easiest way to learn real-world use cases. These labs are carefully designed to prepare you for the certification exams and your next job role. Whether you are starting to learn technology or solving a real-world scenario, our labs will help you learn the core concepts in no time.

IPSpecialist self-paced labs are designed by subject matter experts and provide an opportunity to use products in a variety of pre-designed scenarios and common use cases, giving you hands-on practice in a simulated environment to help you gain confidence. You have the flexibility to choose from topics and products about which you want to learn more.

Companion Guide

Companion Guides are portable desk guides for the IPSpecialist course materials that users (students, professionals, and experts) can access at any time and from any location. Companion Guides are intended to supplement online course material by assisting users in concentrating on key ideas and planning their study time for quizzes and examinations.

Study Cards

IPSpecialist Study Cards offer concise, to-the-point notes designed for efficient memorization of key exam concepts. Aligned with the exam blueprint, each card covers essential technology topics with clear explanations and real-world examples.

Table of Contents

About CEHv13 Course 22

  Key Highlights of the CEHv13 Exam 25

  Key Modules in CEHv13 Exam 25

CEHv13 - Countermeasure 30

Chapter 01: Introduction to Ethical Hacking 31

  Overview...31

    Elements of Information Security 32

    The Security, Functionality, and Usability Triangle 34

    Threats and Attack Vectors 34

    Information Warfare 38

  Hacking Concepts 39

    Hacker 39

    Hacking Phases 40

  Ethical Hacking Concepts 42

    Why Ethical Hacking is Necessary..42

    Scope and Limitations of Ethical Hacking...........................43

    Skills of an Ethical Hacker 44

  Cybersecurity Laws and Regulations 44

    ISO/IEC 27001:2013..46

    Challenges and Ethical Considerations.................................46

    Consequences of Illegal Hacking...47

Chapter 02: Footprinting and Reconnaissance 51

  Introduction 51

  Footprinting Through Online Resources 51

    Footprinting Through Online Resources Countermeasures 51

    Footprinting Through Search Engines..................................52

    Footprinting Through Internet Research Services...............53

    Footprinting Through Social Networking Sites....................54

  Whois Footprinting 55

Whois Footprinting Countermeasures 55
DNS Footprinting 56
    DNS Footprinting Countermeasures 56
Network And Email Footprinting 57
    Network And Email Footprinting Countermeasures 57
Footprinting Through Social Engineering 58
    Footprinting Through Social Engineering Countermeasures 58
Footprinting Through AI 59
    Footprinting Through AI Countermeasures 59

Chapter 03: Network Scanning 63
Introduction 63
Ping Sweep 63
    Ping Sweep Countermeasures 63
Port Scanning 64
    Port Scanning Countermeasures 64
Banner Grabbing 66
    Banner Grabbing Countermeasures 66
IP Spoofing Detection Techniques 68
    IP Spoofing Countermeasures 70

Chapter 04: Enumeration 74
Introduction 74
NetBIOS Enumeration 74
    NetBIOS Enumeration Countermeasures 74
SNMP Enumeration 75
    SNMP Enumeration Countermeasures 75
LDAP Enumeration 77
    LDAP Enumeration Countermeasures 77
NTP Enumeration 79
    NTP Enumeration Countermeasures 79
NFS Enumeration 80
    NFS Enumeration Countermeasures 80
SMTP Enumeration 81

SMTP Enumeration Countermeasures 81

SMB Enumeration 83

SMB Enumeration Countermeasures...83

DNS Enumeration 85

DNS Enumeration Countermeasures...85

Chapter 05: Vulnerability Analysis **90**

Introduction 90

Vulnerability Assessment Concepts.. 90

Vulnerability Assessment Countermeasures 91

Vulnerability Assessment Tools 92

Countermeasures using Vulnerability Assessment Tools............................92

Chapter 06: System Hacking **96**

Introduction 96

Cracking Passwords 96

Countermeasures for Cracking Passwords 96

Vulnerability Exploitation 98

Vulnerability Exploitation Countermeasures 98

Privilege Escalation 99

Privilege Escalation Countermeasures.. 100

Maintaining Access 101

Countermeasures for Maintaining Access 101

Covering Tracks 103

Countermeasures for Covering Tracks...103

Chapter 07: Malware Threats.. **107**

Introduction 107

Trojan Concepts 107

Trojan Countermeasures 107

Backdoor Concepts 109

Backdoor Countermeasures...109

Virus and Worm Concepts 110

Virus and Worm Countermeasures 110

Fileless Malware Concepts 111

Fileless Malware Countermeasures 111

AI-based Malware Concepts 113

AI-based Malware Countermeasures 114

APT Concepts 115

APT Countermeasures 115

Chapter 08: Sniffing **119**

Introduction 119

Sniffing... 119

Defend Against Sniffing 119

Sniffer Detection Techniques 121

Ping Method 121

DHCP Method 122

DNS Method 122

Spoofing 123

ARP Method..123

Countermeasures For Sniffers 124

Chapter 09: Social Engineering **128**

Introduction 128

Social Engineering Concepts 128

Social Engineering Countermeasures 128

Human-based Social Engineering..130

Human-based Social Engineering Countermeasures...............................130

Phishing Attacks 131

Defend against Phishing Attacks 132

Identity Theft 132

Identity Theft Countermeasures 132

Voice Cloning 133

Voice Cloning Countermeasures 134

Deepfake Attack...134

Deepfake Attack Countermeasures..134

Chapter 10: Denial-of-Service **138**

Introduction 138

DoS/DDoS Concept 138

    What is a DoS Attack?..138

    What is a DDoS Attack?...139

    DoS/DDoS Countermeasure 139

DoS/DDoS Attack Techniques 141

    DoS/DDoS Attack Techniques 141

    DoS/DDoS Attack Countermeasures 143

Botnets 145

    Defend Against Botnet 145

Chapter 11: Session Hijacking **148**

Introduction 148

Session Hijacking 148

    Approaches to Prevent Session Hijacking 149

MITM Attack 151

    Approaches to Prevent MITM Attack 151

Session Hijacking Detection Methods..153

    Manual Method 154

    Automatic Method 154

    Protecting against Session Hijacking 154

Web Development Guidelines to Prevent Session Hijacking 157

    Web Guidelines to Prevent Session Hijacking for Users 158

Chapter 12: Evading IDS, Firewalls, and Honeypots **161**

Introduction 161

Evading IDS 161

    Defend against IDS Evasion 161

Evading Firewalls 162

    Defend Against Firewall Evasion..162

Evading Endpoint Security 163

    Defend Against Endpoint Security Evasion..163

Evading NAC 164

    Defend Against NAC Evasion 164

Anti-virus Evasion...165

Defend Against Anti-virus Evasion 165

Honeypot 166

Defend Against Honeypot 166

Chapter 13: Hacking Web Servers 170

Introduction 170

Web Server Attacks 170

Web Server Attack Countermeasures 171

Patch Management 172

Patches and Updates Countermeasures 172

Protocols and Accounts 174

Protocols and Accounts Countermeasures 174

Files and Directories 177

Files and Directories Countermeasures 177

Web Server Hacking Attempts 178

Countermeasures to Defend against Web Server Hacking Attempts 178

HTTP Response-Splitting and Web Cache Poisoning 181

Defend against HTTP Response-Splitting and Web Cache Poisoning 181

DNS Hijacking 182

Defend against DNS Hijacking 182

Chapter 14: Hacking Web Applications 186

Introduction 186

Web Application Attack 186

Web Application Attack Countermeasures 187

Web API and Webhooks 188

Web API and Webhooks Countermeasures 188

Injection Attacks 189

Defend Against Injection Attacks 189

WebSocket Connections 190

Securing WebSocket Connection 190

Chapter 15: SQL Injections 193

Introduction 193

SQL Injection Concepts 193

SQL Injection and Server-Side Technologies 193

HTTP POST Request 194

Normal SQL Query... 194

SQL Injection Query 195

SQL Injection Attack 196

Detecting SQL Injection Attacks... 196

Defending against SQL Injection Attacks.................................... 199

Evasion Techniques 201

Evading IDS 201

Types of Signature Evasion Techniques..202

Evasion Techniques Countermeasures 207

Chapter 16: Hacking Wireless Networks 211

Introduction 211

Wireless Attack 211

Wireless Attack Countermeasures 211

Wireless Security Layer 213

Wireless Security Layer Countermeasures 214

WPA/WPA2/WPA3 Cracking.. 214

Defense Against WPA/WPA2/WPA3 Cracking............................ 214

KRACK Attacks 215

Defense Against KRACK Attacks..215

aLTEr Attacks 216

Defense Against aLTEr Attacks 216

Rogue AP 217

Detection and Blocking of Rogue AP 217

Wireless Intrusion Prevention System 219

Wireless Intrusion Prevention System Countermeasures 219

Chapter 17: Hacking Mobile Platforms 222

Introduction 222

Mobile Platform Attack Vectors 222

Mobile Platform Attack Vectors Countermeasures 224

Bring Your Own Device (BYOD)...224

BYOD Security Guidelines 226
SMS Phishing..229
   SMS Phishing Countermeasures 230
OTP Hijacking...231
   OTP Hijacking Countermeasures..232
Camera/Microphone Capture Attacks...234
   Camfecting Attack...234
   Android Camera Hijack Attack 235
   Camera/Microphone Capture Attacks Countermeasures 236
Critical Data Storage in Android and iOS 237
   Android 237
   iOS..237
   Critical Data Storage in Android and iOS Countermeasures 238
Reverse Engineering...239
   Reverse Engineering Countermeasures 240

Chapter 18: IoT and OT Hacking **244**
Introduction 244
IoT Hacking...244
   IoT Attack Countermeasures 244
OT Hacking 259
   OT Attack Countermeasures 259

Chapter 19: Cloud Computing **272**
Introduction 272
Cloud Computing...272
   Cloud Computing Countermeasures 273
AWS Hacking...274
   Aws Hacking Countermeasures 275
Microsoft Azure Hacking 277
   Microsoft Azure Hacking Countermeasures 277
Google Cloud Hacking..279
   Google Cloud Hacking Countermeasures.....................................279
Container Hacking..280

Container Security Countermeasures 280

Docker Security Countermeasures 281

Cloud Security 283

Cloud Security Countermeasures 283

Kubernetes Vulnerabilities 284

Kubernetes Vulnerabilities Countermeasures 284

Serverless Security Risks 285

Serverless Security Countermeasures 286

Chapter 20: Cryptography 289

Introduction 289

Cryptography Attack..289

Cryptographic Attacks Countermeasures 289

Brute-Force Attack... 291

Brute-Force Attack Countermeasures...292

Blockchain Attacks..293

Defend Against Blockchain Attacks 293

Quantum Computing Attacks..295

Defend Against Quantum Computing Attacks 295

About Our Products...**299**

About CEHv13 Course

This course offers a comprehensive and practical approach to mastering the skills required to pass the Certified Ethical Hacking (CEHv13) 312-50 exam. Developed by IPSpecialist, this course is designed not only to prepare you for the exam but to ensure that you gain hands-on experience with real-world examples and case studies, enabling you to apply your learning in a practical context.

→ Covers complete CEHv13 blueprint
→ Summarized content
→ Case Study based approach
→ Ready to practice labs on VM
→ Pass guarantee
→ Exam tips
→ Mind maps
→ Practice questions

In this course, you will learn the best ethical hacking practices and techniques to prepare for the CEHv13 certification using the latest tools and techniques currently available in the cybersecurity industry. Furthermore, this authoritative guide will remain a valuable resource long after you've passed the exam. Whether you're just starting out or advancing your career, the knowledge you gain here will be essential throughout your professional journey in ethical hacking.

Security Certification Tracks

	University Courses	Marketing/ Management	Information Security		Application Security
Chief Information Security Officer (CISO)					
Expert	MSS		CAT618 CAT616 CAT611 CAT614 CAT612		CAST613
Specialist	BCA BIS	PMITS	PM PM PM PM PM PM		
Advanced	ADCA ADIS	PM CIMP CRM	CEH		PM PM PM PM
Intermediate	DCA DIS		CND		
Fundamental		FPM	FNS FIS FCF		FSP
		Certified Secure Computer User (CSCU)			

How does CEH Certification Help?

A Certified Ethical Hacker is a skilled professional who understands and knows how to look for weaknesses and vulnerabilities in target systems and uses the same knowledge and tools as a clever hacker, but lawfully and legitimately, to assess the security posture of a target system(s). The CEH credential certifies individuals in the specific network security discipline of Ethical Hacking from a vendor-neutral perspective.

The purpose of the CEH credential is to:

→ Establish and govern minimum standards for credentialing professional information security specialists in ethical hacking measures.
→ Inform the public that credentialed individuals meet or exceed the minimum standards.

→ Reinforce ethical hacking as a unique and self-regulating profession.

Prerequisites

CEH requires the candidate to have two years of work experience in the Information Security domain and should be able to provide proof of the same as validated through the application process unless the candidate attends official training.

About the CEHv13 Exam

The Certified Ethical Hacker (CEH) v13 exam by EC-Council is a comprehensive certification that validates a professional's ability to identify vulnerabilities, assess security threats, and defend against various cyberattacks using ethical hacking techniques. CEH v13 has been updated to incorporate cutting-edge technologies such as artificial intelligence (AI), cloud security, and Internet of Things (IoT) vulnerabilities, reflecting the evolving cybersecurity landscape.

Exam Questions	MCQs
Number of Questions	125
Time to Complete	240 minutes
Exam Fee	850 USD
Certification Validity	3 years
Passing Score	70%

With the help of this updated version of the book, you will learn about the most powerful and latest hacking techniques, categorized into four phases.

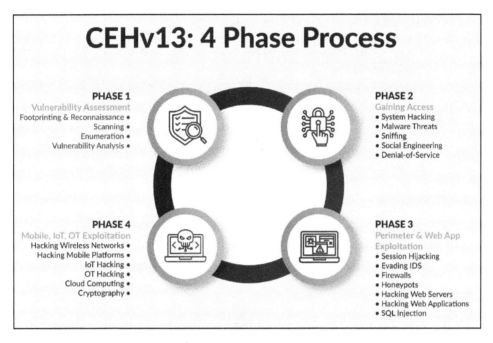

Figure 01: 4 Phases of CEHv13

Key Highlights of the CEHv13 Exam

- **AI-Powered Security Techniques**: CEHv13 introduces a strong emphasis on AI-driven tools for both defense and attack purposes. Candidates will gain knowledge of how to use AI to identify, exploit, and defend against cyber threats.
- **Cloud Security**: The certification updates coverage of cloud-specific vulnerabilities and ethical hacking tools tailored to cloud environments.
- **IoT Security**: With the growth of IoT devices, CEHv13 expands its focus on securing these devices and networks from potential attacks.
- **Modern Cybersecurity Threats**: The exam integrates modern cybersecurity threats, such as machine learning-based attacks, AI-driven malware, and vulnerabilities in AI systems.

Key Modules in CEHv13 Exam

CEHv13 retains the core structure of different modules that cover a wide range of cybersecurity and ethical hacking topics. Below are the key areas:

1. Introduction to Ethical Hacking

- Ethical hacking concepts, methodologies, and lifecycle.
- Overview of cybersecurity frameworks and standards.

2. Information Gathering and Reconnaissance

- Footprinting techniques, social engineering, and OSINT (Open Source Intelligence).
- Tools like Shodan, Maltego, and others are used for gathering intelligence.

3. Scanning Networks

- Network scanning techniques and tools, such as Nmap and Nessus.
- How to identify live hosts, open ports, and network vulnerabilities.

4. Enumeration

- Techniques for obtaining detailed information about systems, users, and network resources.
- Use of tools such as Netcat, SMB enumeration, and SNMP enumeration.

5. System Hacking

- Gaining access to systems through various attack techniques, including password cracking, privilege escalation, and exploiting system vulnerabilities.

6. Malware Threats

- AI-driven malware, including self-learning malware and its defense mechanisms.
- Malware analysis techniques and tools.

7. Sniffing and Social Engineering Attacks

- Using sniffing tools such as Wireshark and tcpdump to capture traffic.
- Mitigating social engineering attacks (phishing, pretexting, baiting).

8. Cloud Security

- Ethical hacking techniques for cloud platforms (AWS, Azure, Google Cloud).
- Addressing vulnerabilities related to cloud configurations, container security, and cloud service misconfigurations.

9. AI-Based Attack Techniques

- Use of machine learning models and AI-powered tools in both attacks and defenses.
- Detecting and mitigating AI-driven threats.

10. IoT Security

- Ethical hacking techniques for securing IoT devices and networks.
- Identifying vulnerabilities in IoT protocols (CoAP, MQTT) and defending against IoT-specific attacks.

11. Web Application Security

- Web application penetration testing (SQL injection, XSS, CSRF).
- Secure coding practices to mitigate common vulnerabilities.

12. Wireless Networks

- Hacking techniques specific to wireless networks (WEP, WPA, WPA2 cracking).
- Securing wireless communications and mitigating risks.

13. Cryptography

- Cryptographic algorithms and their vulnerabilities.
- Implementing strong cryptography practices to protect sensitive data.

14. AI in Vulnerability Detection

- AI-driven vulnerability scanners and their use in identifying system weaknesses.
- Integrating AI tools into security systems for proactive threat management.

Domain	Sub-Domain	No of Questions	Weightage
Information Security and Ethical Hacking Overview	Introduction to Ethical Hacking	8	6%
Reconnaissance Techniques	Footprinting and Reconnaissance	10	21%
	Scanning Networks	10	
	Enumeration	6	
Vulnerability Assessment	Vulnerability Analysis	9	17%
	System Hacking	6	

	Malware Threats	6	
Network and Perimeter Hacking	Sniffing	3	14%
	Social Engineering	5	
	Denial-of-Service	2	
	Session Hijacking	3	
Web Application Hacking	Hacking Web Servers	8	16%
	Hacking Web Applications	8	
	SQL Injections	4	
Wireless Network Hacking	Hacking Wireless Networks	8	6%
Mobile Platform, IoT, and OT Hacking	Hacking Mobile Platforms	4	8%
	IoT and OT Hacking	6	
Cloud Computing	Cloud Computing	7	6%
Cryptography	Cryptography	7	6%

Table 01: Domains

About this Book:

This comprehensive guide goes beyond just exam preparation. It offers a practical, hands-on approach with real-world examples and case studies, ensuring that you gain both theoretical knowledge and practical experience. From operating systems and network security to penetration testing and cyber threat intelligence, every domain essential to the CEHv13 exam is covered in-depth.

What sets this book apart is its focus on both foundational concepts and advanced hacking techniques. Each domain is explained clearly, equipping you with the knowledge and skills needed to tackle the exam and excel in real-world ethical hacking tasks.

How to Access CEHv13 Exam Resources

To access a detailed version of the study guide of the CEHv13 Exam including all topics, navigate to resources present at:

GitHub: https://github.com/IP-Specialist/CEHv13

Scan Me

To access a detailed step-by-step guide of each lab of CEHv13 Exam with the respective screenshots, navigate to resources present at:

GitHub: https://github.com/IP-Specialist/CEHv13---Hands-on-Labs

Scan Me

Other CEHv13 Products

- CEHv13 Study Guide
- CEHv13 Hands-on Labs
- CEHv13 Practice Questions
- CEHv13 Exam Cram Notes
- CEHv13 Glossary Booklet
- CEHv13 Study Cards
- Ethical Hacking Essential Concepts
- Ethical Hacking AI Technologies

CEHv13 - Countermeasure

The CEHv13 Countermeasures guide is a powerful companion tool designed to help learners, cybersecurity professionals, and CEH exam candidates understand and implement real-world security defenses against modern cyber threats. Aligned with the latest CEH v13 exam blueprint, this comprehensive resource breaks down each attack vector and delivers practical countermeasures to mitigate and prevent them, making it an indispensable asset for anyone serious about ethical hacking and information security.

From network and application security to malware analysis and system hardening, this guide emphasizes proactive defense strategies that are critical in today's threat landscape. Readers will gain deep insight into how attacks work, how to detect and respond to them, and most importantly, how to build resilient infrastructures capable of withstanding sophisticated intrusions.

Key Features:

- **CEHv13 Aligned:** Covers all major attack domains and their corresponding defenses as outlined in the CEHv13 syllabus.
- **Attack-to-Countermeasure Mapping:** Directly links each attack method with a tested and proven mitigation strategy.
- **Actionable Guidance:** Includes real-world examples, configuration tips, and step-by-step procedures for implementing security controls.
- **Exam Preparation:** Serves as a high-value resource for CEH candidates aiming to understand both offensive and defensive techniques.

Chapter 01: Introduction to Ethical Hacking

Overview

System security consists of methods and processes for protecting information and information systems from unauthorized access, disclosure, usage, or modification. It ensures the confidentiality, integrity, and availability of information. If an organization lacks security policies and appropriate security rules, its confidential information and data will not be secure, putting it at great risk. Well-defined security policies and procedures help protect an organization's assets from unauthorized access and disclosures.

Millions of users interact with each other every minute in the modern world with the help of the latest technologies and platforms. These sixty seconds can be very vulnerable and costly to private and public organizations due to the presence of various types of old and modern threats present worldwide. The public internet is the most common and rapid option for spreading threats worldwide. Malicious Codes and Scripts, Viruses, Spam, and Malware are constantly waiting to be accessed. This is why security risks to a network or a system can never be eliminated. Implementing a security policy that is effective and efficient, rather than consisting of unnecessary security implementations that can result in a waste of resources and create loopholes for threats, is a continual challenge.

It is necessary to understand some essential cyber security terminology. These terminologies will help in understanding information security concepts.

- **Hack Value:** It refers to the attractiveness, interest, or thing of worth to the hacker. The value describes the target's level of attractiveness to the hacker.

- **Zero-Day Attack:** This refers to threats and vulnerabilities that can be used to exploit the victim before the developer identifies or addresses them and releases a patch for them.

- **Vulnerability:** It refers to a weak point or loophole in any system or network that can be helpful and utilized by attackers to hack into the system. Any vulnerability can be an entry point from which they can reach their target.

- **Daisy Chaining:** It is a sequence of hacking or attacking attempts to gain access to a network or system, one after another, using the same information and the information obtained from the previous attempt.

- **Exploit:** It is a system security breach through vulnerabilities, Zero-Day Attacks, or any other hacking technique.

- **Doxing:** It means publishing information, or a set of information, associated with an individual. This information is collected from publicly available databases, mostly social media and similar sources.

- **Payload:** It refers to the actual section of information or data in a frame as opposed to automatically generated metadata. In information security, a payload is a section or part of a malicious and exploited code that causes potentially harmful activities and actions such as exploiting, opening backdoors, and hijacking.

- **Bot:** It is software that controls the target remotely and executes predefined tasks. It is capable of running automated scripts over the internet. Bots are also known as Internet Bots or Web Robots. These Bots can be used for social purposes, for example, chatterbots and live chats. Furthermore, they can also be used for malicious purposes in the form of malware. Hackers use Malware bots to gain complete authority over a computer.

Elements of Information Security

Confidentiality

The National Institute of Standards and Technology (NIST) defines confidentiality as "Preserving authorized restrictions on information access and disclosure while including means for protecting personal privacy and proprietary information." We always want to make sure that our secret and sensitive data is secure. Confidentiality means that only authorized personnel can work with and see our infrastructure's digital resources. It also implies that unauthorized persons should not have any access to the data. There are two types of data in general. First is data in motion, as it moves across the network and data at rest when the data is in any media storage (such as servers, local hard drives, or the cloud). We need to ensure data encryption before sending it over the network for data in motion. Another option, which we can use along with encryption, is to use a separate network for sensitive data. For data at rest, we can apply encryption on storage media drives so that it cannot be read in the event of theft.

Integrity

The NIST defines integrity as "Guarding against improper information modification or destruction; this includes ensuring information non-repudiation and authenticity". We never want unauthorized persons to modify or manipulate our sensitive and personal data. Data integrity ensures that only authorized parties can modify data. NIST SP 800-56B defines data integrity as a property whereby data has not been altered in an unauthorized manner since it was created, transmitted, or stored. This recommendation states that a cryptographic algorithm "provides data integrity," which means that the algorithm is used to detect unauthorized alterations.

Availability

Ensuring timely and reliable access to and using information applied to systems and data is termed as Availability. Suppose authorized personnel cannot access data due to general network failure or a Denial-of-Service (DoS) attack. In that case, it is considered a critical problem from the point of view of business, as it may result in loss of revenue or of records of some important results.

We can use the term "CIA" to remember these basic yet most important security concepts.

CIA	Risk	Control
Confidentiality	Loss of privacy, Unauthorized access to information and identity theft	Encryption, Authentication, Access Control
Integrity	Information is no longer reliable or accurate. Fraud	Maker/Checker, Quality Assurance, Audit Logs
Availability	Business disruption, Loss of customer confidence, Loss of revenue	Business continuity, Plans, and tests Backup storage, Sufficient capacity

Table 1-01: Cyber Risk and Protection with respect to CIA

Authenticity

Authentication is the process of identifying the credentials of authorized users or devices before granting privileges or access to a system or network and enforcing certain rules and policies. Similarly, authenticity ensures the appropriateness of certain information and whether it has been initiated by a valid user who claims

to be the source of that information. Authenticity can be verified through the process of authentication.

Non-Repudiation

Non-repudiation is one of the Information Assurance (IA) pillars. It guarantees transmitting and receiving information between the sender and receiver via different techniques, such as digital signatures and encryption. Non-repudiation is the assurance of communication and its authenticity so that the sender is unable to deny the sent message. Similarly, the receiver cannot deny what she/he has received. Signatures, digital contracts, and email messages use non-repudiation techniques.

The Security, Functionality, and Usability Triangle

In a system, the level of security is a measure of the strength of a system's Security, Functionality, and Usability. These three components form the Security, Functionality, and Usability triangle. Consider a ball in this triangle, if it is sitting in the center, all three components are stronger. On the other hand, if the ball is closer to Security, it means the system is consuming more resources for Security, and the system's Function and Usability require attention. A secure system must provide strong protection and offer the user complete services, features, and usability.

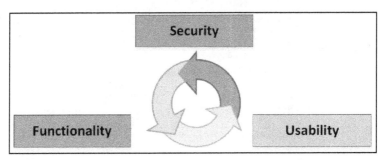

Figure 1-01: Security, Functionality, and Usability Triangle

Implementation of high-level security typically impacts the level of functionality and ease of usability. High-level security will quite often make the system nonuser-friendly and cause a decrease in performance. While deploying security in a system, security experts must ensure a reliable level of functionality and ease of usability. These three components of the triangle must always be balanced.

Threats and Attack Vectors

Motives, Methods, and Vulnerabilities

An attacker attacks the target system to penetrate information security with three attack vectors in mind: motive or objective, method, and vulnerability. These three components are the major blocks on which an attack depends.

- **Motive or Objective:** The reason an attacker focuses on a particular system
- **Method:** The technique or process used by an attacker to gain access to a target system
- **Vulnerability:** These help the attacker in fulfilling his intentions

An attacker's motive or objective for attacking a system may be a thing of value stored in that specific system. It may be ethical, or it may be non-ethical. However, there is always a goal for the hacker to achieve that leads to a threat to the system. Some typical motives behind attacks are information theft, manipulation of data, disruption, propagation of political or religious beliefs, attacks on the target's reputation, or revenge. The method of attack and vulnerability run side by side. To achieve their motives, hackers use various tools and techniques to exploit a system once a vulnerability has been detected.

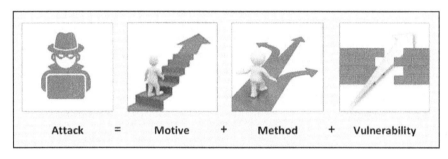

Figure 1-02: Attack Methodology

Top Information Security Attack Vectors

Cloud Computing Threats

Cloud computing has become a popular trend today. Its widespread implementation has exposed it to several security threats. Many of the threats resemble those encountered by traditionally hosted environments. Securing cloud computing is crucial for protecting important and confidential data.

Following are some threats that exist in cloud security:

- In the context of cloud computing, a major threat to cloud security is a single data breach that results in a significant loss. It allows the hacker to

have access to records; hence, a single breach may compromise all the information available on the cloud. It is an extremely serious situation, as the compromise of a single record can lead to multiple records being compromised

- Data loss is one of the most common potential threats to cloud security. Data loss may be due to intended or accidental means. It may be large-scale or small-scale; though massive data loss is catastrophic and costly

- Another major threat to cloud computing is hijacking an account or a service over the cloud. Applications running on a cloud with flaws, weak encryption, loopholes, and vulnerabilities allow the intruder to gain control, manipulate data, and alter the functionality of the service

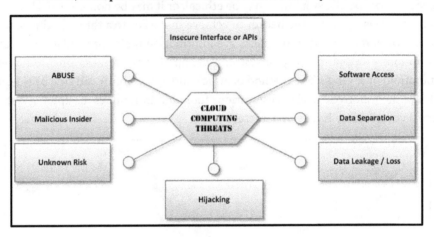

Figure 1-03: Cloud Computing Threats

Furthermore, there are several other threats faced by cloud computing, which are as follows:

- Insecure APIs
- Denial of Services
- Malicious Insiders
- Misconfigurations
- Poorly Secured Multi-Tenancy

Advanced Persistent Threats

An Advanced Persistent Threat (APT) is the process of stealing information through a continuous procedure. An advanced persistent threat usually focuses on private organizations or political motives. The APT process relies upon advanced and sophisticated techniques to exploit vulnerabilities within a system. The term

"persistent" defines the process of an external command and controlling system that continuously monitors and fetches data from a target. The term "threat" indicates the involvement of an attacker with potentially harmful intentions.

The characteristics of APT criteria are:

Characteristics	Description
Objectives	Motive or goal of threat
Timeliness	Time spent in probing & accessing the target
Resources	Level of knowledge & tools
Risk Tolerance	Tolerance to remain undetected
Skills & Methods	Tools & techniques used throughout the event
Actions	Precise action of threat

Table 1-02: APT Criteria Characteristics

Viruses and Worms

The term virus in network and information security describes malicious software. This malicious software is designed to spread by attaching itself to other files. Attaching itself This malicious software is designed to spread by attaching itself to other files, facilitating its transfer to different systems to trigger, infect, and initiate malicious activities on the resident system.

Unlike viruses, worms are capable of replicating themselves. This ability of worms enables them to spread on a resident system very quickly. Worms have been propagated in different forms since the 1980s. A few types of worms that are very destructive and responsible for devastating DoS attacks have emerged.

Mobile Threats

Emerging mobile phone technology, especially smartphones, has raised the focus of attacks on mobile devices. As smartphones became popularly used all over the world, attackers' focus shifted to stealing business and personal information through mobile devices. The most common threats to mobile devices are:

- Data Leakage
- Unsecure Wi-Fi

- Network Spoofing
- Phishing Attacks
- Spyware
- Broken Cryptography
- Improper Session Handling

Insider Threat

An insider can also misuse a system within a corporate network. Users are termed "Insider" and have different privileges and authorization power to access and grant the network resources.

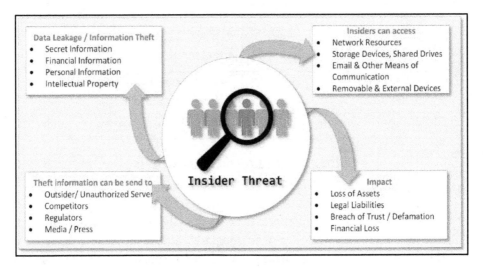

Figure 1-04: Insider Threat

Information Warfare

Information warfare is a concept of warfare over control of information. The term "Information Warfare" or "Info War" describes the use of Information and Communication Technology (ICT) to get a competitive advantage over an opponent or rival. Information warfare is classified into two types:

Defensive Information Warfare

The term Defensive Information Warfare refers to all defensive actions taken to protect oneself from attacks executed to steal information and information-based processes. Defensive Information warfare areas are:

- Prevention
- Deterrence

- Indication and Warning
- Detection
- Emergency Preparedness
- Response

Offensive Information Warfare

Offensive warfare is an aggressive operation that proactively takes against a rival rather than waiting for the attackers to launch an attack. The fundamental concept of offensive warfare is accessing their territory to occupy it rather than lose it. During offensive warfare, the opponent and his strategies are identified, and the attacker makes the decision to attack based on the available information. Offensive Information warfare prevents the information from being used by considering integrity, availability, and confidentiality.

Hacking Concepts

The term hacking in information security refers to exploiting vulnerabilities in a system and compromising the security to gain unauthorized command and control of the system. The purpose of hacking may include altering a system's resources or disrupting features and services to achieve other goals. Hacking can also be used to steal confidential information for any use, such as sending it to competitors or regulatory bodies or publicizing it.

Hacker

A Hacker is a person capable of stealing information such as business data, personal data, financial information, credit card information, username, and password from a system she or he has no authorized access to. An attacker gains access by taking unauthorized control over that system using different techniques and tools. They have great skills and abilities for developing and exploring software and hardware. There can be several reasons for hacking, the most common: being fun, money, thrills, or a personal vendetta.

Hackers usually fall into one of the following categories, according to their activities:

White Hat Hackers

White hat hackers also known as penetration testers are people who apply their hacking expertise for defensive objectives. Nowadays, practically every company has security experts who know how to protect its network and information systems

from harmful attacks by using hacker countermeasures. They have authorization from the owner of the system.

Black Hat Hackers

These are the ones who exploit their exceptional computer skills for malevolent or unlawful ends. This type of hacker frequently engages in illegal activity. Another name for them is crackers.

Gray Hat Hackers

People who work both offensively and defensively at different periods are known as gray hats. Gray hats can assist hackers in identifying different weaknesses in a system or network while also assisting businesses in enhancing their goods (hardware or software) by examining their limitations and enhancing their security.

Hacktivists

Hacktivism is a form of activism in which hackers infiltrate corporate or government computer networks as a form of protest. Hacktivists employ hacking to improve their reputations both online and offline and to raise notice of their social or political agendas. They specifically use hacking to deface or disable websites to further a political cause. Hacktivists have occasionally been known to access and make public sensitive material. Governmental organizations, financial institutions, global enterprises, and any other organization they believe poses a threat are common targets for hacktivists. Unauthorized access is illegal, regardless of the motivations of hacktivists.

Script Kiddies

Script kiddies are inexperienced hackers who use software, tools, and scripts created by professional hackers to compromise systems. Typically, they prioritize the number of attacks they launch over their quality. They just want to become more well-known or demonstrate their technical prowess; they have no particular target or objective in mind when they launch the attack.

Hacking Phases

The following are the five phases of hacking:

1. Reconnaissance
2. Scanning

3. Gaining Access
4. Maintaining Access
5. Clearing Tracks

Reconnaissance

Reconnaissance is an initial preparation phase for the attacker to prepare for an attack by gathering information about the target prior to launching an attack using different tools and techniques. Gathering information about the target makes it easier for an attacker. It helps to identify the target range for large-scale attacks.

In Passive Reconnaissance, a hacker acquires information about the target without directly interacting with the target. An example of passive reconnaissance is searching social media to obtain the target's information.

Active Reconnaissance is gaining information by directly interacting with the target. Examples of active reconnaissance include interacting with the target via calls, emails, help desk, or technical departments.

Scanning

Scanning is a pre-attack phase. In this phase, an attacker scans the network through information acquired during the initial phase of reconnaissance. Scanning tools include dialers, scanners such as port scanners, network mappers, and client tools such as ping and vulnerability scanners. During the scanning phase, attackers finally fetch the ports' information, including port status, Operating System information, device type, live machines, and other information depending on scanning.

Gaining Access

In this hacking phase, the hacker gains control over an Operating System (OS), application, or computer network. The control gained by the attacker defines the access level, whether the Operating System level, application level, or network level. Techniques include password cracking, denial of service, session hijacking, buffer overflow, or other techniques used for gaining unauthorized access. After accessing the system, the attacker escalates the privileges to a point to obtain complete control over services and processes and compromise the connected intermediate system.

Maintaining Access / Escalation of Privileges

The maintaining access phase is the point where an attacker tries to maintain access, ownership, and control over the compromised systems. The hacker usually

strengthens the system in order to secure it from being accessed by security personnel or some other hacker. They use Backdoors, Rootkits, or Trojans to retain their ownership. In this phase, an attacker may either steal information by uploading it to the remote server, download any file on the resident system, or manipulate the data and configuration settings. The attacker uses this compromised system to launch attacks to compromise other systems.

Clearing Tracks

An attacker must hide his identity by clearing or covering tracks. Clearing tracks is an activity that is carried out to hide malicious activities. Suppose attackers want to fulfill their intentions and gain whatever they want without being noticed. In that case, it is necessary for them to wipe all tracks and evidence that can possibly lead to their identity. To do so, attackers usually overwrite the system, applications, and other related logs.

Ethical Hacking Concepts

Ethical hacking and penetration testing are common terms and have been popular in information security environments for a long time. Over the last decade, the increase in cybercrimes and hacking has created a great challenge for security experts, analysts, and regulations. The virtual war between hackers and security professionals has become very common.

Security experts' fundamental challenges include finding weaknesses and deficiencies in running upcoming systems, applications, or software and proactively addressing them. Investigating before an attack occurs is less costly than after facing or dealing with it. For the purpose of security and protection, organizations appoint internal teams as well as external experts for penetration testing. This usually depends on the severity and scope of the attack.

Why Ethical Hacking is Necessary

The rising number of malicious activities and cybercrimes and the appearance of different forms of advanced attacks have created the need for ethical hacking. An ethical hacker penetrates the security of systems and networks in order to determine their security level and advises organizations to take precautions and remediation actions against aggressive attacks. These aggressive and advanced attacks include:

- Denial-of-Services Attacks
- Manipulation of Data
- Identity Theft

- Vandalism
- Credit Card Theft
- Piracy
- Theft of Services

The increase in these types of attacks, hacking cases, and cyber-attacks is mainly due to the increase in the use of online transactions and online services over the last decade. It has become much easier for hackers to steal financial information. Cybercrime law has only managed to slow down prank activities, whereas real attacks and cyber crimes have risen. Ethical hacking focuses on the requirement of a pen-tester, penetration tester in short, who searches for vulnerabilities and flaws in a system before it is compromised.

If you want to win the war against attackers or hackers, you have to be smart enough to think and act like them. Hackers are extremely skilled and possess great knowledge of hardware, software, and exploration capabilities. Therefore, ethical hacking has become essential. An ethical hacker is able to counter malicious hackers' attacks by anticipating their methods. Ethical hacking is also needed to uncover the vulnerabilities in systems and security controls to secure them before they are compromised.

Scope and Limitations of Ethical Hacking

Ethical Hacking is an important and crucial component of risk assessment, auditing, and countering fraud. Ethical hacking is widely used as penetration testing to identify vulnerabilities and risks and highlight loopholes to take preventive action against attacks.

However, there are some limitations to ethical hacking;

- Ethical hackers must operate under legal constraints with permission

- Not all systems may be in scope; legal or operational boundaries may apply

- Cannot guarantee complete security; they identify known vulnerabilities, not future or zero-day threats

In some cases, ethical hacking is insufficient for resolving the issue. For example, an organization must first figure out what it is looking for before hiring an external pentester. This helps achieve goals and save time, as the testing team can then focus on troubleshooting the actual problem and resolving the issues. The ethical hacker also helps to understand an organization's security system better. It is up to the organization to take action recommended by the pentester and enforce security policies over the system and network.

Skills of an Ethical Hacker

An expert ethical hacker has a set of technical and non-technical skills, as outlined below:

Technical Skills

1. Ethical Hackers have in-depth knowledge of almost all Operating Systems, including all popular, widely-used OSes such as Windows, Linux, Unix, and Macintosh.

2. Ethical hackers are skilled at networking, basic and detailed concepts and technologies, and exploring hardware and software capabilities.

3. Ethical hackers have a strong command over security areas, information security-related issues, and technical domains.

4. They must have detailed knowledge of all older, advanced, and sophisticated attacks.

Non-Technical Skills

1. Strong analytical and problem-solving capabilities.

2. Effective communication and report writing skills.

3. High ethical standards and confidentiality.

4. Understanding of laws, regulations, and compliance standards.

Cybersecurity Laws and Regulations

Cybersecurity laws and regulations are essential frameworks established by governments and regulatory bodies to protect information systems, networks, and data from cyber threats. These laws aim to ensure organizations implement adequate security measures, protect individual privacy, and maintain the integrity of critical infrastructures. Below is an overview of key cybersecurity laws and regulations across various regions:

1. United States

The U.S. lacks a singular, comprehensive federal cybersecurity law; instead, it enforces a combination of sector-specific regulations:

- **Health Insurance Portability and Accountability Act (HIPAA):** Enacted in 1996, HIPAA mandates healthcare organizations to implement

measures safeguarding the confidentiality and security of health information.

- **Gramm-Leach-Bliley Act (GLBA):** This act requires financial institutions to protect consumers' personal financial information, enforcing privacy and information security provisions.

- **Federal Information Security Management Act (FISMA):** FISMA obligates federal agencies to develop, document, and implement programs to secure their information systems.

- **Cybersecurity Information Sharing Act (CISA):** Enacted in 2015, CISA facilitates the sharing of cybersecurity threat information between the federal government and private sector entities.

- **California Consumer Privacy Act (CCPA):** Effective in 2020, the CCPA grants California residents rights regarding their personal data, imposing obligations on businesses to ensure data privacy and protection.

Despite these regulations, challenges persist due to overlapping mandates and inconsistent requirements across different sectors and states, complicating compliance efforts for organizations.

2. European Union

The EU has implemented comprehensive regulations to bolster cybersecurity and data protection:

- **General Data Protection Regulation (GDPR):** Effective in 2018, GDPR sets stringent requirements for data protection and privacy, applying to all organizations processing personal data of EU residents, regardless of the organization's location.

- **NIS 2 Directive:** An update to the original Network and Information Security Directive, NIS 2 aims to enhance cybersecurity across the EU by setting stricter security requirements for a broader range of sectors.

- **Cyber Resilience Act (CRA):** Proposed in 2022 and adopted in 2024, the CRA introduces common cybersecurity standards for products with digital elements, such as mandatory incident reporting and automatic security updates.

3. United Kingdom

In 2024, the UK government announced the Cyber Security and Resilience Bill (CS&R), aiming to strengthen the nation's cyber defenses. The proposed legislation seeks to update existing regulations, expand reporting requirements, and empower regulators to proactively address vulnerabilities, thereby enhancing the resilience of critical infrastructure and digital services.

4. Australia

Australia has introduced new cybersecurity laws requiring businesses to report ransomware payments to authorities. These measures aim to improve transparency, assist in understanding vulnerabilities, and facilitate the development of strategies to combat cyber threats. The legislation also enhances the powers of the Cyber Incident Review Board to conduct investigations and share insights with businesses to bolster security.

5. Global Trends

Globally, there is a trend toward implementing more stringent cybersecurity regulations. In 2024, significant new cybersecurity rules were enacted in major economies worldwide, transforming the global regulatory environment. These regulations aim to enhance security, protect individuals' information, and ensure organizations manage threats effectively.

ISO/IEC 27001:2013

The International Organization for Standardization (ISO) and International Electro-Technical Commission (IEC) are organizations that globally develop and maintain their standards. ISO/IEC 2700 1:20 13 standard ensures the requirement for implementation, maintenance, and improvement of an information security management system. This standard is a revised edition (second) of the first edition of ISO/ISE 27001:2005. ISO/IEC 27001:2013 covers the following key points of information security:

- Implementing and maintaining security requirements
- Information security management processes
- Assurance of cost-effective risk management
- Status of information security management activities
- Compliance with laws

Challenges and Ethical Considerations

Organizations encounter significant challenges in navigating the intricate landscape of cybersecurity regulations, particularly when operating across multiple jurisdictions with differing requirements. The absence of regulatory harmonization often results in heightened compliance costs and increased operational complexities. Furthermore, the rapid evolution of cyber threats necessitates the continuous revision of existing laws and the formulation of new regulations to address emerging risks effectively.

Adhering to legal and ethical standards is fundamental in ethical hacking. Practitioners must operate within clearly defined guidelines to ensure that their activities remain both lawful and responsible.

Ethical Considerations

Key ethical considerations include:

- **Permission:** Secure formal authorization before initiating any security assessments or penetration testing.

- **Confidentiality:** Handle sensitive data with the utmost responsibility and ensure that vulnerabilities are disclosed only to authorized parties.

- **Integrity:** Maintain transparency and accuracy in all reports, ensuring that findings are presented fairly and objectively.

Legal Considerations

Ethical hacking must always be performed within legal frameworks:

- Obtain written authorization before any engagement
- Respect confidentiality and do not disclose vulnerabilities without consent
- Adhere to global and regional laws: e.g., CFAA (US), GDPR (EU), IT Act (India)
- Use non-disclosure agreements (NDAs) to protect sensitive data

Consequences of Illegal Hacking

Engaging in illegal hacking, and unauthorized access to or manipulation of computer systems can lead to severe consequences, encompassing legal penalties, financial liabilities, and personal repercussions.

Legal Penalties

In the United States, the Computer Fraud and Abuse Act (CFAA) serves as the primary federal statute addressing unauthorized computer access. Violations under the CFAA can result in both felony and misdemeanor charges, depending on the nature and severity of the offense. For instance, unauthorized access to a protected computer with intent to defraud can lead to significant fines and imprisonment.

Specific offenses and their corresponding penalties under the CFAA include:

- **Trafficking in Passwords or Access Devices:** Knowingly distributing passwords or similar access tools, especially those issued for government or financial institution computers, is illegal. First-time offenders can face fines and up to one year in prison.

- **Trespassing in Government Computers:** Simply accessing a government computer without authorization is considered trespassing, punishable by up to one year of imprisonment for first-time offenders.

Beyond the CFAA, other federal laws impose penalties for specific hacking-related activities. For example, the Electronic Communications Privacy Act (ECPA) addresses unauthorized interception of electronic communications, with violations carrying penalties of up to five years in prison and fines up to $250,000.

Financial Liabilities

Victims of hacking incidents often pursue civil litigation against perpetrators to recover damages. Under statutes like the ECPA, individuals can seek actual damages, punitive damages, and attorney's fees. For instance, in December 2024, a U.S. judge held NSO Group Technologies liable for violating U.S. hacking laws by infecting and surveilling individuals with spyware, leading to potential substantial financial penalties.

Case Studies

- **University Website Breach:** In March 2025, an individual claimed responsibility for hacking the New York University website, replacing its content with apparent test scores and a racial epithet. Such actions not only lead to criminal charges but also civil suits from affected institutions and individuals.

- **Sale of Hacking Tools:** In February 2025, the FBI seized 39 domains associated with selling hacking and fraud tools. Individuals involved in

creating, distributing, or selling such tools face significant legal actions, including asset seizures and criminal charges.

Engaging in illegal hacking activities carries profound legal, financial, and personal risks. Understanding these consequences underscores the importance of ethical behavior in the digital realm and adherence to cybersecurity laws and regulations.

Important Exam Tips for the Certified Ethical Hacker (CEH) Exam on Introduction to Ethical Hacking

Understanding ethical hacking foundations is essential for the CEH exam. Here are key exam tips to help you master this topic:

1. Core Concepts of Cybersecurity

- Understand the **CIA Triad**: Confidentiality, Integrity, and Availability, these are the backbone of information security.

- Know how encryption applies to data Table in motion and at rest.

2. Important Terminologies

- **Hack Value**: Measures how appealing a target is to hackers.

- **Zero-Day Attack**: Exploits vulnerabilities before they're patched.

- **Exploit**: A method to take advantage of system vulnerabilities.

- **Daisy Chaining**: Sequential hacking using credentials or data from prior compromises.

- **Payload**: Malicious part of the exploit used to cause damage.

3. Common Threat Vectors

- **Cloud Computing Threats**: Know risks like insecure APIs, account hijacking, and misconfiguration.

- **Mobile Threats**: Common attacks include data leakage, spyware, and insecure Wi-Fi.

- **Advanced Persistent Threats (APT)**: Long-term, stealthy attacks aimed at stealing data.

- **Viruses vs. Worms**: Viruses attach to files; worms self-replicate and spread.

4. Types of Hackers

- **White Hat**: Ethical hackers with permission.

- **Black Hat**: Malicious, unauthorized hackers.

- **Gray Hat**: Hackers who operate in between ethical and unethical.

- **Script Kiddies**: Inexperienced hackers using pre-made tools.

- **Hacktivists**: Hackers with political or social agendas.

5. Phases of Hacking

- **Reconnaissance**: Gather intel (passive/active).

- **Scanning**: Identify live systems, ports, and services.

- **Gaining Access**: Exploit system to enter (e.g., DoS, password cracking).

- **Maintaining Access**: Use backdoors, trojans, or rootkits.

- **Clearing Tracks**: Erase logs and hide evidence of intrusion.

6. Ethical Hacking

- **Goal**: Identify and fix vulnerabilities before they are exploited.

- **Penetration Testing**: Simulates real-world attacks to assess system defenses.

7. Skills Required for Ethical Hackers

- **Technical Skills**: OS proficiency (Windows, Linux), networking, exploits, cryptography.

- **Non-Technical Skills**: Strong ethics, legal awareness, communication, and problem-solving abilities.

8. Cybersecurity Regulations

- **US Laws:** Know major US laws like- HIPAA, GLBA, FISMA, CISA.

- **Global standards**: GDPR (EU), NIS 2, ISO/IEC 27001:2013.

Chapter 02: Footprinting and Reconnaissance

Introduction

Footprinting and reconnaissance are the first steps in the hacking process, where attackers gather as much information as possible about a target organization or individual. This phase is crucial because it helps attackers map out the target's infrastructure, identify potential vulnerabilities, and plan their attacks. Ethical hackers also use these techniques to assess security risks and strengthen an organization's defenses before real attackers exploit them.

Footprinting involves collecting publicly available data from various sources, such as websites, search engines, social media platforms, Whois databases, DNS records, and network resources. Attackers use both passive and active methods to obtain details like IP addresses, domain names, employee email addresses, server configurations, and technologies in use.

By understanding footprinting and reconnaissance methods, security professionals can proactively identify and mitigate risks, ensuring that their organization's digital assets remain protected from cyber threats.

Footprinting Through Online Resources

Footprinting through online resources is a passive reconnaissance technique used by attackers to gather publicly available information about a target organization. By leveraging search engines, social media, domain registries, company websites, and public databases, attackers can collect critical details such as employee names, email addresses, IP addresses, technologies in use, and network infrastructure. This information helps them craft targeted attacks like phishing, social engineering, and network exploitation. Ethical hackers also use these methods to assess an organization's security posture and identify potential vulnerabilities before they can be exploited.

Footprinting Through Online Resources Countermeasures

- Restrict public exposure of sensitive company details on websites, social media, and forums

- Use Whois privacy protection to hide domain registration details from public databases

- Regularly audit online content to remove unnecessary or outdated information that could be used for reconnaissance

- Educate employees about the risks of oversharing company information on professional and social networking platforms

- Configure robots.txt files to prevent search engines from indexing sensitive directories and internal resources

- Monitor third-party services and data leaks to identify if any company-related information is publicly exposed

- Use disposable or generic email addresses for public registrations instead of internal corporate addresses

- Implement email obfuscation techniques on websites to prevent automated email harvesting

- Use Data Loss Prevention (DLP) solutions to prevent unauthorized sharing of sensitive information online

- Limit the exposure of employee and executive contact details to reduce targeted phishing attacks

- Monitor search engine results and threat intelligence feeds for signs of corporate data being indexed or leaked

- Use anti-scraping tools and CAPTCHAs to prevent automated data extraction from company websites

- Implement Web Application Firewalls (WAFs) to block reconnaissance attempts targeting online resources

- Review metadata in shared documents (PDFs, Word files, images, etc.) before publishing them online to remove hidden details like usernames, file paths, and system information

- Leverage brand protection services to monitor and report impersonation attempts or malicious domains mimicking the organization

Footprinting Through Search Engines

Footprinting through search engines is a passive reconnaissance technique used by attackers to gather publicly accessible information about a target organization. By using advanced search operators (Google Dorking), cached pages, and publicly available documents, attackers can extract employee details, network

infrastructure data, confidential files, and security misconfigurations. Search engines index a vast amount of online data, making them a powerful tool for cybercriminals conducting reconnaissance. Ethical hackers also use these methods to assess an organization's public exposure and mitigate potential risks.

Countermeasures

- Use robots.txt to restrict search engines from indexing sensitive or internal directories

- Apply access controls to online files and directories to limit visibility of confidential content

- Regularly scan for exposed files using Google Dorks to identify and remediate leaks

- Remove or secure outdated or misconfigured web pages that may reveal system or employee information

- Use metadata scrubbers to clean documents before uploading them online

- Monitor indexed data about your organization using tools like Google Alerts or threat intelligence platforms

- Avoid using predictable file names for sensitive documents to reduce discoverability via search

- Deploy Web Application Firewalls (WAFs) to detect and block automated reconnaissance queries

Footprinting Through Internet Research Services

Footprinting through Internet Research Services involves using publicly available online databases, business directories, and professional networking sites to gather intelligence on a target organization. Attackers leverage sources such as Whois records, domain registries, job postings, and financial reports to obtain details about a company's infrastructure, employees, and technologies in use. Cybercriminals use this information to craft social engineering attacks, identify potential entry points, and understand the security posture of a target. Ethical hackers also analyze these sources to assess the organization's exposure and implement mitigation strategies.

Countermeasures

- Use privacy protection services to conceal domain ownership and contact information in Whois databases

- Limit the information disclosed in public job postings and corporate listings

- Review business directory entries regularly to ensure only non-sensitive data is visible

- Avoid sharing specific technology stacks or infrastructure details in press releases or company reports

- Train HR and marketing teams on what technical details should be withheld from public communications

- Leverage brand monitoring tools to detect and mitigate unauthorized mentions or impersonation

- Use generic job titles or aliases for sensitive roles when publishing externally

- Employ Data Loss Prevention (DLP) tools to restrict uploading of confidential documents to third-party platforms

Footprinting Through Social Networking Sites

Footprinting through social networking sites involves gathering intelligence about an individual or organization from platforms like LinkedIn, Facebook, Twitter, Instagram, and other professional or social media networks. Attackers use these sites to collect employee details, job roles, organizational structure, contact information, project details, and security practices. Cybercriminals can exploit this information to craft phishing attacks, impersonation scams, and social engineering campaigns. Ethical hackers also assess social media footprinting to help organizations understand their public exposure and security vulnerabilities.

Countermeasures

- Enforce strict social media policies and awareness programs for all employees

- Encourage employees to limit the amount of professional information shared on public platforms

- Monitor social media for impersonation attempts or suspicious posts referencing the company

- Use privacy settings to control who can view posts, profiles, and contact details

- Educate staff to avoid discussing internal projects, technologies, or security controls online

- Report and take down fake profiles or unauthorized pages using the platform's abuse channels

- Use employee training tools to simulate and prepare for social engineering attacks stemming from social media reconnaissance

- Segment corporate and personal social media use and avoid blending the two, especially for sensitive roles

Whois Footprinting

Whois footprinting is the process of gathering information about a domain using Whois databases, which store domain registration details, owner contact information, IP addresses, name servers, and domain expiration dates. Attackers use Whois lookup services to collect critical details about a target organization's web infrastructure, subdomains, and administrative contacts. This information can be exploited for phishing attacks, social engineering, and domain hijacking. Ethical hackers and security professionals also use Whois footprinting to assess an organization's exposure and security posture.

Whois Footprinting Countermeasures

- Use privacy protection services (such as WhoisGuard or domain privacy protection) to mask domain registrant details

- Register domains using corporate details instead of personal information to prevent targeted attacks

- Ensure that email addresses in Whois records are not publicly accessible to reduce phishing risks

- Use generic contact emails for domain registration instead of personally identifiable addresses

- Regularly monitor Whois records for unauthorized changes that may indicate domain hijacking attempts

- Register domains for longer durations to prevent attackers from exploiting expiration windows

- Use ICANN-accredited registrars that offer security features like two-factor authentication (2FA) for domain management

- Enable domain locking to prevent unauthorized transfers or modifications of domain ownership

DNS Footprinting

Domain Name System (DNS) footprinting is the process of gathering information about a target organization's domain, IP addresses, subdomains, mail servers, and DNS records. Attackers use DNS footprinting techniques to uncover hostnames, network blocks, and server configurations, which can aid in further cyberattacks like phishing, subdomain takeovers, and DDoS attacks. Ethical hackers use DNS footprinting to assess an organization's exposure and recommend security enhancements.

DNS Footprinting Countermeasures

- Restrict access to the DNS resolver to allow queries only from internal hosts and prevent external enumeration

- Disable DNS zone transfers or limit them to authorized secondary name servers to prevent unauthorized access to DNS records

- Use split DNS architecture to separate internal and external DNS records, limiting exposure of sensitive information

- Configure firewall rules to block unauthorized DNS queries and prevent DNS enumeration attempts

- Implement DNSSEC (Domain Name System Security Extensions) to digitally sign DNS records and protect against spoofing attacks

- Audit and remove unused or outdated DNS records to minimize potential attack vectors

- Use randomized source ports and query IDs for outgoing DNS requests to reduce the risk of DNS cache poisoning

- Regularly monitor DNS logs for unusual queries or patterns that may indicate reconnaissance attempts

- Encrypt DNS queries using DNS-over-HTTPS (DoH) or DNS-over-TLS (DoT) to prevent interception and eavesdropping

- Employ rate limiting on DNS queries to prevent brute-force enumeration attempts

Network And Email Footprinting

Network and email footprinting involve gathering information about a target organization's network infrastructure, email servers, and communication protocols. Attackers use these techniques to identify IP addresses, mail servers (MX records), open ports, and network topology, which can be exploited for phishing attacks, email spoofing, and network-based attacks. Ethical hackers analyze network and email footprinting methods to strengthen cybersecurity defenses.

Network And Email Footprinting Countermeasures

- Use firewalls and Intrusion Detection Systems (IDS/IPS) to monitor and block unauthorized network scanning attempts

- Disable ICMP responses to prevent attackers from mapping active hosts using ping sweeps

- Configure Access Control Lists (ACLs) to restrict unauthorized network access and limit exposure of internal infrastructure

- Use Network Address Translation (NAT) to hide internal IP addresses from external attackers

- Employ VPNs and secure tunneling protocols to encrypt sensitive network communications

- Disable unnecessary open ports and services to reduce attack surfaces

- Monitor DNS and MX record queries for signs of enumeration attempts

- Implement email security protocols such as Sender Policy Framework (SPF), DomainKeys Identified Mail (DKIM), and Domain-based Message Authentication, Reporting & Conformance (DMARC) to prevent email spoofing

- Encrypt email communications using TLS or PGP to secure message content from interception

- Regularly audit and remove unused email accounts and mail server configurations to minimize security risks

- Enable logging and anomaly detection for email traffic to detect suspicious activities or phishing attempts

Footprinting Through Social Engineering

Social engineering is a psychological manipulation technique used by attackers to trick individuals into revealing sensitive information such as usernames, passwords, network details, and security policies. It is one of the most effective methods for gathering intelligence about a target organization without using technical tools. Attackers exploit human trust and behavior through various means, including phishing emails, pretexting, baiting, tailgating, and impersonation. Ethical hackers study social engineering techniques to identify potential vulnerabilities and implement security awareness programs to mitigate risks.

Footprinting Through Social Engineering Countermeasures

- Conduct regular cybersecurity awareness training to educate employees about common social engineering attacks and tactics

- Implement strict verification procedures for all requests involving sensitive information, ensuring that callers or email senders are legitimate

- Encourage employees to avoid sharing company or personal details on public platforms, including social media and professional networking sites

- Use multi-factor authentication (MFA) to prevent unauthorized access even if credentials are compromised

- Deploy email filtering solutions to detect and block phishing emails and malicious attachments

- Monitor internal and external communications for unusual requests that may indicate social engineering attempts

- Limit physical access to company premises by enforcing badge-based entry, visitor logs, and escort policies

- Use caller ID verification and callback procedures to confirm the legitimacy of sensitive requests made over the phone

- Restrict employee access to critical information based on job roles, following the Principle of Least Privilege (PoLP)

- Encourage employees to report suspicious interactions immediately to IT security teams for investigation and response

Footprinting Through AI

With advancements in artificial intelligence (AI), attackers can leverage AI-powered tools to automate and enhance footprinting activities. AI can be used to analyze large datasets, identify patterns in publicly available information, and generate detailed profiles of target organizations and individuals. Attackers use AI-driven bots, machine learning algorithms, and natural language processing (NLP) to scrape social media, forums, job postings, and public records for intelligence gathering. AI-powered tools can also simulate human-like conversations, tricking employees into revealing sensitive information through deepfake voice calls or AI-generated phishing emails. Ethical hackers and cybersecurity professionals study AI-based footprinting techniques to develop countermeasures and improve digital security.

Footprinting Through AI Countermeasures

- Implement AI-driven cybersecurity tools to detect and block AI-based reconnaissance attempts

- Use behavioral analytics to identify abnormal network activity and suspicious data access patterns

- Deploy anti-bot protection on websites and applications to prevent AI-driven scraping and automated reconnaissance

- Regularly audit publicly available information to minimize exposure of sensitive details that attackers can exploit

- Enable multi-factor authentication (MFA) for critical systems to prevent AI-powered credential stuffing attacks

- Use advanced email filtering solutions to detect and block AI-generated phishing emails and impersonation attempts

- Train employees to recognize deepfake voice and video scams and implement strict verification policies for sensitive requests

- Monitor social media and online platforms for unauthorized AI-powered data mining or impersonation attempts

- Limit API access and enforce rate limits to prevent AI-based bots from extracting large amounts of data

- Implement privacy-enhancing technologies such as encryption, anonymization, and data masking to safeguard sensitive information

Important Exam Tips for the Certified Ethical Hacker (CEH) Exam on Footprinting and Reconnaissance

Understanding footprinting and reconnaissance is crucial for the CEH exam. Here are key exam tips to help you master this topic:

1. Footprinting Basics

- Footprinting is the first step in the hacking process, used to gather information about a target

- Attackers use footprinting to collect data like IP addresses, domain names, employee details, and security policies

- Ethical hackers perform footprinting to assess an organization's exposure and enhance security

2. Footprinting Through Online Resources

- Involves using search engines, public databases, websites, and social media to collect information

- Attackers use Whois lookups, job postings, DNS records, and metadata from online documents

- **Countermeasures:** Limit publicly available sensitive data, use Whois privacy protection, and monitor online exposure

3. Footprinting Through Search Engines

- Attackers use Google Dorking to find confidential files, login pages, and vulnerable web applications

- Common search operators:

  o site: limits results to a specific domain

- o filetype: searches for specific file formats (PDF, DOC, XLS)

    - o intitle: finds pages with specific keywords in the title

    - o inurl: searches for keywords within URLs

- **Countermeasures:** Use robots.txt to restrict search engine indexing, remove sensitive documents from the web

4. Footprinting Through Internet Research Services

- Involves using business directories, financial reports, and domain registries to gather intelligence

- Attackers use Shodan to find exposed devices and Maltego for link analysis

- **Countermeasures:** Regularly audit publicly available company information and limit data leaks

5. Footprinting Through Social Networking Sites

- Social media platforms like LinkedIn, Twitter, and Facebook can reveal personal and organizational details

- Attackers use social engineering techniques to trick employees into sharing sensitive data

- **Countermeasures:** Educate employees on data privacy, restrict public visibility of work-related information

6. Whois Footprinting

- Whois databases provide details about domain ownership, IP addresses, and contact information

- Attackers use Whois lookups to gather data for phishing attacks and domain hijacking

- **Countermeasures:** Use Whois privacy protection, enable domain locking, and monitor unauthorized changes

7. DNS Footprinting

- DNS footprinting reveals subdomains, mail servers, and network infrastructure

- Attackers use zone transfers and MX record lookups to gather intelligence

- **Countermeasures:** Disable DNS zone transfers, use split DNS, and implement DNSSEC

8. Network and Email Footprinting

- Attackers analyze IP addresses, MX records, and email headers to gather network-related data

- **Countermeasures:** Use firewalls, NAT, VPNs, and SPF/DKIM/DMARC to secure email communications

9. Footprinting Through Social Engineering

- Social engineering exploits human psychology to trick people into revealing sensitive information

- Attackers use phishing, baiting, pretexting, and tailgating

- **Countermeasures:** Conduct employee training, enforce MFA, and implement caller verification protocols

10. Footprinting Through AI

- AI automates footprinting by scraping vast amounts of data and simulating human interactions

- Attackers use deepfake phishing, AI chatbots, and automated reconnaissance tools

- **Countermeasures:** Deploy AI-powered security solutions, anti-bot mechanisms, and behavior analytics

Chapter 03: Network Scanning

Introduction

In ethical hacking, security professionals, often called penetration testers (pen testers), go beyond simply identifying vulnerabilities, they also implement countermeasures to protect networks from real-world attacks. Understanding network security loopholes is ineffective unless proactive steps are taken to defend against threats. This chapter focuses on network scanning techniques, a fundamental part of ethical hacking and malicious cyberattacks.

Network scanning is a reconnaissance technique to identify live hosts, open ports, and running services on a target network. Attackers use scanning methods such as ping sweeps, port scanning, banner grabbing, and IP spoofing to gather intelligence before launching targeted attacks. Conversely, ethical hackers use these same techniques to assess an organization's network security posture and implement necessary defenses.

This topic provides an in-depth understanding of network scanning methodologies and explores defensive strategies to mitigate scanning threats. It also covers essential network security tools used for scanning, detection and prevention, helping organizations safeguard their critical infrastructure against cyber threats.

Ping Sweep

A ping sweep is a method that can establish a range of IP addresses which map to live hosts. The classic tool used for ping sweeps is fping, which traditionally was accompanied by gping to generate the list of hosts for large subnets, although more recent versions of fping include that functionality. Well-known tools with ping sweep capability include nmap for Unix and Windows systems, and the Pinger software from Rhino9 for Windows NT. There are many other tools with this capability, including: Hping, IEA's aping, Simple Nomad's ICMPEnum, SolarWind's Ping Sweep, and Foundstone's SuperScan.

Ping Sweep Countermeasures

Some countermeasures for preventing ping sweep attempts are as follows:

- Configure firewalls to block incoming ICMP echo requests from unknown or untrusted sources

- Deploy Intrusion Detection Systems (IDS) and Intrusion Prevention Systems (IPS) such as Snort to detect and block ping-sweep attempts
- Carefully monitor and evaluate the type of Internet Control Message Protocol (ICMP) traffic passing through enterprise networks
- Terminate connections from any host that sends more than 10 ICMP ECHO requests to prevent scanning attempts
- Use a Demilitarized Zone (DMZ) to allow only specific ICMP commands such as ECHO_REPLY, HOST UNREACHABLE, and TIME EXCEEDED
- Restrict ICMP traffic using Access Control Lists (ACLs) to permit only the ISP's specific IP addresses
- Implement rate limiting for ICMP packets to minimize the effectiveness of ping sweeps and other ICMP-based scanning techniques
- Segment the network into smaller, isolated sections to limit the scope of information an attacker can discover and make lateral movement more difficult if a breach occurs
- Utilize private IP address ranges for internal network devices and apply Network Address Translation (NAT) at the network boundary to conceal internal IP addresses from external visibility

Port Scanning

Port Scanning is the name of the technique used to identify available ports and services on hosts on a network. Security engineers sometimes use it to scan computers for vulnerabilities, and hackers also use it to target victims. It can be used to send connection requests to target computers and then track ports.

Port Scanning Countermeasures

Port scanning provides a large amount of useful information to attackers, such as IP addresses, host names, open ports, and services running on ports. Open ports specifically offer an easy means for an attacker to break into the network. However, there is no cause for concern, provided that the system or network is secured against port scanning by adopting the following countermeasures:

- Configure firewall and Intrusion Detection System (IDS) rules to detect and block probes

- Ensure the firewall can identify probes from attackers using port-scanning tools and examine packet data rather than relying solely on TCP header inspection

- Test the firewall by running port scanning tools against network hosts to verify its ability to detect scanning activity

- Keep router, IDS, and firewall firmware updated with the latest versions to address security vulnerabilities

- Configure commercial firewalls to defend against fast port scans and SYN flood attacks

- Deploy an IDS such as Snort to detect OS fingerprinting attempts by attackers using tools like Nmap

- Minimize the number of open ports and filter the rest to prevent unauthorized access, applying custom firewall rules to block unwanted ports such as 135–159, 256–258, 389, 445, 1080, 1745, and 3268

- Disable unnecessary services running on open ports and ensure all service versions are updated and secure

- Block inbound ICMP message types and outbound ICMP type-3 unreachable messages at border routers before reaching the company's main firewall

- Prevent attackers from using source routing techniques to reach targets by ensuring that firewalls and routers block packets from intermediate hosts

- Strengthen routing and filtering mechanisms at firewalls and routers to prevent bypass attempts using specific source ports or source routing methods

- Conduct TCP and UDP port scans along with ICMP probes to assess network configuration and identify accessible ports

- Verify that anti-scanning and anti-spoofing rules are properly configured to prevent unauthorized access and reconnaissance attempts

- If a commercial firewall is in use, then ensure the following:

  o   It is patched with the latest updates

  o   It has correctly defined anti-spoofing rules

  o   Its fast-mode services are unusable

- Configure TCP wrappers to restrict network access based on domain names or IP addresses

- Utilize proxy servers to block fragmented or malformed packets

- Set firewalls to forward open port scans to empty hosts or honeypots, making port-scanning attempts more difficult and time-consuming for attackers

- Deploy an Intrusion Prevention System (IPS) to detect port scan attempts and blacklist suspicious IP addresses

- Implement port knocking as a method to conceal open ports from unauthorized access

- Use Network Address Translation (NAT) to mask the IP addresses of internal systems, preventing direct exposure

- Apply egress filtering to monitor and control outbound traffic, helping to detect and prevent malicious internal hosts from scanning external targets

- Configure Virtual Local Area Networks (VLANs) to separate different types of network traffic and restrict unauthorized access between them

Banner Grabbing

Banner grabbing is a method used to obtain information about computer systems and services on open ports, providing details such as software type and version. It is used by attackers and security teams for enumeration purposes.

Banner Grabbing Countermeasures

Disabling or Changing Banner

An open port indicates that a service/banner is running on it. When attackers connect to an open port using banner grabbing techniques, the system presents a banner containing sensitive information such as the OS, server type, and version. Using the information gathered, the attacker identifies specific vulnerabilities to exploit and then launches attacks. The countermeasures against banner grabbing attacks are as follows:

- Display false banners to mislead or deceive attackers

- Disable unnecessary services on the network host to minimize information disclosure

- Use server masking tools to modify or disable banner information

- Remove unnecessary HTTP headers and response data while camouflaging the server with false signatures, eliminating file extensions such as .asp and .aspx that indicate a Microsoft server

- For Apache 2.x with the mod_headers module, use a directive in the httpd.conf file to change the banner information header and set the server as a new server name

- Change the ServerSignature line to ServerSignatureOff in the httpd.conf file to prevent exposure of server details

- Disable vendor and version details in banners to reduce attack surface

- Modify the Server Tokens value from Full to Prod in Apache's httpd.conf file to prevent the server version from being disclosed

- Set RemoveServerHeader from 0 to 1 in the UrlScan.ini config file located at C:\Windows\System32\inetsrv\Urlscan to hide the server version

- Trick attackers by changing the AlternateServerName value to options like xyz or myserver

- Disable HTTP methods such as Connect, Put, Delete, and Options on web application servers to limit attack vectors

- Remove the X-Powered-By header using the customHeaders option in the <system.webServer> section of the web.config file to enhance security

Hiding File Extensions from Web Pages

File extensions reveal information about the underlying server technology that an attacker can use to launch attacks. The countermeasures against such banner grabbing attacks are as follows:

- Hide file extensions to mask the web technology

- Replace application mappings such as .asp with .htm, .foo, etc. to disguise the identities of servers

- Apache users can use mod_negotiation directives

Other Banner Grabbing Countermeasures

- Use packet filtering to block or restrict access to ports that might reveal banner information unnecessarily

- Use IDS/IPS systems to monitor and alert on scanning activities that could indicate banner grabbing attempts

- Replace protocols that send clear-text banners (such as HTTP, FTP, and Telnet) with their secure counterparts (HTTPS, SFTP/FTPS, SSH) to encrypt the connection and banner information

- Use Transport Layer Security (TLS) for services to encrypt the banner information during the handshake process, making it more difficult for unauthorized parties to grab banners

IP Spoofing Detection Techniques

Direct TTL Probes

In this technique, you initially send a packet (ping request) to the legitimate host and wait for a reply. Check whether the TTL value in the reply matches that of the packet you are checking. Both will have the same TTL if they are using the same protocol. Although the initial TTL values vary according to the protocol used, a few initial TTL values are commonly used. For TCP/UDP, the values are 64 and 128; for ICMP, they are 128 and 255.

Figure 3-01: IP Spoofing Detection Technique: Direct TTL Probes

If the reply is from a different protocol, then you should check the actual hop count to detect the spoofed packets. Deduct the TTL value in the reply from the initial TTL value to determine the hop count. The packet is spoofed if the reply TTL does not match the TTL of the packet. It will be very easy to launch an attack if the attacker knows the hop count between the source and the host. In this case, the test result is a false negative. This technique is successful when the attacker is in a different subnet from that of the victim.

IP Identification Number

Users can identify spoofed packets by monitoring the IP Identification (IPID) number in the IP packet headers. The IPID increases incrementally each time a system sends a packet. Every IP packet on the network has a unique "IP identification" number, which is increased by one for every packet transmission. To identify whether a packet is spoofed, send a probe packet to the source IP address of the packet and observe the IPID number in the reply. The IPID value in the response packet must be close to but slightly greater than the IPID value of the probe packet. The source address of the IP packet is spoofed if the IPID of the response packet is not close to that of the probe packet.

This method is effective even when both the attacker and the target are on the same subnet.

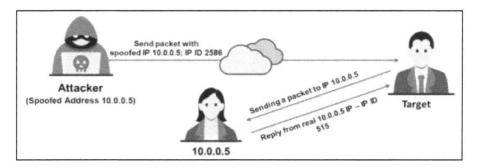

Figure 3-02: IP Spoofing Detection Technique: IP Identification Number

TCP Flow Control Method

The TCP can optimize the flow control on both the sender's and the receiver's end with its algorithm. The algorithm accomplishes flow control using the sliding window principle. The user can control the flow of IP packets by the window size field in the TCP header. This field represents the maximum amount of data that the recipient can receive and the maximum amount of data that the sender can transmit without acknowledgment. Thus, this field helps to control data flow. The sender should stop sending data whenever the window size is set to zero.

In general flow control, the sender should stop sending data once the initial window size is exhausted. The attacker, who is unaware of the ACK packet containing window size information, might continue to send data to the victim. If the victim receives data packets beyond the window size, they are spoofed packets. For effective flow control and early detection of spoofing, the initial window size must be very small.

Most spoofing attacks occur during the handshake, as it is challenging to build multiple spoofing replies with the correct sequence number. Therefore, apply the flow control spoofed packet detection method to the handshake. In a TCP handshake, the host sending the initial SYN packet waits for SYN-ACK before sending the ACK packet. To check whether you are getting the SYN request from a genuine client or a spoofed one, set SYN-ACK to zero. If the sender sends an ACK with any data, it means that the sender is a spoofed one. This is because when SYN-ACK is set to zero, the sender must respond to it only with the ACK packet, without additional data.

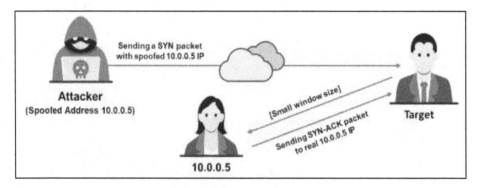

Figure 3-03: IP Spoofing Detection Technique: TCP Flow Control Method

Attackers sending spoofed TCP packets will not receive the target's SYN-ACK packets. Attackers cannot respond to changes in the congestion window size. When the received traffic continues after a window size is exhausted, the packets are most likely spoofed.

IP Spoofing Countermeasures

IP spoofing is a technique adopted by a hacker to break into a target network. Therefore, to protect the network from external hackers, IP spoofing countermeasures should be applied in network security settings. Some IP spoofing countermeasures that can be applied are as follows:

- **Avoid Trust Relationships**: Do not rely on IP-based authentication; always test packets and use password authentication alongside trust relationships to prevent unauthorized access

- **Use Firewalls and Filtering Mechanisms**: Filter both incoming and outgoing packets, deploy firewalls, utilize ACLs, and mitigate insider threats to prevent data loss and unauthorized network access

- **Use Random Initial Sequence Numbers (ISNs)**: Implement random ISNs to prevent attackers from predicting TCP connections and establishing malicious access

- **Implement Ingress Filtering**: Apply ingress filtering on routers using ACLs to block spoofed traffic from entering the network

- **Implement Egress Filtering**: Use egress filtering to block outgoing packets with spoofed source addresses and prevent IP spoofing

- **Use Encryption**: Encrypt all network traffic with IPSec and the latest encryption algorithms to ensure data integrity, confidentiality, and protection against spoofing

SYN Flooding Countermeasures

Countermeasures against SYN flooding attacks can also help avoid IP spoofing attacks.

Other IP Spoofing Countermeasures

- Improve website integrity and confidentiality by migrating from IPv4 to IPv6 during development

- Implement digital certificate authentication mechanisms, including domain and two-way authentication certificate verification

- Use a secure VPN when accessing public Internet services such as free Wi-Fi and hotspots

- Deploy application-specific mitigation devices like Behemoth scrubbers for deep-level packet analysis at speeds of nearly 100 million packets per second

- Utilize dynamic IPv6 address variation with a random address generator to minimize the window of active vulnerability

- Configure routers to send encoded information about fragmented packets entering the network

- Enable routers to verify data packets using their signatures by storing digests of incoming packets

- Modify Network Address Translation (NAT) configurations on routers to conceal intranet hosts from the external network

- Configure internal switches to table DHCP static addresses, filtering out malicious spoofed traffic

- Use secure versions of communication protocols such as HTTPS, SFTP, and SSH to ensure encryption and authentication

---

Important Exam Tips for the Certified Ethical Hacker (CEH) Exam on Network Scanning

Understanding network scanning is crucial for the CEH exam. Here are key exam tips to help you master this topic:

1. Network Scanning Basics

- Network scanning is used to identify live hosts, open ports, and running services on a target network.

- Ethical hackers use scanning techniques to assess security, while attackers use them for reconnaissance.

- Common scanning techniques include ping sweeps, port scanning, and banner grabbing.

2. Ping Sweeps

- Used to identify active hosts on a network by sending ICMP Echo Requests.

- Tools include Nmap, Hping, SolarWinds Ping Sweep, and SuperScan.

3. Port Scanning

- Helps discover open ports and running services.

- Types of port scanning techniques:

    o **TCP Connect Scan** – Completes the 3-way handshake.

    o **SYN Scan (Half-Open Scan)** – Sends SYN packets but does not complete the handshake.

    o **Xmas Scan** – Sends packets with FIN, PSH, and URG flags set.

    o **NULL Scan** – Sends a packet with no flags set.

    o **FIN Scan** – Sends a FIN packet to closed ports.

- **Popular tools:**

    o Nmap (most commonly tested in CEH).

    o Hping, Netcat, SuperScan, Angry IP Scanner.

4. Banner Grabbing

- Attackers extract service information from open ports.

- Can be done using Netcat, Telnet, Nmap, and cURL.

5. IP Spoofing Detection

- Attackers forge source IP addresses to hide their identity.

- Detection techniques:

    o **TTL-based detection:** Compare TTL values to detect inconsistencies.

    o **IP Identification Number Analysis:** Check IP ID sequences.

    o **Reverse Path Filtering (RPF):** Ensures packets come from legitimate sources.

Chapter 04: Enumeration

Introduction

In ethical hacking, enumeration is a crucial phase where attackers and security professionals gather detailed information about a target system, including user accounts, network resources, shared directories, and running services. This information helps attackers plan further exploits, while ethical hackers use it to strengthen network defenses. Enumeration typically follows the network scanning phase, providing deeper insights into vulnerabilities that could be exploited.

This chapter explores various enumeration techniques, including SNMP, LDAP, NFS, SMTP, SMB, and DNS enumeration. Attackers use these methods to extract sensitive details such as user credentials, system configurations, file shares, and network infrastructure. Organizations must know these enumeration threats and implement countermeasures to protect their systems from unauthorized information gathering.

NetBIOS Enumeration

Network Basic Input/Output System (NetBIOS) is a legacy protocol that allows communication between computers on a local network, enabling services such as file sharing, printer sharing, and network name resolution. It operates on ports 137 (name service), 138 (datagram service), and 139 (session service). Attackers exploit NetBIOS enumeration to gather critical information such as machine names, shared resources, user lists, and workgroup details, which can then be used to launch further attacks like brute-force authentication attempts, privilege escalation, or lateral movement within a network. Since NetBIOS is an older protocol, it lacks modern security features, making it an attractive target for cybercriminals. Organizations should assess whether NetBIOS is necessary for their network and implement countermeasures to prevent unauthorized enumeration and potential exploitation.

NetBIOS Enumeration Countermeasures

- Disable NetBIOS if not required, especially on internet-facing systems.

- Block NetBIOS ports (137, 138, 139) at the firewall to prevent unauthorized access.

- Restrict null session access by modifying the Windows registry:

- Set RestrictAnonymous to 1 or 2 under:

    HKEY_LOCAL_MACHINE\SYSTEM\CurrentControlSet\Control\LSA

- Enable strong authentication mechanisms for access to shared resources.

- Limit user account enumeration by disabling anonymous access to user lists.

- Use strong passwords and enforce account lockout policies to mitigate brute-force attacks.

- Regularly audit shared resources and remove unnecessary file or printer shares.

- Implement Access Control Lists (ACLs) to restrict access to shared resources.

- Configure Group Policy settings to disable unnecessary NetBIOS services on Windows systems.

- Use intrusion detection and prevention systems (IDS/IPS) to monitor for suspicious NetBIOS traffic.

- Apply network segmentation to separate critical systems from public or untrusted networks.

- Keep systems updated with the latest patches to fix NetBIOS-related vulnerabilities.

- Use encrypted alternatives like SMBv3 or Kerberos-based authentication to enhance security.

- Monitor NetBIOS-related logs for signs of enumeration or unauthorized access attempts

SNMP Enumeration

SNMP Enumeration refers to the process of using the Simple Network Management Protocol (SNMP) to extract detailed information about devices on a network, including details like system names, user accounts, network interfaces, and running services, by querying the device to identify accessible SNMP resources, essentially providing a comprehensive picture of the network's configuration and devices managed by SNMP.

SNMP Enumeration Countermeasures

- Remove the SNMP agent or disable the SNMP service if it is not required

- If SNMP cannot be turned off, change the default community string names to enhance security

- Upgrade to SNMPv3 to encrypt passwords and messages for secure communication

- Implement the Group Policy security option called "Additional restrictions for anonymous connections" to prevent unauthorized access

- Restrict access to null session pipes, null session shares, and IPsec filtering to minimize security risks

- Block access to TCP/UDP port 161 to prevent unauthorized SNMP requests

- Avoid installing the management and monitoring Windows component unless it is necessary

- Encrypt or authenticate SNMP communications using IPsec for additional security

- Configure the SNMP service correctly to prevent misconfiguration with read-write authorization

- Use Access Control Lists (ACLs) to restrict SNMP connections and allow only legitimate users access to SNMP devices

- Limit SNMP access to specific IP addresses or networks that require it for legitimate management purposes using ACLs on devices or network firewalls

- Conduct regular network traffic audits to identify potential security threats

- Encrypt credentials using the "AuthNoPriv" mode, which utilizes MD5 and SHA for enhanced protection

- Modify the registry settings to restrict or permit access to the SNMP community name based on security policies

- Change the default password and periodically update it to reduce the risk of unauthorized access

- Identify all SNMP devices with read/write permissions and assign read-only permissions to devices that do not require write access

- Avoid using the "NoAuthNoPriv" mode as it does not provide encrypted communication, making it vulnerable to interception

- Implement role-based access control (RBAC) policies to restrict SNMP access based on user roles and responsibilities

- Configure SNMPv3 users within the cluster to enhance security by implementing encryption and authentication

- For devices using SNMPv1 or SNMPv2c, change the default community strings from "public" and "private" to complex, unique values and restrict write access as much as possible

- Maintain management traffic, including SNMP, on a separate, secure VLAN or network segment to minimize exposure to attackers or eavesdroppers

- If SNMP is not required for network management tasks, disable it entirely on devices to eliminate it as a potential attack vector

- Regularly apply manufacturer-released updates to address security vulnerabilities in SNMP implementations and prevent exploitation

- Implement monitoring and anomaly detection tools to identify unusual SNMP traffic patterns that could indicate enumeration or malicious activities

- Enable SNMP logging and conduct regular audits to detect unauthorized access attempts or suspicious activities

LDAP Enumeration

Lightweight Directory Access Protocol (LDAP) is a protocol that enables users to locate data about the organization, users, and other resources like files and devices in a network. LDAP is also used as a central server for authentication. LDAP runs on port 389. By enumerating LDAP, attackers can gather important information like valid usernames, addresses, and other data about an organization that can help as the hack progresses.

LDAP Enumeration Countermeasures

- Since LDAP traffic is transmitted unsecured by default, use Secure Sockets Layer (SSL) or STARTTLS technology to encrypt communications

- Choose a username that is different from the email address and enable account lockout to prevent unauthorized access

- Restrict access to Active Directory (AD) by using software such as Citrix

- Use authentication mechanisms like NT LAN Manager (NTLM), Kerberos, or other basic authentication methods to ensure only legitimate users can access LDAP

- Log all access to Active Directory (AD) services to monitor and detect suspicious activities

- Block users from accessing specific AD entities by modifying object and attribute permissions

- Deploy canary accounts that resemble real accounts to mislead attackers and create decoy groups with "Admin" in the name, as attackers typically search for LDAP admin accounts

- Enable Multi-Factor Authentication (MFA) for accessing LDAP directories to add an extra layer of security and prevent unauthorized access using compromised credentials

- Disable anonymous binds to the LDAP directory unless necessary to ensure only authenticated users can query the LDAP server

- Configure Access Control Lists (ACLs) to restrict authenticated users from viewing or modifying sensitive information beyond their required access level

- Ensure all LDAP queries and modifications are logged and regularly review these logs to detect unusual or unauthorized access patterns that may indicate an enumeration attempt or malicious activity

- Use monitoring tools capable of detecting abnormal LDAP query patterns and alerting administrators to potential enumeration or attack attempts in real time

- Place LDAP servers within a secure network segment, allowing access only to authorized systems and users to reduce the attack surface and prevent unauthorized entry

- Configure firewalls to restrict LDAP traffic to and from authorized systems while blocking unnecessary external access to LDAP services

- Enforce strong password policies for accounts with LDAP access to minimize the risk of brute-force or credential stuffing attacks

NTP Enumeration

Network Time Protocol (NTP) is a networking protocol used to synchronize the clocks of computer systems over packet-switched, variable-latency data networks. It operates on UDP port 123 and plays a crucial role in maintaining accurate time across devices in a network. Attackers exploit NTP enumeration to gather information about a target system's network topology, system uptime, and connected devices, which can aid in reconnaissance and further cyberattacks. Additionally, misconfigured NTP servers can be used for reflection and amplification attacks, leading to Distributed Denial-of-Service (DDoS) attacks. Proper security measures should be implemented to mitigate these risks and prevent unauthorized access to NTP services.

NTP Enumeration Countermeasures

- Disable or restrict NTP service if it is not required to minimize exposure

- Upgrade to NTPv4, which includes enhanced security features such as authentication and encryption

- Restrict access to NTP servers by configuring firewalls and Access Control Lists (ACLs) to allow only trusted hosts and networks

- Disable monlist and query functions in NTP configurations to prevent attackers from retrieving detailed network information

- Enable authentication for NTP queries using cryptographic keys to verify legitimate requests

- Use rate limiting to control the number of incoming NTP requests and prevent abuse

- Regularly patch and update NTP software to mitigate known vulnerabilities

- Monitor NTP logs for unusual traffic patterns that may indicate unauthorized enumeration attempts

- Implement Intrusion Detection and Prevention Systems (IDS/IPS) to detect and block suspicious NTP queries

- Use network segmentation to separate NTP servers from critical infrastructure, reducing potential attack surfaces

- Avoid using public NTP servers for critical systems and instead rely on internal, secured NTP sources

- Implement anti-spoofing measures to prevent forged NTP requests that could manipulate system time

- Deploy DDoS protection mechanisms to safeguard against NTP-based amplification attacks

NFS Enumeration

The Network File System (NFS) is a distributed file system protocol that allows a client to access files over a network as if those files were on the client's local file system. NFS is often used in enterprise environments for file sharing and data access. NFS uses the Transmission Control Protocol (TCP) to provide reliable delivery of data over the network and typically runs on TCP port 2049, which is the default port for NFS over TCP.

NFS Enumeration Countermeasures

- Set proper permissions to restrict read and write access in exported file systems to specific users

- Configure firewall rules to block NFS port 2049

- Ensure proper configuration of files such as /etc/smb.conf, /etc/exports, and /etc/hosts.allow to secure stored data

- Review and update the /etc/exports file to allow access only to authorized hosts

- Use /etc/hosts.allow and /etc/hosts. Deny files to define which hosts or networks can access NFS services

- Log all requests to access system files on the NFS server for security monitoring

- Keep the root_squash option enabled in the /etc/exports file to prevent requests made as root on the client from being trusted

- Implement NFS tunneling through SSH to encrypt NFS traffic over the network

- Apply the principle of least privilege to reduce risks related to data modification, addition, or configuration changes by unauthorized users

- Ensure users are not running suid and sgid on the exported file system

- Require a fully defined hostname in the NIS netgroup to prevent granting higher access to unauthorized hosts

- Configure a Deep Packet Inspection (DPI) firewall to monitor all NFS traffic, regardless of the port number

- Use Kerberos authentication for NFS to establish secure mutual authentication between the client and server, preventing unauthorized access

- Upgrade to NFSv4, which offers stronger security features, including Kerberos-based encryption and authentication

- Keep NFS servers and clients within a secure, segmented network to limit access from unauthorized sources

- Configure firewalls to restrict NFS traffic to and from only authorized systems, preventing unauthorized discovery and access

- Regularly monitor NFS server access logs to detect unusual activity or access attempts from unauthorized hosts

- Use file system auditing tools to track and log access to NFS shares, identifying any unauthorized modifications to sensitive files

- Regularly update and patch NFS server software and client systems to protect against known vulnerabilities that could be exploited during enumeration or attacks

SMTP Enumeration

Simple Mail Transfer Protocol (SMTP) is a set of communication guidelines that allow web applications to perform communication tasks over the internet, including emails. It is a part of the TCP/IP protocol and works on moving emails across the network. SMTP enumeration allows us to identify valid users on the SMTP server.

SMTP Enumeration Countermeasures

SMTP servers should be configured in the following manner:

- Ignore email messages sent to unknown recipients by configuring SMTP servers

- Exclude sensitive information from mail servers and local hosts in mail responses

- Disable the open relay feature to prevent unauthorized email forwarding

- Limit the number of accepted connections from a single source to prevent brute-force attacks

- Disable the EXPN, VRFY, and RCPT TO commands or restrict their use to authenticated users

- Identify spammers using Machine Learning (ML) solutions

- Avoid sharing internal IP addresses, host information, or mail relay system details

- Implement Sender Policy Framework (SPF), Domain Keys Identified Mail (DKIM), and Domain-Based Message Authentication and Reporting & Conformance (DMARC) to enhance email security

- Configure the SMTP server to provide minimal information in error messages, as verbose responses may reveal server configurations or valid user accounts to attackers

- Use Access Control Lists (ACLs) to restrict certain SMTP commands to authorized users or IP addresses, preventing unauthorized enumeration attempts

- Require authentication before allowing access to the SMTP server or granting email-sending permissions

- Encrypt SMTP communications using Transport Layer Security (TLS) to protect data, including authentication credentials, from interception

- Enable logging on the SMTP server to track access attempts and command usage, reviewing logs regularly to detect suspicious activity

- Use security tools to analyze log files and identify unusual patterns, such as a high number of failed login attempts, which may indicate an enumeration attempt

- Control access to the SMTP server using firewalls, allowing only trusted IP addresses or networks to connect

- Implement rate limiting to restrict the number of requests an IP address can send to the SMTP server within a specified timeframe, reducing the risk of brute-force attacks

SMB Enumeration

SMB Enumeration refers to the process of gathering information about a target system's Server Message Block (SMB) shares, including details like available share names, usernames, and potential vulnerabilities, by actively probing the network to identify weaknesses in file sharing configurations, which is a crucial step in penetration testing to assess a network's security posture; essentially, it involves listing and analyzing accessible file shares on a system to identify potential entry points for exploitation.

SMB Enumeration Countermeasures

- **Disable Unused Services**: Common sharing services or unused services can be exploited by attackers, making SMB a high-risk protocol for enumeration

- **Disable SMB on Web and DNS Servers**: Since web and DNS servers do not require SMB, disable it by turning off Client for Microsoft Networks and File and Printer Sharing for Microsoft Networks in Network and Dial-up Connections

- **Disable SMB on Bastion Hosts**: On Internet-facing servers (bastion hosts), disable SMB by deactivating the same properties in the TCP/IP properties dialog box

- **Block SMB Ports**: If disabling SMB entirely is not possible, block TCP ports 139 and 445 to prevent unauthorized SMB access

- **Limit Anonymous Access via Windows Registry**: Configure the Windows Registry to restrict anonymous access to specific files by modifying the RestrictNullSessAccess parameter

- **Modify Registry Key for SMB Restriction**: Set the following registry key to restrict anonymous access:

  HKEY_LOCAL_MACHINE\SYSTEM\CurrentControlSet\Services\Lan manServer\Parameters

  o Set RestrictNullSessAccess to 1 (enabled) to prevent anonymous users from accessing specified network files and shares

The following are additional countermeasures for defending against SMB enumeration.

- Enable Windows Firewall or similar endpoint protection systems on the system

- Install the latest security patches for Windows and third-party software to address vulnerabilities

- Implement a strong authentication mechanism with a robust password policy

- Apply strict permissions to safeguard stored information

- Conduct regular audits of system logs to identify potential security threats

- Continuously monitor systems for any malicious activity

- Use secure VPNs to protect organizational data during remote access

- Deploy file behavioral analysis systems such as Next-Generation Firewalls (NGFWs) to analyze traffic patterns and generate timely reports on SMB resources

- Utilize advanced monitoring systems such as global threat sensors for securing highly sensitive and top-secret data

- Implement digitally signed data transmission and communication for accessing SMB resources

- Block or disable TCP ports 88, 139, and 445 and UDP ports 88, 137, and 138 to prevent SMB attacks

- Enable public profile settings in the firewall for enhanced security

- Block or disable the SMB protocol for Internet-facing servers

- Ensure SMB convention web-facing and DNS mainframes are disabled

- Use SMBv3 or higher for enhanced security features, including encryption, and avoid SMBv1, which is outdated and vulnerable

- Configure ACLs to restrict access to SMB shares only to necessary users and regularly review permissions

- Follow the principle of least privilege to ensure users and services operate with minimal access, reducing the risk of compromised accounts

- Configure SMB servers to log access attempts and track changes to shared resources, regularly reviewing logs for suspicious activity

DNS Enumeration

DNS enumeration is a critical process in cybersecurity that uncovers all DNS records associated with a domain, providing valuable insights for security professionals and cybercriminals alike. By detailing hostnames, IP addresses, and DNS record types, it reveals a domain's footprint and potential vulnerabilities.

DNS Enumeration Countermeasures

Discussed below are various measures to prevent DNS enumeration.

- Restrict resolver access to ensure only internal network hosts can access it, preventing external cache poisoning

- Randomize source ports so request packets use random ports instead of UDP port 53, while also randomizing query IDs and altering the case of domain names to defend against cache poisoning

- Audit DNS zones to identify vulnerabilities in domains and subdomains, addressing any DNS-related issues

- Patch known vulnerabilities by updating and applying security patches to the nameservers, including software like BIND and Microsoft DNS

- Monitor nameservers to detect malicious activities or unusual behaviors as early as possible

- Restrict DNS zone transfers to specific slave nameserver IP addresses, preventing unauthorized access to the master copy of the primary server's database

- Use different servers for authoritative and resolving functions to reduce overload and mitigate Denial-of-Service (DoS) attacks on domains

- Use isolated DNS servers instead of hosting the application server along with the DNS server to minimize the risk of web application attacks

- Disable DNS recursion in the server configuration to restrict queries from other or third-party domains and mitigate DNS amplification and poisoning attacks

- Harden the OS by closing unused ports and blocking unnecessary services

- Use a VPN for secure communication and ensure default passwords are changed

- Implement Two-Factor Authentication (2FA) to provide secure access when a DNS server is managed by a third party

- Use DNS change lock or client lock to restrict unauthorized alterations of DNS settings

- Implement DNSSEC as an additional security layer for DNS servers, allowing only digitally signed DNS requests and mitigating DNS hijacking

- Use premium DNS registration services to hide sensitive information, such as Host Information (HINFO), from public view

- Secure DNS queries by encrypting DNS traffic using DNS-over-HTTPS (DoH) or DNS-over-TLS (DoT) to prevent eavesdropping and man-in-the-middle attacks that could facilitate DNS enumeration

- Enable DNS logging and monitoring to record queries and responses, allowing for regular analysis to identify suspicious patterns that may indicate enumeration attempts

- Employ anomaly detection systems to automatically flag unusual DNS query volumes or patterns, potentially signaling enumeration or other DNS attacks

- Implement rate limiting on DNS servers to restrict the number of accepted queries from individual IP addresses, reducing the effectiveness of brute-force enumeration techniques

- Use split DNS architecture where internal DNS queries are handled by a separate DNS server from external queries, limiting exposure of internal network structure

- Minimize DNS information shared through DNS records by avoiding descriptive subdomain names that reveal internal network details or server purposes

Other countermeasures to defend against DNS enumeration are as follows:

- Ensure private hosts and their IP addresses are not published in the DNS zone files of the public DNS server

- Use standard network admin contacts for DNS registrations to prevent social engineering attacks

- Prune DNS zone files to avoid exposing unnecessary information

- Maintain separate internal and external DNS servers for added security

- Delete old or unused DNS records periodically to reduce vulnerabilities

- Bind request queries using ACLs and configure BIND to run with the least privileges

- Use the /etc/hosts file for developing or staging subdomains instead of relying on DNS records

- Deploy DNS firewalls to block malicious queries and protect against DNS-based threats by leveraging threat intelligence to detect and prevent communication with known malicious domains

- Regularly review and audit DNS configurations to ensure security and limit public exposure of unnecessary DNS information

---

Important Exam Tips for the Certified Ethical Hacker (CEH) Exam on Enumeration

Understanding enumeration is crucial for the CEH exam. Here are key exam tips to help you master this topic:

1. Enumeration Basics

- Enumeration follows network scanning and involves gathering detailed system information such as user accounts, shared resources, and running services.

- Attackers use enumeration to extract sensitive details for further exploitation, while ethical hackers use it to assess and strengthen security.

2. SNMP Enumeration

- Uses Simple Network Management Protocol (SNMP) to extract network configuration, system details, and user accounts.

- Runs on UDP port 161 and is vulnerable if default community strings (e.g., "public" and "private") are not changed.

- **Countermeasures:** Upgrade to SNMPv3, change default community strings, block UDP port 161, and restrict SNMP access via ACLs.

3. LDAP Enumeration

- Uses Lightweight Directory Access Protocol (LDAP) to query Active Directory (AD) for user details, organizational structure, and resources

- Runs on port 389 and is vulnerable if anonymous access is allowed

- **Countermeasures:** Enable SSL/TLS encryption, disable anonymous binds, enforce strong passwords, and **use** Multi-Factor Authentication (MFA)

4. NFS Enumeration

- Network File System (NFS) allows remote file access as if local, using TCP port 2049

- Attackers enumerate exported file systems to access shared data

- **Countermeasures:** Implement firewall rules, enable root_squash, use Kerberos authentication, and monitor NFS access logs

5. SMTP Enumeration

- Uses Simple Mail Transfer Protocol (SMTP) to identify valid email users on a mail server

- Runs on port 25 and allows attackers to exploit EXPN, VRFY, and RCPT TO commands

- **Countermeasures:** Disable EXPN and VRFY, restrict RCPT TO, enforce email authentication (SPF, DKIM, DMARC), and limit SMTP error messages

6. SMB Enumeration

- Server Message Block (SMB) is used for file and printer sharing, running on TCP ports 139 and 445

- Attackers enumerate network shares, user accounts, and system details

- **Countermeasures**: Disable SMB on web and DNS servers, block ports 139/445, enforce ACLs, and upgrade to SMBv3

7. DNS Enumeration

- Attackers query Domain Name System (DNS) records to map internal networks, using tools like nslookup, dig, and host

- **Countermeasures:** Disable DNS zone transfers, use DNSSEC, restrict resolver access, and enable query logging

8. General Enumeration Defense Strategies

- Disable unnecessary services to reduce attack surfaces

- Monitor network logs for unusual activity

- Implement role-based access control (RBAC) for restricting system access

- Use encryption and authentication protocols to secure communications

Chapter 05: Vulnerability Analysis

Introduction

Vulnerability analysis is a critical component of cybersecurity, focusing on identifying, assessing, and mitigating weaknesses within an organization's IT infrastructure. Attackers continuously exploit vulnerabilities in networks, applications, and systems to gain unauthorized access, disrupt operations, or steal sensitive data. Organizations must proactively assess their security posture to minimize risk exposure.

This topic explores the vulnerability analysis countermeasures that organizations can implement to mitigate potential threats and enhance their overall security framework. Ethical hackers and security professionals use these techniques to detect vulnerabilities before cybercriminals can exploit them, ensuring a robust defense against evolving cyber threats.

Vulnerability Assessment Concepts

Vulnerability assessment is the process of systematically identifying, analyzing, and evaluating security weaknesses in an organization's systems, networks, applications, and processes. These vulnerabilities could be due to outdated software, misconfigurations, weak passwords, open ports, or coding flaws that can be exploited by cyber attackers to gain unauthorized access or disrupt operations.

The goal of vulnerability assessment is to proactively detect potential security gaps before they can be exploited and to prioritize remediation efforts based on risk severity. Assessments may be conducted manually or through automated tools such as vulnerability scanners and configuration analyzers.

Types of vulnerability assessments include:

- **Network-based assessments**: Scanning for vulnerabilities in wired and wireless networks

- **Host-based assessments**: Reviewing individual systems for weaknesses like unpatched software or insecure configurations

- **Application assessments**: Identifying flaws in web applications and APIs.

- **Database assessments**: Detecting misconfigurations, weak permissions, or outdated database systems

- **Cloud-based assessments**: Evaluating cloud configurations and services for compliance and security risks

Vulnerability Assessment Countermeasures

- Conduct regular vulnerability scans using automated tools to continuously scan systems and networks for new vulnerabilities

- Patch management ensures operating systems, applications, and firmware are updated with the latest security patches

- Implement configuration management by following security best practices for system and network configurations to reduce exposure

- Prioritize remediation based on risk by addressing high-risk vulnerabilities first, especially those with known exploits or affecting critical systems

- Use firewalls and IDS/IPS to protect against exploitation of known vulnerabilities through traffic monitoring and filtering

- Perform penetration testing to simulate real-world attacks and identify exploitable weaknesses while testing the effectiveness of security measures

- Establish a vulnerability management program with a structured process for identifying, tracking, and resolving vulnerabilities

- Use secure coding practices where developers follow coding standards that minimize security flaws and perform code reviews

- Apply the Principle of Least Privilege (PoLP) by restricting user and system access to only what is necessary to reduce potential attack surfaces

- Enable logging and monitoring to keep detailed logs and monitor systems for signs of attempted exploitation or unusual behavior

- Segment networks by dividing them into zones to limit lateral movement of attackers and contain potential breaches

- Regularly audit and assess assets by maintaining an updated inventory of all hardware and software and evaluating their security status

- Train employees on security awareness to recognize signs of system vulnerabilities, phishing attempts, and poor security practices

- Use encryption and secure protocols to protect sensitive data in transit and at rest with strong encryption standards

- Establish incident response procedures with a clear plan to respond quickly and effectively if a vulnerability is exploited

Vulnerability Assessment Tools

Vulnerability Assessment Tools are security solutions designed to identify, analyze, and prioritize weaknesses in IT systems, networks, applications, and infrastructure. These tools help organizations detect misconfigurations, outdated software, and exploitable vulnerabilities before attackers can exploit them. They use automated scanning, manual testing, and compliance checks to enhance security posture.

Countermeasures using Vulnerability Assessment Tools

- Use Nessus to perform comprehensive vulnerability scans across systems, networks, and applications to detect misconfigurations and outdated software

- Deploy OpenVAS (Open Vulnerability Assessment System) for open-source scanning of IT infrastructure and vulnerability management

- Utilize QualysGuard for cloud-based vulnerability management, compliance monitoring, and asset discovery

- Implement Nmap to perform network mapping, port scanning, and identify hosts and services that may be vulnerable

- Use Nikto to scan web servers for dangerous files, outdated versions, and configuration issues

- Employ Burp Suite for web application security testing, including vulnerability scanning, crawling, and manual testing tools

- Run Acunetix to identify security issues in web applications such as SQL injection, XSS, and other common web threats

- Use Metasploit Framework to validate vulnerabilities through controlled exploitation and simulate real-world attacks

- Utilize Wireshark for network traffic analysis to identify potential vulnerabilities and suspicious communications

- Implement OpenSCAP for automated vulnerability assessment, policy compliance checks, and configuration validation

- Integrate Retina CS for vulnerability management, configuration assessment, and patching across enterprise networks

- Use GFI LanGuard to scan networks, detect vulnerabilities, and assess patch status and security configurations

- Apply Aircrack-ng for wireless network vulnerability assessment and testing the strength of Wi-Fi security protocols

- Use OWASP ZAP (Zed Attack Proxy) for open-source web application scanning and penetration testing

- Perform patch verification and remediation to ensure discovered vulnerabilities are resolved promptly and verified

- Enable automated alerts and reporting to receive immediate notifications of detected vulnerabilities and generate actionable reports

- Conduct regular tool updates to keep scanning engines current with the latest vulnerability signatures and threat intelligence

- Train security teams on correct tool usage to avoid misconfigurations and false positives during assessments

- Combine multiple tools and techniques for comprehensive coverage and cross-validation of results

- Incorporate manual testing and expert validation alongside automated scans for deeper insights and prioritization of findings

---

Important Exam Tips for the Certified Ethical Hacker (CEH) Exam on Vulnerability Analysis

Understanding Vulnerability Analysis is crucial for the CEH exam. Here are key exam tips to help you master this topic:

1. Fundamentals of Vulnerability Analysis

- Vulnerability analysis involves identifying, assessing, and mitigating security weaknesses in networks, applications, and systems.

- Ethical hackers use vulnerability assessments to find security flaws before cybercriminals exploit them.

- Organizations implement vulnerability management programs to systematically track and remediate security risks.

2. Vulnerability Assessment Tools

- **Nessus:** Comprehensive vulnerability scanning tool for networks and applications.

- **OpenVAS:** Open-source vulnerability scanner for security assessments.

- **QualysGuard:** Cloud-based vulnerability management and compliance monitoring tool.

- **Nmap:** Used for network mapping, port scanning, and host discovery.

- **Nikto:** Web server scanner for outdated versions and misconfigurations.

- **Burp Suite:** Tool for web application security testing and manual penetration testing.

- **Metasploit:** Framework for vulnerability validation through controlled exploitation.

3. Risk-Based Vulnerability Prioritization

- High-risk vulnerabilities should be addressed first, especially those with known exploits.

- Common Vulnerability Scoring System (CVSS) is used to prioritize vulnerabilities based on severity.

- Automated tools help categorize vulnerabilities based on their impact and exploitability.

4. Secure Coding and Application Security

- Developers should follow secure coding practices to prevent vulnerabilities in software.

- Regular code reviews and security testing help identify coding flaws.

- Web applications should be tested for common vulnerabilities like SQL injection and cross-site scripting.

5. Incident Response and Remediation

- Organizations must have an incident response plan to address security breaches.

- Logs and monitoring systems help detect unauthorized access and suspicious activity.

- Security audits and compliance checks ensure adherence to industry standards.

Chapter 06: System Hacking

Introduction

System hacking is a critical phase in cybersecurity where attackers attempt to gain unauthorized access to computer systems, networks, or sensitive data by exploiting security weaknesses. This process involves various attack techniques, including password cracking, vulnerability exploitation, privilege escalation, maintaining access, and covering tracks. Cybercriminals use these methods to infiltrate systems, steal confidential information, and disrupt operations, often leaving minimal traces of their activities.

Understanding system hacking techniques is essential for cybersecurity professionals, ethical hackers, and IT administrators to strengthen security defenses. By identifying and mitigating vulnerabilities before attackers exploit them, organizations can protect their critical assets from cyber threats.

This chapter focuses on the techniques attackers use to perform system hacking and the countermeasures that can be implemented to detect, block, and prevent them. Topics covered include password cracking techniques, how vulnerabilities are exploited, privilege escalation strategies, persistence mechanisms, and anti-forensic techniques used to cover tracks. Additionally, it provides best practices and security measures to defend against these threats, ensuring robust protection for IT environments.

Cracking Passwords

Cracking Passwords is the process of attempting to gain unauthorized access to systems, accounts, or encrypted data by breaking or guessing passwords. Attackers use various techniques such as brute force attacks, dictionary attacks, rainbow table attacks, credential stuffing, and keylogging to crack passwords and exploit user credentials. Weak or reused passwords increase the risk of successful password cracking attempts.

Countermeasures for Cracking Passwords

- Use strong, unique passwords that include a mix of uppercase and lowercase letters, numbers, and special characters to make cracking difficult

- Implement Multi-Factor Authentication to require additional verification beyond just a password

- Enforce password length and complexity policies requiring at least 12-16 characters with no common words or patterns

- Enable account lockout policies to temporarily disable accounts after multiple failed login attempts and prevent brute force attacks

- Utilize password managers to generate and store complex passwords securely without needing to memorize them

- Implement rate limiting and CAPTCHA to slow down automated password guessing attempts on login pages

- Regularly update and rotate passwords to reduce the risk of compromised credentials being exploited

- Store passwords securely using strong hashing algorithms like bcrypt, Argon2, or PBKDF2 with proper salting

- Monitor for credential leaks and password breaches using services like "Have I Been Pwned" and enforce password resets if exposed

- Educate employees on password security best practices to avoid using weak, common, or reused passwords

- Restrict password reuse across multiple accounts to prevent attackers from exploiting the same password on different services

- Implement Privileged Access Management (PAM) to limit access to critical systems and enforce strict authentication controls

- Use biometric authentication such as fingerprint or facial recognition for enhanced security where applicable

- Deploy endpoint protection solutions to detect and block keyloggers, malware, and credential-stealing attacks

- Conduct regular security audits and penetration testing to assess password policies and identify weaknesses

- Encourage passphrase-based authentication using longer phrases instead of complex but short passwords

- Implement Single Sign-On (SSO) solutions to reduce password fatigue while maintaining strong authentication controls

- Require encrypted storage and transmission of credentials to prevent interception during authentication

- Monitor login attempts and unusual authentication patterns to detect and respond to unauthorized access attempts

- Enforce automatic logout and session expiration policies to reduce the risk of unauthorized access from idle sessions

Vulnerability Exploitation

Vulnerability Exploitation is the process of attackers taking advantage of security weaknesses in software, hardware, or network systems to gain unauthorized access, execute malicious code, or disrupt operations. Exploits can target unpatched vulnerabilities, misconfigurations, weak access controls, and outdated systems. Attackers use methods such as buffer overflows, SQL injection, remote code execution, and privilege escalation to exploit vulnerabilities and compromise systems.

Vulnerability Exploitation Countermeasures

- Conduct regular vulnerability scans to detect and address security weaknesses before attackers exploit them

- Apply security patches and updates promptly for operating systems, applications, and firmware to fix known vulnerabilities

- Use IDS/IPS to identify and block exploitation attempts in real-time

- Implement web application firewalls (WAFs) to filter and block malicious traffic targeting web-based vulnerabilities

- Enforce the PoLP to minimize the permissions available to users and services

- Perform penetration testing regularly to identify exploitable weaknesses and assess security defenses

- Deploy endpoint protection and endpoint detection and response (EDR) solutions to detect and prevent malware that exploits vulnerabilities

- Harden system configurations by disabling unnecessary services, ports, and default accounts

- Use secure coding practices to prevent application vulnerabilities like SQL injection and buffer overflow attacks

- Monitor security logs and alerts for signs of exploitation attempts or unusual system behavior

- Isolate critical systems using network segmentation to limit an attacker's ability to move laterally within the network

- Implement multi-factor authentication to reduce the risk of unauthorized access even if a vulnerability is exploited

- Encrypt sensitive data in transit and at rest to prevent attackers from accessing critical information

- Conduct security awareness training to educate employees on recognizing and reporting potential exploitation attempts

- Establish an incident response plan to detect, contain, and remediate security breaches efficiently

- Limit the use of third-party applications and plugins to reduce exposure to software vulnerabilities

- Use threat intelligence services to stay informed about emerging vulnerabilities and available mitigations

- Enforce Secure Software Development Lifecycle (SDLC) practices to identify and fix vulnerabilities during development

- Implement automated remediation tools to quickly patch or mitigate vulnerabilities in large-scale environments

- Monitor and control privileged accounts to prevent unauthorized privilege escalation attacks

Privilege Escalation

Privilege Escalation is a cyberattack technique where attackers exploit system vulnerabilities, misconfigurations, or weak access controls to gain higher privileges than originally granted. This allows them to access restricted data, execute malicious commands, or take complete control of a system. Privilege escalation is classified into vertical escalation, where attackers gain higher privileges (e.g., from user to admin), and horizontal escalation, where they access other user accounts with similar privileges. Attackers use methods such as exploiting unpatched

software, misconfigured permissions, credential theft, and kernel vulnerabilities to escalate privileges.

Privilege Escalation Countermeasures

- Apply security patches and updates promptly to fix vulnerabilities that could be exploited for privilege escalation

- Implement the PoLP to restrict user and system access to only necessary permissions

- Use multi-factor authentication to prevent unauthorized access, even if credentials are compromised

- Regularly audit and review user privileges to identify and revoke unnecessary elevated permissions

- Implement strong password policies to prevent credential-based privilege escalation attacks

- Deploy EDR solutions to monitor and detect privilege escalation attempts

- Use Role-Based Access Control (RBAC) to ensure users only have access relevant to their job functions

- Restrict execution of scripts and unauthorized binaries to prevent privilege escalation exploits

- Enforce secure configuration management to prevent system misconfigurations that allow privilege escalation

- Monitor security logs and alerts for unusual user activity or unauthorized access attempts

- Limit the use of administrative accounts and require users to log in with standard accounts for daily operations

- Disable unnecessary services and ports to reduce the attack surface for privilege escalation exploits

- Use application whitelisting to allow only authorized applications to execute on critical systems

- Implement sandboxing and process isolation techniques to limit the impact of privilege escalation attacks

- Conduct regular penetration testing to identify privilege escalation vulnerabilities before attackers do

- Restrict local administrator privileges on workstations to prevent malware from escalating privileges

- Use Privileged Access Management (PAM) solutions to control and monitor privileged account usage

- Enable security event logging and auditing to track privilege escalation attempts in real-time

- Prevent kernel exploits by disabling unnecessary kernel modules and enabling kernel security features

- Educate employees on privilege escalation risks to recognize suspicious activities and insider threats

Maintaining Access

Maintaining Access is the process attackers use to ensure continued control over a compromised system or network. Once initial access is gained, attackers deploy various techniques to maintain persistence, evade detection, and prevent removal. Common methods include creating backdoors, installing rootkits, leveraging scheduled tasks, modifying system configurations, and abusing legitimate credentials. Maintaining access allows attackers to conduct long-term espionage, data theft, or further attacks on an organization.

Countermeasures for Maintaining Access

- Conduct regular security audits to identify unauthorized accounts, scheduled tasks, and services that may be used for persistence

- Use EDR solutions to monitor system behavior and detect persistent threats

- Disable unnecessary services and ports to reduce potential entry points for attackers to maintain access

- Implement multi-factor authentication to prevent attackers from reusing stolen credentials for long-term access

- Enforce strict access control policies to ensure only authorized users can modify system settings and configurations

- Monitor system and application logs to detect unusual access patterns and persistence mechanisms

- Regularly update and patch operating systems and applications to prevent attackers from exploiting known vulnerabilities

- Use behavioral analysis tools to detect unauthorized remote access and persistence techniques

- Restrict administrative privileges to limit the attacker's ability to create backdoors or modify security settings

- Conduct regular malware and rootkit scans to detect hidden malicious software that facilitates persistent access

- Implement network segmentation to prevent attackers from moving laterally after gaining access

- Monitor and restrict the use of remote access tools like RDP, SSH, and VPNs to prevent unauthorized access

- Use IDS/IPS to identify and block malicious activities

- Harden authentication mechanisms by implementing strong password policies and rotating credentials regularly

- Disable unused user accounts and remove outdated or inactive accounts to prevent exploitation by attackers

- Apply application whitelisting to prevent unauthorized execution of persistence tools and malware

- Monitor registry and system changes to detect unauthorized modifications related to persistence techniques

- Enable secure boot and firmware protections to prevent rootkits and bootkits from maintaining access at a low level

- Implement deception techniques like honeypots and fake credentials to detect and mislead attackers attempting to maintain access

- Conduct regular penetration testing and red team exercises to identify weaknesses in persistence defenses before attackers exploit them

Covering Tracks

Covering Tracks is the process attackers use to erase evidence of their activities and evade detection after gaining unauthorized access to a system or network. This includes modifying or deleting logs, clearing command history, disabling security tools, using anti-forensic techniques, and hiding malicious files. By covering their tracks, attackers make it harder for security teams to detect, investigate, and respond to incidents, increasing the chances of long-term persistence within a compromised environment.

Countermeasures for Covering Tracks

- Implement centralized logging solutions like Security Information and Event Management (SIEM) to collect and analyze logs from multiple sources, making tampering more difficult

- Use immutable log storage to prevent attackers from modifying or deleting critical system logs

- Enable logging and audit trails on all systems and applications to monitor security events and unauthorized activities

- Restrict access to log files by applying strict access control measures to prevent unauthorized modifications

- Monitor for log tampering and anomalies such as sudden log deletions, missing logs, or unusual patterns in log data

- Use EDR tools to track malicious activities, even if attackers attempt to erase evidence

- Enable secure audit policies to log user activities, process execution, file changes, and privilege escalations

- Deploy File Integrity Monitoring (FIM) solutions to detect unauthorized changes to critical system files and logs

- Monitor system commands and shell history to detect attackers attempting to cover their tracks

- Use honeytokens and deception techniques to lure attackers into triggering alerts when they attempt to erase logs

- Implement strict security policies for privileged access to reduce the chances of attackers gaining control over log management

- Enable tamper-proof logging mechanisms that prevent logs from being altered or deleted

- Regularly review log retention policies to ensure logs are stored for an appropriate duration for forensic investigations

- Enforce network segmentation to isolate security monitoring tools from systems attackers might compromise

- Utilize forensic analysis tools to recover deleted logs and traces of attacker activities

- Monitor unauthorized process execution to identify attackers running anti-forensic tools or scripts

- Educate employees on security best practices to recognize and report suspicious activities related to log tampering

- Conduct regular security audits and penetration testing to detect vulnerabilities that attackers could exploit to cover their tracks

- Enforce strict access logging for security tools to track who accesses log files and forensic data

- Ensure logs are securely backed up to a separate location to prevent attackers from erasing all traces of their actions

> 💡 **Important Exam Tips for the Certified Ethical Hacker (CEH) Exam on System Hacking**
>
> Understanding System Hacking is crucial for the CEH exam. Here are key exam tips to help you master this topic:
>
> **1. Fundamentals of System Hacking**
>
> - **Definition:** System hacking involves gaining unauthorized access to systems, networks, or applications by exploiting vulnerabilities and weaknesses.
>
> - **Ethical Hackers Role:** Ethical hackers use system hacking techniques to identify and mitigate weaknesses before malicious attackers can exploit them.

- **Key Phases:** The hacking process generally follows five key stages: gaining access, escalating privileges, maintaining access, covering tracks, and reconnaissance.

2. Techniques Used in System Hacking

- **Password Cracking:** Attackers use various methods to crack weak passwords, such as brute force, dictionary attacks, and rainbow table attacks.

- **Exploiting Vulnerabilities:** Hackers may exploit vulnerabilities like buffer overflows, SQL injection, or weak configurations to gain access.

- **Privilege Escalation:** Once inside the system, attackers seek to escalate their privileges to gain administrator or root-level access.

- **Maintaining Access:** Techniques like installing backdoors or rootkits ensure attackers can maintain access to the compromised system.

- **Covering Tracks:** Attackers remove traces of their activities by clearing logs or deleting command histories to avoid detection.

3. System Hacking Tools

- **John the Ripper:** A popular password cracking tool used for brute force and dictionary attacks.

- **Metasploit:** A powerful framework for identifying, exploiting, and validating vulnerabilities in systems.

- **Nmap:** A network scanner used to discover open ports and services, often the first step in system hacking.

- **Cain and Abel:** A password recovery tool that includes features like sniffing and cracking passwords.

- **Hydra:** A fast and flexible password cracker that supports multiple protocols for cracking passwords.

- **Netcat:** A network utility that can be used for backdoor access and connecting to remote systems.

4. Countermeasures for System Hacking

- **Strong Authentication:** Use multi-factor authentication (MFA) to protect against unauthorized access, even if passwords are compromised.

- **Patch Management:** Ensure all software, operating systems, and applications are up to date to minimize vulnerabilities.

- **Least Privilege Principle:** Apply the least privilege principle by giving users and systems only the permissions they need to perform their tasks.

- **Firewalls & IDS/IPS:** Use firewalls to filter malicious traffic and IDS/IPS systems to detect and block unauthorized access.

- **Regular Audits:** Conduct regular security audits to check for unauthorized access, backdoors, or rootkits that attackers may have left behind.

- **Security Monitoring:** Continuously monitor logs and system activities for suspicious behavior or indicators of compromise.

5. Privilege Escalation Techniques

- **Vertical Privilege Escalation:** Gaining higher privileges within the system, such as moving from a regular user account to an administrator account.

- **Horizontal Privilege Escalation:** Accessing other users' accounts or data with the same level of privileges as the attacker's initial access.

- **Exploiting Vulnerabilities:** Attackers exploit system misconfigurations, software bugs, or weak access control to escalate privileges.

- **Countermeasures:** Use role-based access control (RBAC), secure configurations, and regular privilege audits to minimize escalation risks.

6. Incident Response and Remediation

- **Incident Response Plan:** Establish a robust incident response plan to handle breaches and mitigate further damage quickly.

- **Forensic Analysis:** After a breach, forensic analysis helps determine how attackers gained access, what actions they took, and how to prevent future incidents.

- **Real-Time Monitoring:** Implement real-time monitoring solutions to detect unusual activities or intrusions on critical systems.

- **Security Patching:** Ensure all systems are promptly patched to address known vulnerabilities that could be exploited in future attacks.

Chapter 07: Malware Threats

Introduction

Malware threats are among the most persistent and evolving dangers in cybersecurity, impacting organizations and individuals worldwide. Malware, short for malicious software, is designed to disrupt, damage, or gain unauthorized access to computer systems. Attackers use various forms of malware, including Trojans, backdoors, viruses, worms, fileless malware, and AI-based malware, to exploit system vulnerabilities and compromise sensitive data.

This chapter explores different types of malwares, their attack methodologies, and the countermeasures organizations can implement to defend against these threats. It provides insights into how ethical h

ackers analyze and test malware defense mechanisms, using penetration testing techniques to identify security gaps before malicious actors can exploit them.

Trojan Concepts

Trojan concept refers to a type of malicious software designed to deceive users by appearing as a legitimate program, allowing attackers to gain unauthorized access to a system once the user unknowingly installs or executes it, essentially acting like a "backdoor" to infiltrate the network; ethical hackers utilize this concept by creating controlled Trojan programs to test a system's security vulnerabilities by simulating real-world attacks, but always with explicit permission from the system owner to assess and remediate potential risks.

Trojan Countermeasures

Some countermeasures against Trojans are as follows:

- Avoid opening email attachments from unknown senders

- Block unnecessary ports at the host and use a firewall

- Refrain from accepting programs transferred via instant messaging

- Strengthen weak default configurations and disable unused functionalities, including protocols and services

- Monitor internal network traffic for unusual ports or encrypted transmissions

- Avoid downloading and executing applications from untrusted sources

- Install patches and security updates for the OS and applications regularly

- Restrict permissions within the desktop environment to prevent the installation of malicious applications

- Avoid executing commands blindly or using pre-fabricated programs and scripts without verification

- Manage local workstation file integrity through checksums, auditing, and port scanning

- Run host-based antivirus, firewall, and intrusion detection software

- Avoid clicking on unsolicited pop-ups and banners

- Exercise caution when using peer-to-peer file-sharing services

- Choose ISPs that provide network security and employ robust anti-spam techniques

- Disable the autorun option for external devices such as USB drives and hard drives

- Verify Secure Socket Layer (SSL) authenticity before accessing e-commerce websites to prevent information sniffing

- Establish strong and unique passwords, updating them frequently

- Utilize web browser security features and extensions for enhanced protection

- Install host-based intrusion prevention systems on endpoints to monitor and prevent malicious activities, such as file system changes and process injections linked to Trojan infections

- Deploy File Integrity Monitoring (FIM) solutions to detect unauthorized modifications to critical system files, configuration files, and application binaries

- Enable memory protection mechanisms like Data Execution Prevention (DEP) and Address Space Layout Randomization (ASLR) to mitigate buffer overflow and code injection attacks commonly used by Trojans to execute arbitrary code

Backdoor Concepts

A backdoor refers to a hidden, unauthorized access point within a computer system or network that allows an attacker to bypass normal authentication procedures and gain privileged access without detection, essentially creating a covert entry point to manipulate the system remotely, often used for penetration testing to assess vulnerabilities and identify potential security risks.

Backdoor Countermeasures

Some common countermeasures against backdoors are as follows:

- Most commercial antivirus products can automatically scan and detect backdoor programs before they can cause damage.

- Educate users to avoid installing applications from untrusted Internet sites and email attachments

- Avoid untrusted software and ensure every device is protected by a firewall

- Use antivirus tools like Bitdefender and Kaspersky to detect and eliminate backdoors

- Monitor open-source projects entering the enterprise from untrusted external sources such as open-source code repositories

- Inspect network packets using protocol monitoring tools

- If a computer is infected with backdoors, restart it in safe mode with networking

- Run registry monitoring tools to identify malicious registry entries added by the backdoor

- Remove or uninstall programs or applications installed by the backdoor Trojan or virus

- Delete malicious registry entries added by the backdoor Trojan

- Remove all malicious files associated with the backdoor Trojan

- Ensure the device has auto-update enabled to receive the latest security patches

- Implement the pipeline emission analysis method to detect and analyze hardware-based backdoors that may have been inserted during manufacturing

- Avoid hardware components from untrusted shopping sites or black markets, where attackers can easily inject backdoors into devices

- If abnormal behavior is detected, restore the device to factory settings and reconfigure it with new credentials

- Check user ratings and reviews before installing or granting permissions to any product, even if downloaded from trusted sources

- Use file integrity monitoring software to detect unauthorized changes to critical system files and settings

- Disable services and close unnecessary ports to reduce potential entry points for backdoors

Virus and Worm Concepts

A virus refers to a malicious code that attaches itself to existing files or programs, requiring user interaction (like opening an infected file) to spread, while a worm is a standalone malicious program that can self-replicate and spread across a network without any user action needed, essentially crawling from computer to computer on its own, exploiting vulnerabilities in systems to propagate.

Virus and Worm Countermeasures

Some countermeasures against viruses and worms are as follows:

- Install antivirus software capable of detecting and removing infections as they occur

- Develop an antivirus policy for safe computing and distribute it to staff

- Carefully follow instructions when downloading files or programs from the Internet

- Keep antivirus software updated regularly

- Avoid opening attachments from unknown senders, as viruses often spread through email attachments

- Perform regular data backups to prevent data loss from virus infections

- Schedule routine scans for all drives after installing antivirus software

- Check all disks or programs with the latest antivirus software before accepting them

- Ensure that all executable code used within the organization is approved

- Avoid booting the machine with an infected bootable system disk

- Stay updated on the latest virus threats

- Enable pop-up blockers and use an Internet firewall for added protection

- Perform disk clean-up and run a registry scanner once a week

- Run anti-spyware or anti-adware software weekly

- Do not open files with multiple file type extensions

- Exercise caution with files received through instant messaging applications

- Conduct regular reviews of installed programs and stored data

- Use an effective email filter and scan emails consistently

- Disable the AutoRun feature to prevent automatic execution of malicious programs from external media

- Implement strong, unique passwords for all accounts and change them periodically

Fileless Malware Concepts

Fileless malware refers to a type of malicious code that operates entirely within a computer's memory, utilizing legitimate system tools and scripts to execute harmful actions, meaning no malicious files are downloaded or stored on the hard drive, making it significantly harder to detect with traditional antivirus software; essentially, it leverages native system functions to achieve its malicious goals without leaving a traceable file footprint.

Fileless Malware Countermeasures

Some countermeasures against fileless malware attacks are as follows:

- Remove administrative tools and limit access using Windows Group Policy or Windows AppLocker

- Disable PowerShell and WMI when not needed

- Turn off macros and allow only digitally signed, trusted macros

- Deploy whitelisting solutions like McAfee Application Control to prevent unauthorized applications and code execution

- Educate employees on identifying phishing emails and emphasize never enabling macros in MS Office documents

- Prevent PDF readers from automatically running JavaScript

- Disable Flash in browser settings

- Require Two-Factor Authentication (2FA) for accessing critical systems and network resources

- Implement a multi-layered security approach to detect and mitigate memory-resident malware

- Use User Behavior Analytics (UBA) to identify hidden threats within data

- Ensure system tools like PowerShell and WMIC, along with whitelisted application scripts, are monitored for security risks

- Conduct regular antivirus scans to detect infections and maintain updated antivirus software

- Install browser protection tools and disable automatic plugin downloads

- Perform routine security checks for applications and apply patches as needed

- Keep the operating system updated with the latest security patches

- Analyze all active programs for malicious activity or suspicious signatures and heuristics

- Enable endpoint security with continuous monitoring to protect remote network access

- Monitor Indicators of Compromise (IoCs) across the system and network

- Regularly review security logs, particularly when large amounts of data are transferred out of the network

- Restrict administrative privileges and apply the principle of least privilege to prevent privilege escalation attacks

- Use application control to block internet browsers from launching script interpreters like PowerShell and WMIC

- Closely monitor deviations from baseline system behavior

- Implement Next-Generation Antivirus (NGAV) with Machine Learning (ML) and Artificial Intelligence (AI) to counter polymorphic malware

- Utilize baselines and identify common Tactics, Techniques, And Procedures (TTPs) employed by cyber adversaries

- Leverage Managed Detection And Response (MDR) services for proactive threat hunting

- Deploy tools like Blackberry Cylance and Microsoft Enhanced Mitigation Experience Toolkit (EMET) to combat fileless attacks

- Disable unnecessary applications and services

- Remove unneeded software to reduce attack surfaces

- Block all incoming network traffic or files with the .exe format

- Inspect drives and the \TEMP folder for hidden PowerShell scripts

- Use projects like AltFS to gain insights into how fileless malware operates on targeted devices

- Deploy security solutions that utilize behavioral analysis to detect suspicious activities linked to fileless malware, such as unusual PowerShell execution or registry modifications

- Implement advanced Endpoint Protection Platforms (EPPs) that monitor memory and script execution behaviors to detect fileless malware

- Apply network segmentation to restrict the lateral movement of fileless malware across systems and networks

AI-based Malware Concepts

AI-based malware is a malicious software that utilizes Artificial Intelligence (AI) techniques to enhance its capabilities, such as automatically adapting to target systems, evading detection, and learning from previous attacks, making it a more sophisticated and harder-to-counter threat than traditional malware; ethical hackers often study and analyze such AI-powered malware to identify vulnerabilities and develop defensive strategies against real-world cyberattacks.

AI-based Malware Countermeasures

Some common countermeasures against AI-based malware are as follows:

- Scan for anomalous patterns such as unusual data transmission or system modifications

- Deploy AI-powered security solutions such as Next-Generation Antivirus (NGAV), Endpoint Detection and Response (EDR), and Network Traffic Analysis (NTA) to detect and mitigate AI-based malware threats

- Frequently perform anomaly detection methods, including statistical analysis, clustering algorithms, and unsupervised learning techniques

- Develop and deploy Explainable AI (XAI) techniques to enhance the transparency and interpretability of AI-based security solutions

- Implement automated response mechanisms, such as threat hunting algorithms and orchestration platforms

- Ensure compliance with relevant cybersecurity regulations and standards, such as GDPR, HIPAA, and NIST guidelines that address AI-based malware threats

- Equip the Security Operations Center (SOC) with advanced monitoring tools and automated response capabilities to detect and respond to AI-based malware threats in real time

- Leverage threat intelligence feeds and services that provide real-time updates on emerging AI-based malware threats and associated Indicators of Compromise (IoCs)

- Promote cybersecurity awareness training programs to empower employees in defending against AI-driven threats

- Regularly assess and audit compliance regulations and standards to identify vulnerabilities that may expose organizations to AI-based malware risks

- Carefully read end-User License Agreements (EULAs) and installation screens to opt out of any bundled software that could be adware

- Choose advanced or custom installation options when installing software to deselect any additional, potentially unwanted programs

- Adjust web browser privacy settings to reduce tracking and data collection

- Utilize system clean-up tools to remove unused files and software that could be vulnerable to adware

- Regularly review installed programs and remove any that were not authorized or are no longer needed

APT Concepts

APT stands for Advanced Persistent Threat, referring to a sophisticated cyber-attack strategy where a malicious actor gains unauthorized access to a target network and maintains a hidden presence for an extended period, stealthily exfiltrating sensitive data without detection, often used in highly targeted attacks against specific organizations or individuals with valuable information; ethical hackers simulate APT attacks to identify and address potential vulnerabilities within a system by mimicking the tactics, techniques, and procedures used by real-world attackers.

APT Countermeasures

Some important countermeasures against APT threats are as follows:

- Utilize a zero-trust security model to verify and authorize all users and devices.

- Conduct regular risk assessments to identify and mitigate potential threats.

- Segment the network into isolated zones to minimize lateral movement by Advanced Persistent Threats (APTs).

- Deploy Next-Generation Antivirus (NGAV) and endpoint detection and response (EDR) solutions for enhanced threat detection.

- Strengthen email security by implementing spam filters, authentication protocols (SPF, DKIM, DMARC), and email encryption to prevent malware infiltration.

- Engage in proactive threat hunting to detect early signs of APT activity.

- Encrypt sensitive data both in transit and at rest to prevent unauthorized access.

- Enforce Data Loss Prevention (DLP) controls and establish data classification policies to safeguard critical information.

- Regularly update security controls and threat intelligence sources to stay ahead of evolving APT Tactics, Techniques, And Procedures (TTPs).

- Keep operating systems, applications, and firmware up to date with the latest security patches.

- Implement Multi-Factor Authentication (MFA) for accessing sensitive systems.

- Continuously monitor network traffic for abnormal activity that may indicate an APT presence.

- Utilize Security Information and Event Management (SIEM) tools and anomaly detection solutions to automate the identification of suspicious behavior.

- Adopt a zero-trust approach, assuming no user or device is inherently trustworthy without verification.

- Deploy deception technologies, such as honeypots and decoys, to mislead attackers and detect intrusions early

---

Important Exam Tips for the Certified Ethical Hacker (CEH) Exam on Malware Threats

Understanding malware threats is crucial for the CEH exam. Here are key exam tips to help you master this topic:

1. Understanding Malware Threats

- Malware is any malicious software designed to harm, exploit, or compromise computer systems

- Common types include Trojans, backdoors, viruses, worms, fileless malware, AI-based malware, and APTs (Advanced Persistent Threats)

- Ethical hackers analyze malware using penetration testing techniques to identify vulnerabilities and enhance security

2. Trojan Malware

- A Trojan appears as legitimate software but secretly executes malicious actions

---

- Attackers use it to create backdoors for persistent access to compromised systems

- **Countermeasures:** Avoid downloading from untrusted sources, use firewalls, restrict unnecessary privileges, and implement Intrusion Detection Systems (IDS)

3. Backdoor Attacks

- Backdoors allow attackers to bypass authentication and gain hidden access

- These are often installed through Trojans or exploited vulnerabilities in software

- **Countermeasures:** Use firewalls, run registry monitoring tools, remove malicious programs, and enable system auto-updates

4. Virus and Worms

- Viruses attach to files and spread when executed, while worms self-replicate across networks

- **Countermeasures:** Install updated antivirus, enable firewalls, disable AutoRun, and conduct regular security audits

5. Fileless Malware

- Fileless malware operates in memory without creating malicious files, making it harder to detect

- Uses legitimate system tools like PowerShell, WMI, and registry modifications to execute attacks

- **Countermeasures:** Disable PowerShell & macros, **restrict** script execution, **monitor** behavioral anomalies, and use advanced endpoint protection (EPPs)

6. AI-Based Malware

- AI-powered malware adapts to security measures, evades detection, and learns from previous attacks

- **Countermeasures:** Deploy AI-powered cybersecurity tools, implement anomaly detection, use Explainable AI (XAI) for transparency, and conduct continuous threat assessments

7. Advanced Persistent Threats (APTs)

- APTs are stealthy, long-term attacks aimed at exfiltrating sensitive data

- Attackers maintain persistent access using sophisticated techniques like lateral movement, data exfiltration, and command-and-control (C2) communication

- **Countermeasures:** Implement zero-trust security, use multi-factor authentication (MFA), enforce network segmentation, and deploy SIEM tools for continuous monitoring

8. General Malware Defense Strategies

- Regular security updates for OS, applications, and firmware

- Deploy Endpoint Detection and Response (EDR) solutions to monitor and respond to threats

- Implement security awareness training to prevent phishing and social engineering attacks

- Encrypt sensitive data both in transit and at rest

- Use deception technologies (honeypots) to lure attackers and detect APT activities

Chapter 08: Sniffing

Introduction

Sniffing is a network attack technique used to intercept and monitor network traffic, allowing attackers to capture sensitive data such as login credentials, financial information, and confidential communications. Cybercriminals deploy sniffers, specialized hardware or software tools, to eavesdrop on unencrypted network packets, gaining unauthorized access to critical information without detection.

Sniffing attacks are categorized into passive sniffing and active sniffing. Passive sniffing occurs when an attacker monitors network traffic without interfering, typically in networks using hubs. Active sniffing involves manipulating network protocols, such as ARP poisoning or MAC flooding, to redirect or capture traffic in switched networks. Attackers use various techniques, including packet sniffing, MAC spoofing, DHCP attacks, DNS poisoning, and Man-In-The-Middle (MITM) attacks, to exploit network vulnerabilities.

Sniffing

Sniffing is a technique used to intercept and monitor network traffic to capture sensitive data such as login credentials, emails, and confidential communications. Attackers deploy sniffers, software, or hardware tools to eavesdrop on unencrypted network packets, allowing them to extract valuable information without detection.

Defend Against Sniffing

Organizations can strengthen their defenses against sniffing attacks by applying the following countermeasures:

- Restrict physical access to network media to prevent unauthorized installation of packet sniffers

- Use end-to-end encryption to secure confidential information during transmission

- Permanently add the MAC address of the gateway to the ARP cache to prevent spoofing

- Use static IP addresses and ARP tables to block attackers from adding spoofed ARP entries

- Disable network identification broadcasts and limit network access to authorized users to prevent discovery through sniffing tools

- Use IPv6 instead of IPv4, as IPv6 mandates IPsec implementation for better security

- Replace vulnerable protocols with encrypted alternatives such as SSH instead of Telnet, SCP instead of FTP, and SSL for email connections

- Use HTTPS instead of HTTP to protect usernames and passwords from being intercepted

- Use network switches instead of hubs to ensure data packets are delivered only to intended recipients

- Secure file transfers with SFTP instead of FTP to prevent unauthorized access

- Utilize PGP, S/MIME, VPN, IPsec, SSL/TLS, SSH, and one-time passwords (OTPs) for enhanced security

- Download emails using POP2 or POP3 instead of POP to reduce security risks

- Manage networked devices with SNMPv3 instead of SNMPv1 or SNMPv2 for better encryption and authentication

- Encrypt wireless traffic using strong encryption protocols such as WPA2 or WPA3

- Retrieve MAC addresses directly from NICs rather than the OS to prevent MAC address spoofing

- Use detection tools to check if any NICs are operating in promiscuous mode

- Implement access control lists (ACLs) to allow access only to a fixed range of trusted IP addresses

- Change default passwords to complex, unique passwords to strengthen security

- Avoid broadcasting SSIDs to reduce the risk of unauthorized access to wireless networks

- Enable MAC filtering on routers to limit network access to trusted devices

- Deploy network scanning and monitoring tools to detect malicious intrusions, rogue devices, and sniffers

- Avoid connecting to unsecured networks and open Wi-Fi to prevent data interception

- Use VLANs and network segmentation techniques to create smaller, more secure network segments, reducing the impact of sniffing attacks

- Continuously monitor and audit network traffic for unusual patterns that may indicate sniffing activities

- Use VPNs to establish a secure tunnel for data transmission over public networks, safeguarding sensitive information

- Deploy intrusion detection and prevention systems (IDS/IPS) to identify and mitigate sniffing attempts and other malicious activities

- Regularly audit network traffic logs to detect suspicious behavior and ensure logging is comprehensive

Sniffer Detection Techniques

Ping Method

To detect a sniffer on a network, identify the system on the network running in promiscuous mode. The ping method is useful in detecting a system that runs in promiscuous mode, which in turn helps to detect sniffers installed on the network.

Just send a ping request to the suspected machine with its IP address and incorrect MAC address. The Ethernet adapter will reject it because the MAC address does not match, whereas the suspect machine running the sniffer responds to it, as it does not reject packets with a different MAC address. Thus, this response will identify the sniffer in the network.

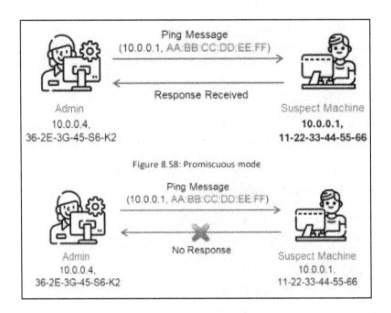

Figure 8.58: Promiscuous mode

Figure 8-01: Non-Promiscuous Mode

DHCP Method

The Dynamic Host Configuration Protocol (DHCP) method is a technique used to detect the presence of sniffers on a network. Since sniffers operate in promiscuous mode, they passively capture packets and do not actively communicate with the network. However, by leveraging DHCP behavior, network administrators can identify rogue devices running sniffing tools.

When a device connects to a network, it typically sends a DHCP request to obtain an IP address. A legitimate device will respond to DHCP lease offers and communicate normally with the network. A sniffer, on the other hand, remains passive and does not generate DHCP requests or responses. By analyzing devices that receive packets but do not request an IP address, security professionals can detect potential sniffers operating in stealth mode.

DNS Method

The reverse DNS lookup is the opposite of the DNS lookup method. Sniffers using reverse DNS lookup increase network traffic. This increase in network traffic can be an indication of the presence of a sniffer on the network. The computers on this network are in promiscuous mode.

Users can perform a reverse DNS lookup remotely or locally. Monitor the organization's DNS server to identify incoming reverse DNS lookups. The method of sending ICMP requests to a non-existing IP address can also monitor reverse

DNS lookups. The computer performing the reverse DNS lookup would respond to the ping, thus identifying it as hosting a sniffer.

For local reverse DNS lookups, configure the detector in promiscuous mode. Send an ICMP request to a non-existing IP address and view the response. If the system receives a response, the user can identify the responding machine as performing reverse DNS lookups on the local machine. A machine generating reverse DNS lookup traffic will most likely be running a sniffer.

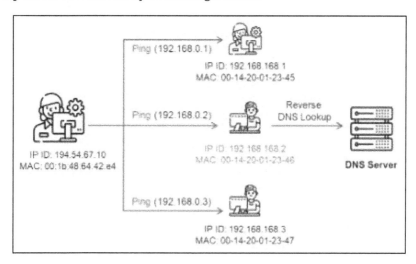

Figure 8-02: Sniffing Detection using the DNS Method

Spoofing

Spoofing is a technique used in sniffer detection to identify unauthorized sniffers on a network. Since sniffers operate in promiscuous mode, they silently capture all network traffic without directly interacting with the network. By sending crafted packets designed to trigger a response from a sniffer, security professionals can detect its presence.

Spoofing techniques rely on manipulating network protocols to trick a sniffer into revealing itself. These methods exploit the way sniffers process packets but remain undetectable to regular hosts operating in non-promiscuous mode.

ARP Method

This technique sends a non-broadcast ARP to all the nodes in the network. The node that runs in promiscuous mode on the network will cache the local ARP address. Then, it will broadcast a ping message on the network with the local IP address but a different MAC address. In this case, only the node that has the MAC

address (cached earlier) will be able to respond to your broadcast ping request. A machine in promiscuous mode replies to the ping message, as it has the correct information about the host that is sending ping requests in its cache; the remaining machines will send an ARP probe to identify the source of the ping request. This will detect the node on which the sniffer is running.

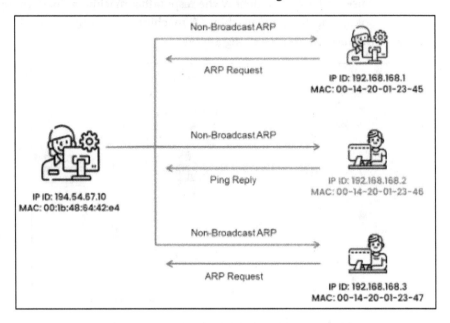

Figure 8-03: Detecting Sniffing via the ARP Method

Countermeasures For Sniffers

- Use TLS, SSL, IPsec, or VPNs to encrypt all sensitive communications

- Enable end-to-end encryption for emails, VoIP calls, and file transfers

- Implement DNS over HTTPS (DoH) or DNS over TLS (DoT) to secure DNS queries

- Replace hubs with network switches to prevent sniffers from capturing broadcast traffic

- Implement port security features on switches to restrict unauthorized devices

- Use VLAN segmentation to isolate traffic and prevent sniffers from accessing internal data

- Use Dynamic ARP Inspection (DAI) to block ARP spoofing attacks

- Deploy ARPWatch to monitor and detect unusual ARP traffic

- Configure static ARP entries for critical network devices

- Use Intrusion Detection Systems to monitor network activity for signs of sniffing

- Deploy Intrusion Prevention Systems to block malicious traffic in real time

- Configure IDS/IPS tools like Snort, Zeek (Bro), and Suricata to detect sniffing attempts

- Use VLANs to separate sensitive data from general traffic

- Restrict network access based on user roles and permissions

- Isolate critical infrastructure using firewall rules and access controls

- Analyze traffic using Wireshark, NetFlow, and Splunk to detect unauthorized packet captures

- Monitor for unusual ARP, DNS, and DHCP activity that could indicate sniffing

- Use honeypots and decoys to identify attackers attempting to intercept network traffic

- Use Multi-Factor Authentication to prevent unauthorized access

- Enforce strong password policies to protect against credential theft

- Utilize certificate-based authentication for critical network services

- Disable open and WEP-based Wi-Fi networks, as they are vulnerable to sniffing

- Use WPA3 encryption for wireless security

- Disable SSID broadcasting and implement MAC address filtering

- Perform penetration testing to identify vulnerabilities in network configurations

- Audit firewall rules, network device settings, and access logs regularly

- Simulate sniffing attacks in a controlled environment to test detection capabilities

- Disable unnecessary network protocols like Telnet, SMBv1, and FTP, which are prone to sniffing

- Block unauthorized DHCP, DNS, and SNMP traffic to prevent reconnaissance

- Restrict ICMP (ping) requests from untrusted sources

Important Exam Tips for the Certified Ethical Hacker (CEH) Exam on Sniffing

Understanding sniffing is crucial for the CEH exam. Here are key exam tips to help you master this topic:

1. Sniffing Basics

- Sniffing is the act of intercepting and capturing network traffic to steal sensitive data.

- Sniffers can be software-based (Wireshark, Tcpdump, Ettercap) or hardware-based (network taps, packet analyzers).

- Attackers use sniffing to steal login credentials, emails, financial data, and session cookies.

- Ethical hackers use sniffing techniques to test network security and detect vulnerabilities.

2. Types of Sniffing Attacks

- **Passive Sniffing**: Captures traffic without altering it (used in hubs and unencrypted Wi-Fi networks).

- **Active Sniffing**: Involves manipulating network traffic using ARP poisoning, MAC flooding, and DHCP attacks.

3. Sniffer Detection Techniques

- **Ping Method**: Sends a ping with an incorrect MAC address; sniffers in promiscuous mode will still respond.

- **DHCP Method**: Identifies devices that receive packets but do not request an IP address.

- **DNS Method**: Monitors network traffic for excessive reverse DNS lookups, which indicate sniffing activity.

- **ARP Method**: Sends a non-broadcast ARP request; sniffers capture and respond, revealing their presence.

- **Spoofing Techniques**: Uses specially crafted packets to trigger responses from sniffers in promiscuous mode.

5. Tools Commonly Tested in CEH for Sniffing

- **Wireshark**: Packet analysis and traffic monitoring.

- **Tcpdump**: Command-line packet sniffer for Unix/Linux.

- **Ettercap**: ARP poisoning and MITM attacks.

- **Cain & Abel**: Sniffing, ARP poisoning, and password cracking.

- **Dsniff**: Captures passwords from unencrypted network traffic.

Chapter 09: Social Engineering

Introduction

Social engineering is a psychological manipulation technique used by attackers to exploit human behavior and deceive individuals into revealing sensitive information, granting unauthorized access, or performing actions that compromise security. Unlike traditional hacking methods that target software vulnerabilities, social engineering preys on human emotions such as trust, fear, curiosity, or urgency to achieve malicious objectives.

Cybercriminals use various social engineering tactics, including phishing, pretexting, baiting, tailgating, impersonation, and voice cloning, to extract confidential information such as login credentials, financial data, and internal security details. The rise of AI-based attacks, deepfake technology, and voice cloning has further enhanced the effectiveness of social engineering scams, making them harder to detect.

Social Engineering Concepts

Social engineering is a tactic where attackers manipulate individuals into disclosing confidential information, granting unauthorized access, or taking actions that undermine security. Rather than targeting technical flaws, social engineering exploits human emotions such as trust, curiosity, fear, or urgency to achieve malicious goals. Common methods include phishing emails, pretexting, baiting, tailgating, and impersonation. Attackers may use various communication channels, including emails, phone calls, social media, or direct interactions, to obtain sensitive data like login credentials, financial information, or proprietary company details.

Social Engineering Countermeasures

- Conduct regular security awareness training to educate employees on recognizing and responding to social engineering attacks

- Implement a strict verification process for any request involving sensitive data or system access

- Encourage employees to verify unexpected emails, calls, or messages through official channels before responding

- Use email security tools such as spam filters, anti-phishing protection, and email authentication protocols like SPF, DKIM, and DMARC

- Avoid clicking on unknown links or downloading attachments from unsolicited emails

- Train employees to recognize common social engineering tactics such as phishing, pretexting, baiting, tailgating, and impersonation

- Establish policies that prohibit sharing sensitive information over phone calls or emails unless identity verification is performed

- Use multi-factor authentication (MFA) to add an extra layer of security for system logins and sensitive accounts

- Implement role-based access control (RBAC) to ensure employees only have access to the data necessary for their job functions

- Encourage a culture of skepticism, where employees are cautious about unsolicited requests for sensitive information

- Deploy endpoint protection and advanced threat detection systems to identify and block social engineering-based malware

- Monitor and audit employee access logs for unusual activities that may indicate insider threats or unauthorized access attempts

- Conduct simulated phishing exercises to test employees' awareness and improve their ability to detect real threats

- Enforce a strict password policy, requiring complex passwords and regular password updates to prevent credential theft

- Restrict access to social media and external communication platforms from company networks if not required for business purposes

- Educate employees on the dangers of oversharing company information on social media, as attackers can use it for reconnaissance

- Implement visitor access control measures to prevent unauthorized individuals from physically entering restricted areas

- Encourage employees to report suspicious emails, phone calls, or interactions immediately to the IT security team

- Use caller ID verification and block unknown or suspicious numbers to prevent vishing (voice phishing) attacks

- Establish incident response protocols to handle social engineering attempts and mitigate potential damage efficiently

Human-based Social Engineering

Human-based social engineering involves direct interaction between an attacker and the target to manipulate individuals into revealing sensitive information or granting unauthorized access. Unlike technical hacking methods, this approach relies on deception, impersonation, and psychological manipulation. Attackers may pose as employees, IT support personnel, vendors, or executives to gain trust and extract confidential data. Common human-based social engineering tactics include pretexting, impersonation, tailgating, shoulder surfing, and dumpster diving.

Human-based Social Engineering Countermeasures

- Conduct employee training on recognizing and responding to social engineering tactics such as impersonation, pretexting, and tailgating

- Enforce strict identity verification procedures for anyone requesting sensitive information or system access

- Implement visitor management protocols, requiring all guests to check in and wear identification badges

- Educate employees on the risks of sharing sensitive company details with unknown individuals in person or over the phone

- Restrict physical access to critical areas using biometric authentication, smart cards, or access control systems

- Use security guards and surveillance cameras to monitor restricted areas and prevent unauthorized access

- Implement a clean desk policy to ensure sensitive documents are not left exposed when unattended

- Train employees to verify the identity of unexpected visitors, contractors, or service personnel before granting access

- Enforce policies that prohibit employees from discussing confidential work-related matters in public places

- Secure all printed documents, shred discarded papers, and properly dispose of confidential information to prevent dumpster diving

- Require employees to lock their computers and workstations when stepping away to prevent shoulder surfing

- Regularly conduct security awareness drills and social engineering penetration tests to evaluate employees' preparedness

- Establish a company culture where employees feel comfortable reporting suspicious activities without fear of retaliation

- Implement least-privilege access policies, ensuring employees only have access to data necessary for their job roles

- Use multi-factor authentication (MFA) for secure access to company systems and sensitive information

- Monitor and audit access logs to detect unusual login attempts or unauthorized data access

- Encourage employees to challenge and report individuals who attempt to bypass security protocols or claim authority without verification

- Restrict information sharing on social media and train employees on the risks of oversharing professional details online

- Establish clear escalation procedures for handling suspicious interactions and social engineering attempts

- Provide regular updates on emerging social engineering tactics and techniques to ensure employees remain vigilant

Phishing Attacks

Phishing attacks are a form of social engineering where attackers trick individuals into revealing sensitive information, such as login credentials, financial details, or personal data, by masquerading as a trusted entity. These attacks often occur through emails, text messages, phone calls, or fake websites that appear legitimate. Phishing is widely used in credential theft, financial fraud, and malware distribution. Common phishing techniques include spear phishing (targeted attacks), whaling (high-profile targets like executives), vishing (voice phishing), and smishing (SMS phishing).

Defend against Phishing Attacks

- Implement advanced email filtering tools to detect and block phishing attempts before they reach users

- Enable Multi-Factor Authentication to add an extra layer of security, reducing the impact of stolen credentials

- Provide regular training to users on recognizing phishing attempts and how to avoid falling victim to them

- Encourage users to verify any suspicious communications, especially those asking for sensitive information, through independent channels

- Use Domain-Based Message Authentication (DMARC) to authenticate email senders and prevent domain spoofing

- Monitor for phishing websites and employ tools that detect and block fake websites

- Ensure users check for HTTPS encryption and verify URLs before entering sensitive information

- Deploy and regularly update anti-malware software to block malicious attachments or links in phishing emails

- Limit the sharing of personal information on public platforms to reduce the likelihood of targeted phishing attacks

- Establish clear incident response plans to report and respond to phishing attacks swiftly, minimizing potential damage

Identity Theft

Identity theft occurs when cybercriminals steal personal or financial information to impersonate an individual, commit fraud, or gain unauthorized access to sensitive accounts. Attackers use various methods such as phishing, data breaches, social engineering, malware, and credential stuffing to obtain personal details, including names, addresses, Social Security numbers, and banking information.

Identity Theft Countermeasures

- Create complex passwords for different accounts and use password managers to store them securely

- Add an extra layer of security by requiring authentication beyond just a password

- Regularly review bank and credit card statements for unauthorized transactions

- Place a credit freeze or fraud alert with credit bureaus to prevent unauthorized access to credit files

- Avoid clicking on suspicious links or providing personal information via email, phone, or text messages

- Shred sensitive documents before disposing of them and store important documents in a secure location

- Ensure websites use HTTPS and use VPNs when accessing public Wi-Fi networks

- Keep operating systems, browsers, and antivirus software updated to patch vulnerabilities

- Avoid sharing sensitive personal details such as birthdates, addresses, and vacation plans publicly

- Confirm legitimacy before sharing sensitive details over email or phone

- Consider subscribing to identity monitoring services that alert users of suspicious activity

- Enable screen locks, biometric authentication, and remote wipe capabilities to protect against data theft

- If affected by a data breach, change compromised passwords immediately and monitor affected accounts for fraud

- If identity theft is suspected, report it to the appropriate authorities such as the FTC, local law enforcement, and financial institutions

Voice Cloning

Voice cloning is a technology that enables attackers to replicate a person's voice using artificial intelligence and deep learning models. This technique can be exploited for malicious purposes such as impersonation, fraud, social engineering attacks, and misinformation campaigns. Attackers use voice cloning to bypass voice authentication systems, conduct phone-based phishing scams (vishing), and manipulate recorded conversations to deceive victims.

Voice Cloning Countermeasures

- Avoid relying solely on voice authentication and implement additional security measures like PINs, passwords, or biometric authentication

- If a caller sounds suspicious or makes unusual requests, verify their identity through alternate communication channels

- Avoid sharing voice recordings on public platforms and social media where attackers can easily collect samples for cloning

- Use AI-powered voice recognition systems that can detect anomalies in speech patterns and flag potential deepfake voice attempts

- Raise awareness about voice cloning threats and train individuals to recognize and handle suspicious voice-based requests

- Encrypt voice calls and use secure VoIP solutions to prevent unauthorized interception and manipulation

- Set up alerts for unusual transactions and require additional verification for large or sensitive financial activities

- Establish a pre-agreed verification phrase between family members or employees to authenticate voice-based requests

- Ensure organizations review and update security policies to include protections against AI-generated voice threats

- If targeted by a voice cloning attack, report it to the relevant authorities, financial institutions, and cybersecurity teams to prevent further exploitation

Deepfake Attack

A Deepfake Attack involves the use of Artificial Intelligence (AI) and deep learning algorithms to create highly realistic but falsified images, videos, or audio recordings. Attackers use deepfake technology to manipulate digital content, impersonate individuals, spread misinformation, and commit fraud. Deepfake attacks pose significant risks in social engineering, cybersecurity, politics, and financial scams, as they can be used to mimic executives, alter public speeches, or deceive individuals into believing fake content is real.

Deepfake Attack Countermeasures

- Always cross-check videos and images with trusted sources before accepting them as real

- Implement advanced deepfake detection software that analyzes inconsistencies in facial movements, voice patterns, and lighting anomalies

- Raise awareness about deepfake threats and train employees to recognize manipulated media

- Do not rely solely on voice or video authentication, use additional verification methods such as PINs, biometrics, or passcodes and MFA

- Organizations should monitor high-level executive or financial transactions that could be manipulated using deepfake impersonations

- Blockchain-based digital signatures can help verify the authenticity of media files and detect alterations

- Reduce exposure by avoiding excessive sharing of personal videos, speeches, or voice recordings on public platforms

- If a deepfake attack is detected, report it to relevant authorities, cybersecurity teams, and affected individuals to prevent further damage

- Update security frameworks to include deepfake awareness and preventive measures against AI-generated fraud

- Support legal initiatives and policies aimed at regulating deepfake technology and punishing its malicious use

💡 Important Exam Tips for the Certified Ethical Hacker (CEH) Exam on Social Engineering

Understanding Social Engineering is crucial for the CEH exam. Here are key exam tips to help you master this topic:

1. Social Engineering Basics

- Social engineering manipulates human psychology to deceive individuals into revealing confidential information.

- Attackers exploit trust, urgency, fear, or curiosity to bypass security controls.

- Common attack vectors include emails, phone calls, social media, and face-to-face interactions.

2. Types of Social Engineering Attacks

- **Phishing**: Fraudulent emails designed to trick victims into disclosing credentials.

- **Spear Phishing**: Targeted phishing attacks aimed at specific individuals or organizations.

- **Whaling**: Phishing attacks targeting high-profile executives or decision-makers.

- **Vishing**: Voice phishing via phone calls to manipulate victims.

- **Smishing**: Phishing via SMS or mobile messaging apps.

- **Baiting**: Luring victims with fake offers or malware-infected USB drives.

- **Pretexting**: Attackers impersonate authority figures to extract information.

- **Tailgating**: Gaining unauthorized physical access by following authorized personnel.

- **Shoulder Surfing**: Observing a victim's screen or keystrokes to capture sensitive data.

- **Dumpster Diving**: Retrieving confidential documents from trash bins to gather intelligence.

3. Identity Theft and Prevention

- Use strong, unique passwords for different accounts.

- Regularly monitor financial statements and credit reports for unauthorized activity.

- Enable MFA on all sensitive accounts.

- Avoid oversharing personal details on social media.

- Secure personal documents and shred sensitive paperwork before disposal.

4. Voice Cloning Threats

- Attackers use AI-powered deep learning models to impersonate voices.

- Verify suspicious callers through a secondary communication method before acting on their requests.

- Implement AI-based detection tools to analyze speech patterns for anomalies.

- Use safe words or pre-agreed authentication phrases for verification.

5. Deepfake Attacks

- Attackers use deepfakes for fraud, misinformation, and impersonation of executives.

- Use deepfake detection tools to analyze inconsistencies in facial movements and voice patterns.

- Implement blockchain-based media verification to ensure digital content authenticity.

6. Incident Response to Social Engineering Attacks

- Establish clear incident response procedures for handling social engineering attempts.

- Create dedicated reporting channels for employees to report suspected scams.

- Conduct forensic investigations on successful attacks to identify security gaps.

- Regularly update security policies and training materials based on emerging threats.

Chapter 10: Denial-of-Service

Introduction

Denial-of-Service (DoS) and Distributed Denial-of-Service (DDoS) attacks are cybersecurity threats that disrupt the availability of online services, networks, or applications. These attacks aim to overwhelm a target's resources, rendering it inaccessible to legitimate users. A DoS attack is launched from a single source, while a DDoS attack leverages multiple compromised devices (botnets) to flood the target with malicious traffic.

DoS/DDoS attacks exploit vulnerabilities in network infrastructure, server configurations, and application-level protocols to consume system resources and cause service disruptions. Attackers use various techniques, such as traffic flooding, protocol abuse, and application-layer attacks, to cripple systems. The consequences of these attacks include operational downtime, financial losses, reputational damage, and data security risks.

Organizations must implement proactive security measures to detect and mitigate these threats. Effective countermeasures include deploying DDoS protection services, firewalls, Intrusion Prevention Systems (IPS), load balancers, and Web Application Firewalls (WAF). Additionally, monitoring network traffic, configuring rate limits, and engaging with Internet Service Providers (ISPs) help minimize the impact of attacks. Understanding DoS/DDoS attack techniques, mitigation strategies, and the role of botnets is essential for strengthening cybersecurity defenses.

DoS/DDoS Concept

Denial-of-Service (DoS) and Distributed Denial-of-Service (DDoS) attacks are malicious attempts to disrupt the availability of a network, service, or application by overwhelming it with excessive traffic or resource consumption. In a DoS attack, a single source targets a system, while in a DDoS attack, multiple compromised devices (botnets) coordinate to flood the target with traffic, making it inaccessible to legitimate users. These attacks exploit vulnerabilities in network protocols, server configurations, or application weaknesses to exhaust system resources and cause downtime.

What is a DoS Attack?

A DoS attack is an attack on a computer or network that reduces, restricts, or prevents access to system resources for legitimate users. In a DoS attack, attackers flood a victim's system with nonlegitimate service requests or traffic to overload its resources and bring down the system, leading to the unavailability of the victim's website or at least significantly reducing the victim's system or network performance. The goal of a DoS attack is to keep legitimate users from using the system, rather than to gain unauthorized access to a system or to corrupt data.

DoS attacks have various forms and target various services. The attacks may cause the following:

- Consumption of resources

- Consumption of bandwidth, disk space, CPU time, or data structures

- Actual physical destruction or alteration of network components

- Destruction of programming and files in a computer system

What is a DDoS Attack?

A DDoS attack is a large-scale, coordinated attack on the availability of services on a victim's system or network resources, and it is launched indirectly through many compromised computers (botnets) on the Internet. As defined by the World Wide Web Security FAQ, "A Distributed Denial-of-Service (DDoS) attack uses many computers to launch a coordinated DoS attack against one or more targets. Using client/server technology, the perpetrator is able to multiply the effectiveness of the denial of service significantly by harnessing the resources of multiple unwitting accomplice computers, which serve as attack platforms." The flood of incoming messages to the target system essentially forces it to shut down, thereby denying service to legitimate users.

DoS/DDoS Countermeasure

- Use DDoS mitigation services to detect and filter malicious traffic before it reaches the target system

- Deploy firewalls and intrusion prevention systems to block known attack patterns and malicious IP addresses

- Enable rate limiting and traffic filtering to prevent excessive requests from overloading servers

- Implement load balancing to distribute traffic across multiple servers and reduce the impact of an attack

- Use Web Application Firewalls (WAF) to protect against HTTP-based attacks, such as application-layer DDoS attacks

- Configure network devices to block spoofed traffic and implement ingress and egress filtering to prevent IP spoofing

- Monitor network traffic with real-time analytics to detect abnormal spikes in requests that indicate a potential attack

- Enable automated response mechanisms to quickly mitigate attacks by adjusting security policies or rerouting traffic

- Use Anycast DNS routing to distribute traffic across multiple geographically dispersed servers

- Keep systems and applications updated to patch vulnerabilities that could be exploited in DoS/DDoS attacks

- Harden server configurations to withstand high-traffic situations and reduce attack impact

- Implement SYN flood protection mechanisms such as SYN cookies to prevent TCP handshake abuse

- Utilize Content Delivery Networks (CDNs) to cache content and absorb attack traffic before it reaches the origin server

- Monitor and restrict application-layer requests to prevent excessive API calls or bot-driven attacks

- Enable blackhole routing to divert attack traffic away from the main network infrastructure

- Educate employees on DoS/DDoS attack indicators to ensure quick detection and response

- Deploy rate-based access control to limit connections from a single source and prevent excessive resource consumption

- Establish an incident response plan to quickly react to ongoing DoS/DDoS attacks and minimize service disruption

- Engage with Internet Service Providers (ISPs) and cloud security providers for additional DDoS mitigation support

DoS/DDoS Attack Techniques

Denial-of-Service (DoS) and Distributed Denial-of-Service (DDoS) attacks are methods used to disrupt the normal functioning of a server, service, or network by overwhelming it with traffic or requests. These attacks aim to exhaust resources, leading to slowdowns, outages, or total service disruption.

DoS/DDoS Attack Techniques

- **UDP Flood Attack:** An attacker sends a large number of UDP packets to random ports on a target system, causing the system to check for applications at those ports and respond with ICMP "Destination Unreachable" messages, consuming resources

- **ICMP Flood Attack:** Also known as a ping flood, this attack overwhelms the target with ICMP Echo Request (ping) packets, exhausting bandwidth and processing power

- **PoD Attack:** the Ping of Death (PoD) attack sends malformed or oversized ping packets to a system, which can crash or freeze when trying to process them due to buffer overflows

- **Smurf Attack:** An attacker sends ICMP requests with the victim's spoofed IP address to a network's broadcast address, causing all devices in the network to respond to the victim and overwhelm it

- **Pulse Wave Attack:** A high-volume attack that alternates between short bursts and inactivity, overwhelming the target during pulses and causing systems to repeatedly scale up and down, destabilizing defenses

- **Zero-day Attack:** Exploits an unknown or unpatched vulnerability in a system or application, allowing attackers to crash or disable services before defenses can react

- **NTP Amplification Attack:** Abuses Network Time Protocol (NTP) servers by sending small queries with the victim's spoofed IP, causing large responses to flood the victim's network

- **SYN Flood Attack:** An attacker sends a series of TCP SYN requests to a server but never completes the handshake, causing the server to use up resources waiting for responses

- **Fragmentation Attack:** Sends fragmented packets to confuse the target system's reassembly process, consuming resources or exploiting reassembly vulnerabilities

- **ACK Flood Attack:** Sends TCP ACK packets to the target to overwhelm firewalls or intrusion prevention systems that must process each ACK, exhausting resources

- **TCP State Exhaustion Attack:** Attempts to deplete the target's ability to maintain TCP connections by keeping many connections in a half-open or open state

- **Spoofed Session Flood Attack:** Uses fake IP addresses to flood a server with traffic that appears to come from many legitimate sessions, making it hard to trace and filter

- **HTTPS GET/POST Attack:** Targets the application layer by sending seemingly legitimate HTTPS GET or POST requests in high volumes, overloading web servers

- **Slowloris Attack:** Keeps many HTTP connections open by sending partial requests very slowly, exhausting the web server's connection pool without requiring high bandwidth

- **UDP Application Layer Flood Attack:** Targets specific UDP-based applications (like DNS or VoIP) with floods at the application layer, rather than just the transport layer

- **Multi-Vector Attack:** Combines several attack methods (e.g., SYN flood + DNS amplification + HTTP GET flood) to attack different layers at once, making mitigation harder

- **Peer-to-Peer Attack:** Exploits peer-to-peer networks by tricking many peers into sending traffic to a target system, overwhelming it with seemingly legitimate traffic

- **Permanent DoS (PDoS) Attack:** Also called "phlashing," this attack damages a system so severely (e.g., corrupting firmware) that it requires hardware replacement to recover

- **Distributed Reflection DoS (DRDoS) Attack:** Combines spoofing and amplification: an attacker sends spoofed requests to many servers, which reflect large responses to the victim, amplifying the attack

- **TCP SACK Panic Attack:** Targets a vulnerability in the TCP Selective Acknowledgment (SACK) feature, causing a kernel panic or crash in certain systems (notably Linux)
- **DDoS Extortion Attack:** Threatens to launch (or continues) a DDoS attack unless the target pays a ransom, often combined with smaller demo attacks to prove intent

DoS/DDoS Attack Countermeasures

Protect Secondary Victims

- Increase security awareness to avoid becoming part of a DDoS network
- Install and regularly update antivirus and anti-Trojan software
- Apply timely software patches for known vulnerabilities
- Disable unnecessary services and remove unused applications
- Scan all external files before opening
- Configure and regularly update built-in OS-level defenses
- Use dynamic pricing models to incentivize customers to maintain secure systems

Detect and Neutralize Handlers

- Analyze network traffic for communication between handlers, clients, and agents
- Identify and disable DDoS handlers to disrupt attack coordination
- Detect spoofed source addresses to block malicious packets

Mitigating Potential Threats

- Block spoofed outbound packets to prevent unauthorized traffic from leaving the network
- Restrict outbound connections to stop compromised systems from communicating with attackers
- Prevent exploit payloads from being effective by limiting unauthorized outbound traffic
- Block incoming packets with invalid or spoofed source IP addresses

- Trace incoming traffic to its true source to identify potential attackers

- Intercept SYN packets to protect servers from SYN-flood attacks

- Establish and manage connections on behalf of both client and server to prevent fake requests

- Merge validated half-connections to ensure only legitimate traffic reaches the server

- Control network traffic at layers 4 and 5 of the OSI model to prevent overload

- Limit the rate of incoming requests to reduce the impact of traffic spikes during DDoS attacks

Deflecting Attacks (Using Honeypots)

- Deploy honeypots to attract and monitor attacker behavior

- Use honeynets to replicate full network environments for analysis

- Utilize deception technology like **Blumira Honeypot Software** to:

  o Detect unauthorized access

  o Block malicious IPs at switch/firewall level

Mitigating Attacks

- Increase available bandwidth during DDoS attacks to prevent server downtime

- Use replicated servers to distribute traffic and balance the load

- Limit incoming traffic rates with server-centric routers to prevent overload

- Differentiate between legitimate user requests and malicious DDoS traffic

- Manage high volumes of traffic to reduce the risk of server shutdowns

- Drop excess traffic automatically when server load reaches critical levels

- Require users to complete computational puzzles to discourage compromised systems from participating in the attack

Post-Attack Forensics

- Analyze post-attack traffic logs to identify attacker behavior

- Develop new filtering strategies based on detected patterns

- Reverse-trace attack traffic to its original source

- Implement targeted blocks and create new countermeasures

- Use logs from honeypots, firewalls, and intrusion detection systems to trace attackers

- Identify the type and method of attack for future defense

- Collaborate with ISPs and law enforcement to trace attacker IPs and gather evidence

Botnets

Botnets are networks of compromised devices controlled by an attacker, often without the knowledge of the device owners. These devices can include computers, routers, and other IoT devices that have been infected with malware. Once infected, the devices, or "zombies," can be used to perform various malicious activities such as launching DDoS attacks, sending spam, or stealing sensitive data.

Defend Against Botnet

- Implement ACL filters to block traffic with spoofed source IP addresses based on RFC 3704 guidelines

- Ensure only packets from valid, allocated IP address space are allowed into the network

- Regularly update and maintain a bogon list to identify and drop packets from unallocated or reserved IP ranges

- Confirm with the ISP whether they perform RFC 3704 filtering before traffic reaches your system; if not, manage your own filtering or consider switching ISPs

- Use source IP reputation filtering tools, like Cisco Global Correlation and SensorBase Network, to identify and block traffic from known malicious sources.

- Integrate threat intelligence into intrusion prevention systems to enhance early detection and mitigation of DoS attacks

- Apply black hole filtering to silently discard unwanted traffic, particularly from botnets, before it reaches the target network

- Configure Remotely Triggered Black Hole (RTBH) filtering in coordination with the ISP, using BGP to route malicious traffic to a null interface

- Leverage DDoS mitigation services from ISPs or third-party providers to scrub and clean traffic in the cloud, preventing link saturation

- Enable features like IP Source Guard on routers and switches to block spoofed packets based on DHCP snooping or static IP bindings

---

💡 **Important Exam Tips for the Certified Ethical Hacker (CEH) Exam on Denial-of-Service (DoS) and Distributed Denial-of-Service (DDoS) Attacks**

Understanding DoS/DDoS attacks is crucial for the CEH exam. Here are key exam tips to help you master this topic:

1. DoS and DDoS Concepts:

Understand the difference between DoS (single-source attack) and DDoS (multi-source/botnet attack). Both aim to exhaust system or network resources, leading to downtime and service unavailability.

2. DoS/DDoS Attack Techniques:

Familiarize yourself with attack types such as SYN Flood, UDP Flood, ICMP Flood, Smurf Attack, Slowloris, NTP Amplification, TCP SACK Panic, and Multi-vector attacks. Know how they function and the specific layers they target (network, transport, or application).

3. Botnets:

Recognize the role of botnets (zombie networks) in DDoS attacks. Understand how compromised devices are controlled by attackers to perform large-scale attacks.

4. Common Tools for DoS/DDoS:

Be familiar with tools like Low Orbit Ion Cannon (LOIC), Low Orbit Ion Cannon (HOIC), and botnets such as Mirai. Know how attackers use these for launching DoS/DDoS campaigns.

5. Countermeasures and Defenses:

Learn mitigation strategies including the use of firewalls, Intrusion Prevention Systems (IPS), load balancers, rate limiting, SYN cookies, Web Application Firewalls (WAFs), and Content Delivery Networks (CDNs).

6. Advanced Defense Mechanisms:

Understand blackhole routing, Anycast DNS, IP reputation filtering, Remotely Triggered Black Hole (RTBH) filtering, and the use of AI/ML-based anomaly detection systems to detect and respond to attacks.

7. Application-Layer DDoS Attacks:

Know about HTTP GET/POST floods, API abuse, and Slowloris attacks. Learn how WAFs, request throttling, and secure configurations help mitigate these attacks.

8. Incident Response and Planning:

Understand the importance of having an incident response plan that includes attack detection, escalation procedures, communication protocols, and system recovery processes.

9. ISP and Cloud Provider Collaboration:

Be aware of the benefits of working with ISPs and cloud-based DDoS mitigation services to filter and scrub attack traffic before it reaches your infrastructure.

Chapter 11: Session Hijacking

Introduction

In ethical hacking, security professionals, also known as penetration testers or pen testers, go beyond merely identifying vulnerabilities, they proactively implement countermeasures to defend networks against real-world attacks. Session hijacking, a type of attack where an attacker takes control of a valid user session, poses significant risks to both users and organizations. Identifying the threat is only part of the solution; effective countermeasures are essential to mitigate such attacks and protect sensitive data. This chapter focuses on session hijacking and its countermeasures, offering insights into how ethical hackers can safeguard systems from such threats.

Session Hijacking

Session hijacking can take many forms, with attackers utilizing methods like Man-in-the-Middle (MITM) attacks, session fixation, and cookie stealing to gain unauthorized access. Understanding these attack vectors is critical for ethical hackers to implement the appropriate countermeasures. This topic will cover key strategies to prevent session hijacking, including approaches to defend against MITM attacks, methods for detecting session hijacking attempts, and essential guidelines for both web developers and users to follow.

In session hijacking an attacker takes control of an active Transmission Control Protocol (TCP) session between two systems. Because most authentication mechanisms occur only at the beginning of a session, an attacker can exploit this by gaining unauthorized access while the session is still ongoing. By intercepting the TCP traffic, the attacker may perform actions such as identity theft, data theft, or fraudulent transactions.

This attack typically exploits vulnerabilities in the session-token generation process or weaknesses in how tokens are secured. An attacker may steal or predict a valid session ID, which uniquely identifies an authenticated user, and use it to establish an unauthorized connection with the target server. Mistaking the attacker for a legitimate client, the server processes the attacker's requests as if they originated from the authenticated user.

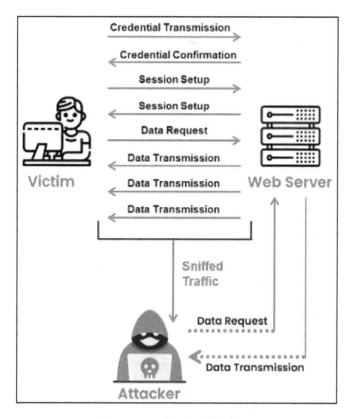

Figure 11-01: Session Hijacking

Approaches to Prevent Session Hijacking

Preventing session hijacking involves implementing security measures that protect session tokens from being intercepted, guessed, or reused by unauthorized parties. Below are key approaches used to prevent session hijacking attacks:

HTTP Strict Transport Security (HSTS)

- HSTS is a web security policy that protects HTTPS websites from Man-In-the-Middle (MITM) attacks

- It forces web browsers to communicate with the server using only HTTPS

- All insecure HTTP requests are automatically upgraded to HTTPS

- Ensures that communication between the browser and server is encrypted

- Guarantees that responses are exchanged only with an authenticated server

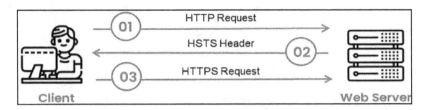

Figure 11-02: Implementation of HSTS

Token Binding

- A session ID (token) is generated when a user logs into a web application and is stored in a cookie

- The session token is used by the client to access resources on the server

- Attackers may attempt to hijack the session by capturing and reusing a valid session token

- Token binding secures communication by binding the session to the client's unique key pair

- The client generates a public-private key pair for each server connection

- The client signs the connection using its private key and sends the signature with the public key

- The server verifies the signature using the client's public key

- This ensures only the legitimate client can authenticate the session

- Even if an attacker captures the signature, they cannot reuse it or regenerate it for a different connection

- A new public-private key pair is created for each new connection

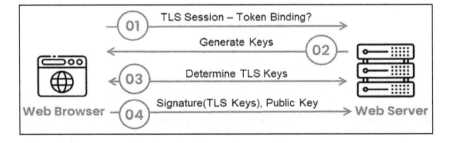

Figure 11-03: Implementation of Token Binding

MITM Attack

Attackers can leverage session hijacking to carry out various malicious activities, including Man-in-the-Middle (MITM) and Denial-of-Service (DoS) attacks. In a Man-in-the-Middle (MITM) attack, an attacker intercepts and potentially alters the communication between two parties, typically between a client and a server. By hijacking an active session, the attacker positions themselves between the client and the server, enabling them to monitor, intercept, or manipulate the data being transmitted. Both the client and server are often unaware of the presence of the attacker, believing they are communicating directly with each other. This allows the attacker to eavesdrop on sensitive data such as login credentials, personal information, and financial details, which can then be exploited for malicious purposes. In addition to capturing sensitive information, the attacker can inject malicious data into the conversation, potentially altering commands, responses, or data being transferred between the two parties. The attacker may use the MITM position to disrupt the communication or even launch additional attacks.

Approaches to Prevent MITM Attack

Man-in-the-middle (MITM) attacks are among the most prevalent types of cyberattacks, where attackers intercept communication between two endpoints. The victim is often unaware of the attack, as it is typically passive. Due to the difficulty in detecting MITM attacks, prevention requires implementing various protective measures. Below are some strategies to guard against MITM attacks:

DNS over HTTPS

- Encrypts DNS queries using the HTTPS protocol over port 443

- Prevents ISPs and attackers from monitoring DNS lookups

- Routes queries through secure HTTPS tunnels, hiding them within regular web traffic

- Only sends essential parts of the domain name to improve privacy

- Supported by major browsers like Chrome, Firefox, and Edge

- Reduces the risk of session hijacking and DNS spoofing

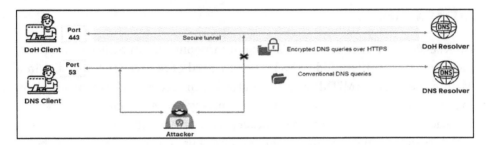

Figure 11-04: DNS over HTTPS

WPA3 Encryption

- Enhances wireless network security with stronger encryption protocols

- Prevents unauthorized users from accessing Wi-Fi networks

- Mitigates the risk of credential brute-force attacks and wireless MITM attacks

VPN

- Creates a secure, encrypted tunnel over public networks

- Safeguards data in transit between endpoints

- Prevents interception or decryption by unauthorized users

Two-Factor Authentication

- Adds a secondary verification step to user login processes

- Prevents unauthorized account access even if credentials are compromised

- Effective against session hijacking and brute-force attempts

Password Manager

- Securely stores user credentials in an encrypted format

- Generates strong, unique passwords for different accounts

- Reduces the risk of password interception and credential reuse in MITM attacks

Zero-Trust Principles

- Enforces authentication for every user and device, regardless of location

- Assumes no implicit trust, even for users within the network perimeter

- Ensures continuous verification and monitoring of access requests

Public Key Infrastructure (PKI)

- Uses digital certificates to validate the identity of communication parties

- Certificates are issued by trusted Certificate Authorities (CAs)

- Helps detect and prevent the use of forged or fraudulent certificates

Network Segmentation

- Divides the network into isolated segments or zones

- Limits the scope of access and lateral movement by attackers

- Reduces the potential impact and spread of MITM attacks within the network

Session Hijacking Detection Methods

Session hijacking attacks are often extremely difficult to detect, and users typically remain unaware unless the attacker causes noticeable disruption or damage. Some common indicators of a session hijacking attack include:

- Sudden spikes in network traffic that degrade overall system performance

- Increased server load caused by simultaneous requests from both the legitimate user and the attacker

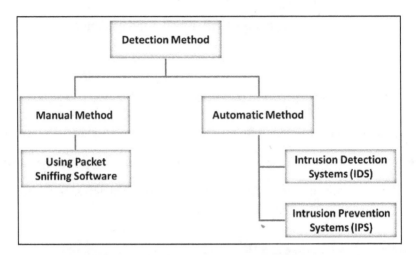

Figure 11-05: Session Hijacking Detection Methods

Manual Method

The manual method involves using packet sniffing tools like Wireshark and SteelCentral Packet Analyzer to monitor and detect session hijacking attacks. These tools capture packets transmitted over the network, which can then be analyzed using various filtering techniques to identify suspicious activity.

Forced ARP Entry

A forced ARP entry involves altering the MAC address of a compromised device in the server's ARP cache and replacing it with a different MAC address to reroute network traffic to the compromised device. This technique is useful in situations where:

- There are repeated ARP updates

- Frames are sent between the client and server with mismatched MAC addresses

- ACK storms are detected

Automatic Method

The automatic method utilizes Intrusion Detection Systems (IDS) and Intrusion Prevention Systems (IPS) to monitor incoming network traffic. If a packet matches any attack signatures in the system's internal database, the IDS triggers an alert, while the IPS proactively blocks the traffic from entering the network.

Protecting against Session Hijacking

Session hijacking is a serious threat as it exposes the victim to risks such as identity theft, fraud, and the loss of sensitive information. All networks utilizing TCP/IP are susceptible to various types of session hijacking attacks. However, adhering to the following practices can help protect against such attacks:

- Use Secure Shell (SSH) to establish a secure communication channel

- Pass authentication cookies over HTTPS connections

- Implement log-out functionality to end the user session

- Generate a session ID after a successful login and only accept session IDs generated by the server

- Ensure data in transit is encrypted and implement defense-in-depth mechanisms

- Utilize strings or long random numbers as session keys

- Use different usernames and passwords for each account

- Educate employees and minimize remote access

- Implement a timeout mechanism to destroy expired sessions

- Avoid including session IDs in the URL or query string

- Switch from a hub network to a switch network to reduce risks of ARP spoofing and other hijacking attacks

- Ensure client-side and server-side protection software are active and up-to-date

- Use strong authentication methods (e.g., Kerberos) or peer-to-peer VPNs

- Configure appropriate spoofing rules on gateways for internal and external traffic

- Utilize IDS products or ARPwatch to monitor ARP cache poisoning

- Utilize encrypted protocols in the OpenSSH suite

- Use firewalls and browser settings to confine cookies

- Protect authentication cookies with SSL

- Regularly update platform patches to address TCP/IP vulnerabilities (e.g., predictable packet sequences)

- Use IPsec to encrypt session data

- Enable browsers to verify website authenticity with network notary servers

- Implement DNS-based authentication of named entities

- Disable compression mechanisms in HTTP requests

- Restrict cross-site scripting to prevent CSRF attacks on the client side

- Upgrade web browsers to the latest versions

- Use vulnerability scanners to identify insecure HTTPS session settings on sites

- Enable the HTTPOnly property to prevent user scripts from accessing cached cookies

- Use SFTP, AS2-managed file transfer, or FTPS to send encrypted data with digital certificates

- Employ Microsoft SMB signing to enable traffic signing

- Apply SSL or TLS to reduce the likelihood of successful hijacks

- Implement IPsec to secure IP communications

- Use encrypted VPNs like PPTP and L2TP for secure remote connections

- Use multifactor authentication (MFA) to reduce unauthorized access risks, even with compromised session tokens

- Use the SameSite cookie attribute to prevent browsers from sending cookies with cross-site requests

- Monitor session activity for unusual patterns like multiple simultaneous logins from different locations, which could indicate a hijacked session

- Educate users on logging out from applications, especially on public or shared computers, and the importance of strong, unique passwords

- Bind the session to the user's IP address

- Leverage behavioral biometrics such as typing rhythms, mouse movements, and navigation patterns for continuous authentication

- Implement a challenge-response mechanism (e.g., CAPTCHA) when suspicious activity is detected

- Enforce an absolute timeout when the user is inactive, regardless of the session timeout

Web Development Guidelines to Prevent Session Hijacking

Attackers typically hijack sessions by exploiting vulnerabilities in the mechanisms used for session establishment. Web developers often overlook security, but they should follow these guidelines during development to reduce or eliminate the risk of session hijacking:

- Create session keys with long strings or random numbers to make it difficult for attackers to guess a valid session key

- Reinitialize the session ID following a successful login to mitigate the risk of session fixation attacks

- Encrypt data and session keys exchanged between the user and web servers

- Use SSL to encrypt all data in transit over the network

- Ensure the session expires immediately when the user logs out

- Prevent eavesdropping within the network

- Limit the lifespan of sessions or cookies

- Use restrictive cache directives (e.g., "Cache-Control: no-cache, no-store" and "Pragma: no-cache") in HTTP headers or equivalent META tags on all or at least sensitive web pages

- Avoid creating sessions for unauthenticated users unless necessary

- Enable HTTPOnly for cookies that store session IDs

- Use the secure flag to send cookies only over HTTPS and encrypt them before transmission

- Verify that all requests for the current session come from the same IP address and user agent

- Implement continuous device verification to confirm that the user who initiated the session is still in control

- Apply risk-based authentication at different levels before granting access to sensitive information

- Perform authentication and integrity checks between VPN endpoints

- Destroy sessions on the server side instead of relying solely on session expiration when a user is unauthenticated

- Ensure the web application can redirect HTTP requests to HTTPS via server settings or redirection techniques

- Require user re-authentication and the creation of new sessions before allowing access to sensitive functions

- Use secure web frameworks that provide strong session ID management instead of creating your own session handling

- Enforce HTTPS across all pages of the web application, not just the login page

Web Guidelines to Prevent Session Hijacking for Users

Here are some guidelines for web users to protect against session hijacking:

- Avoid clicking on links received through emails or Instant Messages (IMs)

- Use firewalls to block malicious content from entering the network

- Configure firewalls and browser settings to restrict cookie access

- Ensure the website is certified by trusted certifying authorities

- Clear browser history, offline content, and cookies after every sensitive transaction

- Prioritize HTTPS over HTTP when transmitting sensitive data

- Always log out using the logout button instead of closing the browser

- Review and disable add-ons from untrusted sites, enabling them only when necessary

- Use one-time passwords for critical transactions, such as credit card payments

- Regularly update antivirus signatures to prevent malware from stealing cookies

- Avoid conducting sensitive activities or financial transactions over public Wi-Fi

- Disable auto-connect to open Wi-Fi networks

- Keep your operating system, web browsers, and plugins up to date

- Use encrypted messaging and email services for confidential communications

- Avoid saving passwords in browsers

- Use incognito mode when browsing on shared computers

- Be cautious about granting apps access to sensitive information or features on your device

- Implement custom session handlers for securely storing and managing session tokens

---

💡 Important Exam Tips for the Certified Ethical Hacker (CEH) Exam on Session Hijacking

Understanding session hijacking is crucial for the CEH exam. Here are key exam tips to help you master this topic:

1. Session Hijacking

- Session hijacking involves an attacker taking control of a valid session between a client and a server

- Common methods include stealing session tokens, session fixation, and exploiting weak session management

- **Countermeasures:** Use secure session tokens, implement session expiration, and enforce HTTPS

2. MITM Attack

- Attackers intercept and manipulate traffic between two parties

- **Countermeasures:** Use TLS/SSL for encryption, implement HSTS, and secure DNS with DNS over HTTPS (DoH)

3. Session Hijacking Detection Methods

- **Manual Method**

    - Use packet sniffing tools like Wireshark and SteelCentral Packet Analyzer to capture and analyze network packets for signs of session hijacking

    - Filters and analysis are applied to identify unusual or suspicious activity, such as altered session tokens or abnormal traffic patterns

- **Forced ARP Entry**

    - Replace the MAC address in the ARP cache of the server to redirect traffic to a compromised machine

    - This method helps detect hijacking when issues such as repeated ARP updates, mismatched MAC addresses, or ACK storms occur

    - **Countermeasures:** Monitor and secure ARP tables to avoid unauthorized entries

- **Automatic Method**

    - Use Intrusion Detection Systems (IDS) and Intrusion Prevention Systems (IPS) to automatically monitor network traffic

    - IDS generates alerts for traffic matching known attack signatures, while IPS can block malicious traffic in real-time

    - **Countermeasures:** Regularly update attack signatures and ensure proper configuration of IDS/IPS to respond to threats promptly

4. Web Development Guidelines to Prevent Session Hijacking

- Use secure cookies with HttpOnly and Secure flags, regenerate session IDs after login

- Implement session expiration, use strong session identifiers, and enforce HTTPS for all pages

- Avoid exposing session IDs in URLs, use token binding, and apply regular session checks

Chapter 12: Evading IDS, Firewalls, and Honeypots

Introduction

In cybersecurity, attackers constantly develop techniques to bypass security mechanisms such as Intrusion Detection Systems (IDS), firewalls, endpoint security, and honeypots. These evasion tactics allow threat actors to avoid detection while infiltrating networks, exfiltrating data, or launching attacks. Understanding these methods and implementing robust countermeasures is essential to maintaining a secure environment. This chapter explores common evasion techniques and effective strategies to mitigate them.

Evading IDS

Intrusion Detection Systems (IDS) monitor and analyze network traffic to detect suspicious activity. Attackers evade IDS by using techniques such as fragmentation (splitting malicious payloads across multiple packets), encryption (hiding attack payloads in encrypted traffic), and polymorphic malware (modifying code to avoid signature detection). They may also inject junk data or alter packet headers to confuse the IDS, making it difficult to identify real threats.

Defend against IDS Evasion

- Disable switch ports linked to known malicious hosts
- Conduct a thorough examination of ambiguous network traffic to identify potential threats
- Utilize TCP FIN or Reset (RST) packets to terminate malicious TCP connections
- Detect and mitigate polymorphic shellcode by identifying nop opcodes beyond 0x90
- Educate users on attack patterns and maintain regular system and network device updates
- Strategically deploy IDS based on network topology, traffic characteristics, and host count
- Implement a traffic normalizer to eliminate ambiguities before traffic reaches the IDS
- Ensure IDS processes fragmented packets correctly and reassembles them in the right order
- Set up a DNS server for client resolvers within routers or similar network devices

- Strengthen security measures on communication devices, including modems and routers
- If feasible, block ICMP TTL expired packets at the external interface and adjust the TTL value to ensure end hosts receive packets properly
- Frequently update the antivirus signature database
- Utilize traffic normalization tools within IDS to prevent evasions
- Log attack-related details such as attacker IP, victim IP, and timestamp for future analysis
- Properly configure Snort rules to prevent DoS attacks caused by false positives.
- Regularly check Snort rule directories for injected malicious scripts
- Adopt a hybrid exploit protection method combining signature-based detection with advanced statistical and behavioral analysis to counter zero-day exploits
- Configure IDS rules to identify tunneling and obfuscation tactics
- Apply heuristic or behavioral analysis to detect polymorphic threats
- Discard packets with spoofed or invalid source IP addresses
- Deploy high-interaction honeypots that mimic real services
- Configure IDS to effectively manage overlapping packet fragments
- Use IDS solutions capable of reconstructing fragmented sessions

Evading Firewalls

Firewalls filter incoming and outgoing traffic based on predefined security rules. Attackers bypass firewalls using techniques like IP spoofing (disguising their real IP address), tunneling (hiding malicious traffic within legitimate protocols like DNS or ICMP), and port hopping (switching between open ports to maintain access). Another method is manipulating application-layer traffic, such as sending malformed HTTP requests, to exploit firewall misconfigurations.

Defend Against Firewall Evasion

- Configure the firewall to block intruder IP addresses
- Set firewall rules to deny all traffic by default and allow only necessary services
- If possible, assign a dedicated user ID for running firewall services instead of using an administrator or root account
- Set up a remote syslog server and implement strict security measures to protect it from malicious access
- Regularly monitor firewall logs and investigate any suspicious activities
- Disable all FTP connections to and from the network by default
- Maintain a record of all inbound and outbound traffic permitted through the firewall and periodically review it

- Conduct routine risk assessments to identify and eliminate weak firewall rules
- Monitor user access to the firewall and restrict configuration modifications to authorized personnel
- Inform the security policy administrator about firewall modifications and maintain proper documentation
- Limit physical access to firewall hardware to prevent unauthorized tampering
- Perform regular backups of firewall rulesets and configuration files
- Schedule periodic firewall security audits to ensure continued protection
- Enable integrated HTTPS/TLS inspection to detect and prevent evasion techniques
- Utilize HTTP Evader for automated testing of potential firewall evasions
- Implement deep packet inspection at the application layer for enhanced security
- Restrict the number of concurrent connections allowed per IP address
- Filter traffic based on geographical locations to minimize risk
- Design firewall rules based on user behavior patterns rather than relying solely on IP addresses
- Implement a zero-trust security framework that assumes no inherent trust for internal or external traffic

Evading Endpoint Security

Endpoint security solutions, including antivirus and behavior-based detection tools, protect individual devices from threats. Attackers evade these defenses by using fileless malware (executing malicious code directly in memory), rootkits (hiding malware deep in the system), and process injection (injecting malicious code into legitimate system processes). They also use obfuscation techniques to disguise malware as legitimate files, making it harder to detect.

Defend Against Endpoint Security Evasion

- Ensure antivirus solutions utilize advanced detection techniques, including behavioral analysis, machine learning, and cloud-based threat intelligence
- Keep all operating systems and applications updated to patch security vulnerabilities
- Implement network segmentation to prevent malicious activity from spreading across endpoints
- Apply the principle of least privilege to limit malware propagation risks
- Define specific roles with designated privileges, allowing only authorized users to have administrative access

- Enable Multi-Factor Authentication (MFA) for accessing critical systems and sensitive data to enhance security
- Use VPNs and other secure access methods for remote connections to endpoints
- Deploy decoys or honeypots to mislead attackers and detect threats
- Maintain comprehensive logs of all network activities and leverage SIEM solutions for analysis
- Use code signing certificates to validate the authenticity of executable files and scripts
- Conduct regular security audits and penetration tests to assess the effectiveness of endpoint security measures
- Implement MAC address filtering to restrict network access to authorized devices only
- Perform real-time network monitoring to identify abnormal activities
- Utilize security techniques like Address Space Layout Randomization (ASLR), Data Execution Prevention (DEP), and Control Flow Integrity (CFI) to safeguard endpoint memory
- Deploy File Integrity Monitoring (FIM) solutions to track changes in critical system files and directories
- Enforce USB security policies to prevent malware infiltration through external storage devices
- Use Data Loss Prevention (DLP) tools to monitor and control sensitive data movement within and outside the organization
- Establish policies restricting the transfer of confidential information via removable media or email

Evading NAC

Network Access Control (NAC) restricts unauthorized devices from connecting to a network. Attackers evade NAC by MAC address spoofing (impersonating an authorized device), VLAN hopping (abusing network segmentation to access restricted areas), and rogue DHCP servers (spoofing legitimate network services to trick devices into connecting). Some sophisticated attacks involve using compromised credentials to gain access to network resources.

Defend Against NAC Evasion

- Establish clear policies defining access controls, authentication requirements, and remediation procedures for noncompliant devices
- Implement device profiling to detect and classify devices attempting to connect, helping identify unauthorized or suspicious activity

- Require Multi-Factor Authentication (MFA) for accessing sensitive network resources to minimize unauthorized access risks
- Apply Role-Based Access Control (RBAC) to restrict resource access based on user roles, preventing lateral movement by attackers
- Segregate critical network resources into isolated segments to reduce the impact of NAC evasion
- Utilize Virtual Local Area Networks (VLANs) to confine devices to specific network segments
- Conduct routine security audits and vulnerability assessments to identify and address weaknesses in the NAC system
- Enforce MAC address filtering to permit only authorized devices on the network
- Adopt a zero-trust security model, requiring verification of every user and device at every access point
- Deploy endpoint security solutions that provide antimalware, antiphishing, and firewall protection
- Use RBAC to uphold the principle of least privilege, ensuring users only access what is necessary
- Share threat intelligence with the security community to strengthen collective defenses against NAC evasion and cyber threats
- Integrate NAC solutions with SIEM platforms to correlate NAC events with firewall logs, IDS/IPS alerts, and endpoint security data
- Implement advanced authentication mechanisms such as certificate-based authentication or biometrics for enhanced NAC security
- Conduct proactive threat-hunting activities to detect and mitigate NAC evasion attempts

Anti-virus Evasion

Antivirus software detects and removes known threats based on signatures and behavior analysis. Attackers evade antivirus by using polymorphic and metamorphic malware (altering code structure to avoid signature detection), packers and crypters (encrypting malicious payloads to bypass scanning), and disabling security services. Some attackers also use steganography (hiding malware within legitimate files, such as images or PDFs) to remain undetected.

Defend Against Anti-virus Evasion

- Deploy antivirus software that utilizes behavior-based detection, machine learning, and heuristic analysis to detect and block unknown threats

- Keep antivirus software up to date to ensure it includes the latest threat intelligence, detection algorithms, and malware signatures
- Enable real-time protection in antivirus solutions to guard against malware and other security threats
- Segment the network to limit malware outbreaks and restrict unauthorized lateral movement across sensitive systems
- Educate users about the risks of downloading files from untrusted sources, clicking suspicious links, and opening attachments from unknown senders
- Ensure operating systems, applications, and firmware are regularly updated to patch known vulnerabilities
- Use application whitelisting to allow only approved programs to run, reducing the attack surface
- Deploy monitoring tools to detect suspicious activities such as unauthorized file modifications, process injections, and abnormal network traffic
- Utilize sandbox environments to safely execute and analyze potentially malicious files in isolation
- Implement SIEM solutions to centralize log collection and detect abnormal activities or evasion attempts across the network
- Use tools to analyze scripts in real-time to identify and block malicious documents and attachments
- Strengthen security by integrating multiple layers of defense, including firewalls, Intrusion Detection Systems (IDS), and Intrusion Prevention Systems (IPS)
- Deploy signature-less detection techniques, such as anomaly detection and AI-based threat identification, to detect novel malware behavior without relying on known signatures
- Enforce the principle of least privilege, granting users only the access necessary for their roles to limit the potential impact of malware
- Use secure remote access methods, such as VPNs, to minimize exposure to external threats

Honeypot

Honeypots are security traps designed to lure attackers and study their behavior. Skilled attackers detect and evade honeypots by analyzing system responses, checking for unrealistic network behavior (such as unused services being active), or probing for inconsistencies in system configurations. Some attackers even deploy fake attacks or trigger false positives to mislead security analysts and waste their resources.

Defend Against Honeypot

- Measure response times of network services; honeypots often introduce additional latency due to logging and monitoring overhead
- Observe outbound traffic patterns, honeypots may communicate with monitoring systems differently than legitimate systems
- Be cautious when interacting with well-known honeypot ports (e.g., 2222 for Cowrie SSH honeypot) to avoid detection
- Employ strong encryption (TLS, SSH, VPNs) to prevent honeypots from capturing sensitive data in plaintext
- Test system behaviors, some honeypots may not perfectly replicate real systems and could have abnormal responses to commands
- Reduce excessive port scanning or reconnaissance activities to avoid triggering honeypots designed to detect such actions
- Check system uptime and logs, honeypots are often newly deployed or frequently restarted, which can be a red flag
- Deploy IDS/IPS evasion strategies such as fragmented packets or encrypted payloads to bypass honeypots that rely on deep packet inspection
- Refrain from engaging with suspicious or non-critical systems that could be set up as honeypots
- Validate DNS and reverse DNS lookups, some honeypots use deceptive DNS entries; checking if a system's hostname and reverse DNS match can help detect inconsistencies
- Instead of aggressive scanning, use passive reconnaissance techniques like packet sniffing to avoid triggering honeypots
- Some honeypots emulate services without having an actual underlying file system, which can be detected by attempting to access system files
- Use tools like Nmap and pof to compare OS and service fingerprints against expected configurations to identify anomalies
- Some honeypots are used for malware analysis, advanced malware can use sandbox detection techniques to avoid executing in these environments

Important Exam Tips for the Certified Ethical Hacker (CEH) Exam on Evading IDS, Firewalls, and Honeypots

It is important to know about common evasion techniques and effective strategies to mitigate them. Here are key exam tips to help you master this topic:

1. **Evading IDS**

- Intrusion Detection Systems (IDS) monitor network traffic for suspicious activities

- Attackers evade IDS using techniques like fragmentation, encryption, polymorphic malware, or obfuscation to disguise malicious traffic
- **Countermeasure:** Ensure packets originate from IDS-protected paths; otherwise, conduct deep inspections on non-IDS paths

2. **Evading Firewalls**

- Firewalls control incoming and outgoing network traffic based on security rules
- Attackers bypass firewalls using methods like tunneling, spoofing, and encrypted payloads
- **Countermeasure:** Define specific source and destination IP addresses, along with corresponding ports, in firewall rules

3. **Evading Endpoint Security**

- Endpoint security solutions detect and block malware or unauthorized access
- Attackers evade these protections using fileless malware, rootkits, and code injection techniques
- **Countermeasure:** Implement application whitelisting to ensure only approved applications can run on network devices

4. **Evading NAC**

- Network Access Control (NAC) ensures only authorized devices can access a network
- Attackers bypass NAC using MAC address spoofing, rogue DHCP servers, or exploiting weak authentication methods
- **Countermeasure:** Ensure NAC policies are enforced dynamically, allowing real-time adjustments based on security threats or changing requirements

5. **Anti-virus Evasion**

- Traditional antivirus solutions rely on signature-based detection
- Attackers evade antivirus by using polymorphic malware, packers, and encryption to modify malicious code dynamically
- **Countermeasure:** Implement endpoint protection (EPP) solutions that offer additional security layers beyond traditional antivirus, including Endpoint Detection and Response (EDR)

6. **Honeypot**

- Honeypots are decoy systems designed to lure attackers and study their behavior
- Attackers recognize and evade honeypots by analyzing system responses, checking for inconsistencies, or avoiding interaction with suspicious hosts
- **Countermeasure:** Regularly scan the network for unauthorized or unexpected services that might indicate a honeypot

Chapter 13: Hacking Web Servers

Introduction

In ethical hacking, penetration testers play a vital role in identifying and addressing security weaknesses to protect networked systems. One of the most critical components to secure is the web server, which is responsible for hosting websites and services accessible over the internet. These servers are prime targets for attackers due to their visibility and the sensitive information they often handle.

Web servers are critical components in delivering web-based services, making them prime targets for cyberattacks. This chapter explores the various techniques attackers use to exploit vulnerabilities in web servers, including direct attacks, misconfigurations, and protocol abuse. The chapter also provides detailed countermeasures for securing web servers through patch management, proper configuration, input validation, and monitoring practices.

Web Server Attacks

Web servers are frequent targets for attackers because they are publicly accessible and often store or process sensitive information. When misconfigured or left unpatched, web servers can become vulnerable entry points for a variety of cyberattacks. Understanding these attacks is essential for both defending web infrastructure and learning how hackers exploit them.

One common type of attack is directory traversal, where an attacker attempts to access restricted directories and files outside the web root by manipulating file paths in the URL. For example, using sequences like ../../ can allow access to sensitive files such as system passwords or configuration files. Denial-of-Service (DoS) and Distributed Denial-ofService (DDoS) attacks aim to overwhelm a web server with excessive traffic or requests, making the server crash or become unresponsive, thereby disrupting business operations and availability.

Code injection attacks are also prevalent. These include SQL injection, which targets databases by inserting malicious SQL commands through input fields, and command injection, which involves executing system-level commands through a vulnerable web application. Such attacks can lead to data theft, unauthorized access, or full control over the server.

Cross-Site Scripting (XSS) is another major threat, where attackers inject malicious scripts into web pages viewed by users. These scripts can steal session cookies or

trick users into performing unintended actions. Similarly, Cross-Site Request Forgery (CSRF) involves tricking users into submitting requests unknowingly, such as changing passwords or making transactions, by exploiting the trust a web application has in the user's browser.

File inclusion attacks, such as Local File Inclusion (LFI) and Remote File Inclusion (RFI), involve tricking the server into executing malicious files. LFI includes files already on the server, while RFI fetches and runs remote malicious scripts. Both can result in code execution and system compromise. Authentication bypass techniques, including brute-force attacks, session hijacking, or exploiting logic flaws, are used to gain unauthorized access to secure parts of a web application.

In some cases, attackers manage to upload a web shell, which is a malicious script (often PHP) that provides remote command-line access to the server. This can give the attacker full control over the system. Web server misconfigurations are also a major security risk. Leaving default credentials unchanged, enabling directory listing, or running in debug mode can expose sensitive data or make the server easier to compromise.

Man-in-the-Middle (MitM) attacks occur when attackers intercept communication between the client and the web server, often due to a lack of HTTPS or improper SSL/TLS configuration. This can lead to the theft of login credentials, sensitive information, or even session hijacking.

Web Server Attack Countermeasures

Some countermeasures for preventing web server attacks are as follows:

- Configure firewalls to block suspicious incoming traffic from known malicious IP addresses or geographies

- Deploy Intrusion Detection Systems (IDS) and Intrusion Prevention Systems (IPS) such as Snort to detect and block web server attack attempts, including SQL injection, XSS, and others

- Monitor web traffic patterns closely to identify abnormal behaviors such as excessive requests to login or search pages, indicating a possible DoS attack

- Implement access controls to limit IP addresses or subnets that can access certain parts of the server (e.g., administrative panels or sensitive databases)

- Use secure coding practices and input validation to prevent attacks such as SQL injection and Cross-Site Scripting (XSS)

- Configure Content Security Policy (CSP) to mitigate the risk of XSS attacks by restricting what scripts can run on web pages

- Restrict file uploads to trusted formats and ensure proper file validation to prevent malicious code from being executed on the server

- Regularly patch and update software to fix vulnerabilities that attackers might exploit. Apply updates to server software, web applications, and any plugins or frameworks used

- Implement rate limiting for HTTP requests to reduce the impact of brute force attacks and automated script attacks, such as login attempts

- Encrypt sensitive data transmitted via HTTPS to protect data in transit and prevent man-in-the-middle (MITM) attacks

- Configure Web Application Firewalls (WAFs) to filter out malicious traffic targeting known vulnerabilities in web applications

- Segment the network into smaller isolated zones so that if an attack compromises one section, it does not spread easily to others

- Utilize private IP addresses for internal networks and implement Network Address Translation (NAT) to hide internal IP addresses from external visibility

Patch Management

Patch Management refers to the process of identifying, acquiring, testing, and installing software patches or updates to systems, applications, and networks. These patches typically address security vulnerabilities, fix bugs, or improve the functionality of the software. The goal of patch management is to ensure that systems are up-to-date, secure, and operating efficiently.

Patches and Updates Countermeasures

Some countermeasures for implementing secure and effective patch management are as follows.

- Define a formal policy that includes roles, responsibilities, and procedures for identifying, evaluating, and deploying patches consistently across all systems

- Apply a risk-based approach by prioritizing critical security patches for high-risk systems such as internet-facing web servers or systems handling sensitive data

- Keep a current list of all hardware and software assets, endpoints, services, and dependencies to ensure full patch coverage

- Conduct an extensive risk assessment to determine which network segments are most vulnerable or at high risk and should be patched first

- Leverage tools like Microsoft WSUS, SCCM, SolarWinds Patch Manager, or similar systems to automate detection, testing, and deployment of patches

- Automation ensures timely updates and reduces human error

- Deploy an alerting system to notify about patch availability or failures

- Before deploying patches to production, test them on a representative non-production environment to avoid disrupting business-critical systems

- Read and peer-review all relevant documentation before applying any hotfix or security patch

- Ensure consistency in patch levels across systems, especially domain controllers (DCs)

- Schedule server outages for patching, and make sure a complete set of backup tapes and emergency repair disks is available

- Always perform system backups before applying patches to allow for recovery if issues occur

- Keep a back-out plan to restore systems to their previous state in case of failed patch implementation

- Implement a regular patching schedule (e.g., monthly or bi-weekly), with flexibility for emergency patching needs

- For zero-day vulnerabilities or actively exploited threats, deploy out-of-band patches immediately without waiting for the regular cycle

- Regularly monitor vendors' security bulletins and mailing lists for vulnerability disclosures and patch releases

- Conduct regular audits to verify that patches have been successfully applied

- Use reporting tools to monitor patch status across systems

- Apply all updates, regardless of type, on an "as-needed" basis, based on impact and urgency

- Disable all unused script extension mappings

- Avoid using default configurations shipped with web servers

- Use virtual patches to provide additional identification and logging capabilities where physical patching isn't possible

- Establish a disaster recovery plan to handle patch management failures

- Train IT personnel on how to evaluate and deploy patches safely

- Ensure that patching is part of post-incident remediation to close exploited vulnerabilities and prevent recurrence

- Make patch management and security update methodology a standardized part of the software development lifecycle (SDLC)

- Reduce exposure to third-party risks by limiting the number of different software versions in use

Protocols and Accounts

Protocols and accounts are fundamental to secure communication and access control in networked systems. Protocols such as HTTP, HTTPS, FTP, SSH, and SMTP define how data is exchanged between devices and applications across the network. Accounts represent users or services that require authentication and authorization to access systems or resources. Improperly configured protocols or poorly managed accounts can expose systems to attacks such as unauthorized access, data breaches, and privilege escalation.

Securing these components is essential to maintaining the integrity, confidentiality, and availability of the IT infrastructure.

Protocols and Accounts Countermeasures

Countermeasures: Protocols

The following are various countermeasures for using secure protocols on web servers:

- Block all unnecessary ports, ICMP traffic, and unnecessary protocols

- Harden the TCP/IP stack and consistently apply the latest software patches and updates to system software

- If insecure protocols such as Telnet, SMTP, and FTP are used, then take appropriate measures to provide secure authentication and communication, for example, by using IPsec policies

- If remote access is needed, ensure that remote connections are secured properly by using tunneling and encryption protocols

- Use secure protocols such as Transport Layer Security (TLS)/SSL for communicating with the web server

- Ensure that unidentified FTP servers operate in an innocuous part of the directory tree that is different from the web server's tree

- Ensure that the HTTP service banner is properly configured to cover the details of the host device like OS version and type

- Isolate the supporting servers such as LDAP servers from the local subnet to filter out the traffic through a firewall before entering the local network

- Ensure that all the file transfer applications through the web server are done through FTPS for better data encryption and protection

- Redirect all HTTP traffic to HTTPS to ensure data is encrypted in transit

- Use HSTS headers to force browsers to use secure connections, preventing downgrade attacks

- Automate the renewal process for SSL/TLS certificates to avoid the use of expired certificates

- Implement rate-limiting to mitigate DDoS attacks that target the SSL/TLS handshake process

Countermeasures: Accounts

The following countermeasures can be adopted to secure user accounts on a web server:

- Remove all unused modules and application extensions

- Disable unused default user accounts created during the installation of an OS

- When creating a new web root directory, grant the appropriate (least possible) NTFS permissions to anonymous users of the IIS web server to access the web content

- Eliminate unnecessary database users and stored procedures and follow the principle of least privilege for the database application to defend against SQL query poisoning

- Use secure web permissions, NTFS permissions, and .NET Framework access control mechanisms, including URL authorization

- Slow down brute-force and dictionary attacks with strong password policies and implement audits and alerts for login failures

- Run processes using least privileged accounts as well as least privileged services and user accounts

- Limit the administrator or root-level access to the minimum number of users and maintain a record of the same

- Maintain logs of all user activity in an encrypted form on the web server or in a separate machine on the intranet

- Disable all noninteractive accounts that should exist but do not require an interactive login

- Use secure VPN networks such as OpenVPN while accessing multi-server platforms or accessing data from cross-server network models, which helps use one account for multiple server access

- Use password managers such as KeePass to maintain a proper password policy for multiple user accounts

- Enable the Separation of Duties (SoD) feature on the server config settings

- Force users to periodically change passwords for their accounts by creating a password expiry policy

- Enable the user account locking feature by setting a limit on the number of failed login attempts

- Implement 2FA or MFA as an additional layer of security for user accounts

- Use CAPTCHA challenges on login and registration pages to prevent automated bot attacks

- Use security questions with unpredictable answers as an additional authentication factor or for account recovery

- Use strong, one-way hashing algorithms such as bcrypt, scrypt, or Argon2 to securely store passwords

- Design secure account recovery processes that verify a user's identity without exposing the account to takeover risks

Files and Directories

Files and directories are essential components of operating systems and web applications, used to store, organize, and manage data and code. Improper permissions, directory exposure, or lack of input validation can make these elements vulnerable to attacks such as directory traversal, unauthorized file access, and malicious file uploads. Attackers may exploit insecure file handling to access sensitive information, execute arbitrary code, or gain control over a system. Securing files and directories is crucial to maintaining system integrity and preventing data leakage or compromise.

Files and Directories Countermeasures

The following countermeasures can be adopted for securing files and directories on a web server:

- Eliminate unnecessary files within .jar files

- Eliminate sensitive configuration information within the byte code

- Avoid mapping virtual directories between two different servers or over a network

- Monitor and check all network services logs, website access logs, database server logs (e.g., Microsoft SQL Server, MySQL, and Oracle), and OS logs frequently

- Disable the serving of directory listings

- Eliminate non-web files such as archive files, backup files, text files, and header/include files

- Disable the serving of certain file types by creating a resource map

- Ensure that web applications or website files and scripts are stored in a partition or drive separate from that of the OS, logs, and any other system files

- Run the web server within a sandbox directory for preventing access to system files

- Avoid all non-web file types from being referenced in a URL

- Run the web server processes with the least required privileges and give access only to the necessary directories

- Exclude meta characters while processing user inputs to ensure proper filtering of inputs

- Employ file integrity checkers to verify web content and intrusion detection

- If an application allows file uploads, the uploaded files are scanned for malware and stored outside the web root

- Use WAF to protect against common web-based attacks such as SQL injection, which can lead to unauthorized file access

- Use SFTP instead of FTP to encrypt file transfers

- Ensure that the configuration files (e.g., .htaccess, web.config) are secure and not accessible from the Web

- Implement version control for web application files to track changes and revert to previous versions if necessary

Web Server Hacking Attempts

Web servers are frequent targets for attackers due to their accessibility over the internet and their potential to host valuable or sensitive data. Hackers attempt to exploit vulnerabilities in web servers through various techniques such as brute force attacks, exploiting misconfigurations, or taking advantage of unpatched vulnerabilities. Common methods of web server hacking include directory traversal, DoS/DDoS attacks, code injection, Cross-Site Scripting (XSS), and file inclusion attacks. Proper protection and monitoring of web servers are essential to prevent unauthorized access, data theft, or server compromise.

Countermeasures to Defend against Web Server Hacking Attempts

Some countermeasures for protecting against web server hacking attempts are as follows:

Port Management

- Monitor all ports regularly to prevent unauthorized or unnecessary traffic

- Do not allow unrestricted public access to port 80 (HTTP) or port 443 (HTTPS)

- Restrict and encrypt intranet traffic to protect internal communications

- Use firewall rules or blackhole routing to block traffic from spoofed IP addresses

Server Certificates

- Use direct validation of certificates

- Use protocols that don't rely on third-party validation

- Allow domains to securely inspect their certificates using trusted credentials

- Use strong cryptographic methods to enhance server identity validation

- Ensure certificate date ranges are valid and aligned with intended use

- Verify that certificates haven't been revoked and that chains lead to a trusted root

Machine.config Hardening

- Map protected resources to HttpForbiddenHandler and remove unused HttpModules

- Disable tracing and debug modes (<trace enable="false"/>)

- Prevent detailed ASP.NET errors from being sent to the client

- Review and secure session state settings

Code Access Security

- Apply secure coding practices to prevent source-code disclosure and input-based attacks

- Restrict code execution permissions from the internet or intranet sources

- Block path traversal using IIS configurations and restrict access to system utilities with ACLs

- Regularly install patches and updates to close vulnerabilities

System and File-Level Protections

- Apply restricted ACLs and block remote registry administration

- Secure the SAM database (for stand-alone servers)

- Lock down access to the metabase file with NTFS permissions

- Remove unnecessary ISAPI filters and script mappings

- Eliminate unused file shares and administration shares

- Relocate sites and virtual directories to non-system partitions

- Use IIS permissions to restrict access to site resources

- Enable auditing and secure log files with NTFS permissions

Infrastructure and Deployment Best Practices

- Use a dedicated machine for web hosting

- Avoid installing IIS on a domain controller

- Physically secure the web server in a restricted location

- Don't connect the server to the internet before hardening it

- Limit local login to administrators only

- Configure separate anonymous accounts for each hosted application

- Limit server capabilities to only required web technologies

- Store website files and scripts on a separate partition or drive

Session and User Control

- Use server-side session tracking with timestamps, IPs, and connection metadata

- Implement role-based access control (RBAC) and the principle of least privilege

Traffic Filtering and Network Security

- Screen and filter all incoming traffic

- Implement firewalls to manage traffic flow based on defined rules

- Use anti-bot tools such as DataDome to detect and stop botnets

- Use VPNs, HTTPS, and network segmentation to protect communications

- Deploy Intrusion Detection and Prevention Systems (IDPS) to detect malicious activity

HTTP Response-Splitting and Web Cache Poisoning

HTTP Response-Splitting and Web Cache Poisoning are two related attacks that exploit vulnerabilities in web servers and web applications. HTTP Response-Splitting occurs when an attacker injects malicious headers into the response sent by the server, effectively splitting the response into multiple parts. This can lead to various consequences, including cache poisoning, cross-site scripting (XSS), and redirecting users to malicious websites. Web Cache Poisoning involves manipulating the cache of a proxy server or CDN by injecting harmful content, which can then be served to other users who request the same resource. Both attacks rely on improperly sanitized or validated user input and can be used to bypass security measures or deceive users.

Defend against HTTP Response-Splitting and Web Cache Poisoning

Some countermeasures for defending against HTTP Response-Splitting and Web Cache Poisoning are as follows:

- Validate and sanitize all user inputs, especially those that influence HTTP headers or response content, to prevent malicious data from being injected into responses

- Ensure that user-generated data is encoded or escaped properly before being included in HTTP headers to avoid unintended header manipulations

- Configure web servers and proxy caches to reject or discard suspicious or malformed responses that could be exploited for splitting or poisoning

- Use secure, modern HTTP response headers and ensure that cookies, redirects, and other sensitive data are handled appropriately to prevent injection attacks

- Avoid placing user-controlled input directly into HTTP headers such as Location, Set-Cookie, or Content-Type without proper validation and sanitization

- Implement cache-control headers such as Cache-Control: no-store to prevent sensitive information from being cached at intermediate proxies and CDNs

- Use web application firewalls (WAFs) to detect and block malicious traffic aimed at exploiting response-splitting vulnerabilities

- Regularly audit and monitor web traffic for abnormal behavior, such as unexpected redirects or changes in cached content

- Ensure that cache configurations on proxy servers and CDNs are properly set to prevent unauthorized content from being cached or served to users

- Use input validation libraries or frameworks that automatically handle escaping, encoding, and sanitizing data to reduce the risk of HTTP response-splitting

- Apply strict validation and checking of HTTP response codes to avoid inadvertently allowing malicious responses to be cached

DNS Hijacking

DNS Hijacking, also known as DNS redirection, is an attack where a malicious actor intercepts or alters the Domain Name System (DNS) resolution process. This attack redirects users from legitimate websites to fraudulent or malicious ones without their knowledge. It can be performed by compromising DNS servers, modifying local DNS settings on a user's device, or through malware infections. DNS hijacking is used for phishing, malware distribution, credential theft, or surveillance, and can affect individuals, enterprises, and service providers.

Defend against DNS Hijacking

The following techniques can be used to defend against DNS hijacking:

- Choose a registrar accredited by the Internet Corporation for Assigned Names and Numbers (ICANN) and encourage them to set REGISTRAR-LOCK on the domain name.

- Safeguard the registrant's account information.

- Include DNS hijacking in incident response and business continuity planning.

- Use DNS monitoring tools/services to monitor the IP address of the DNS server and set alerts.

- Avoid downloading audio and video codecs and other downloaders from untrusted websites.

- Install an antivirus program and update it regularly.

- Change the default router password.

- Restrict zone transfers and use script blockers in the browser.

- Domain Name System Security Extensions (DNSSEC) adds an extra layer to DNS that prevents it from being hacked.

- Strong password policies and user management further enhances security.

- When signing up for DNS servers with DNS service providers, learn who to contact when an issue occurs, how to receive good-quality reception and support, and whether the DNS server's infrastructure is hardened against attacks.

- Use a master–slave DNS and configure the master without Internet access. Maintain two slave servers so that even if an attacker hacks a slave, it will update only when it receives an update from the master.

- The constant monitoring of DNS servers ensures that a domain name returns the correct IP address.

- Change the default username and password of the router. Keep the firmware up-to-date for ensuring safety from new vulnerabilities.

- VPN service establishes VPN-encrypted tunnels for secure private communication over the Internet. This feature protects messages from eavesdropping and unauthorized access.

- Use firewall protection services to safeguard the original DNS resolvers and filter out the rogue DNS resolver traffic.

- Maintain proper protection systems such as MFA and hardware security to ensure controlled access to the DNS server.

- Install script blocker extensions in the browser.

- Use only secured and reputed VPN networks instead of free VPN services, which can track your activities and record them for future use.

- Use ACLs to restrict who can query DNS servers, thereby reducing the risk of malicious queries leading to hijacking

💡 **Important Exam Tips for the Certified Ethical Hacker (CEH) Exam on Hacking Web Servers**

Understanding how to hack web servers is crucial for the CEH exam. Here are key exam tips to help you master this topic:

1. Fundamentals of Web Server Hacking: Web servers are prime targets, so ethical hackers assess them to prevent data theft, defacement, or full compromise.

- **Common Web Server Vulnerabilities:** Typical flaws include misconfigurations, injection attacks, XSS, file inclusion, weak authentication, and DoS risks.

- **Web Server Attack Techniques:** Attackers use directory traversal, web shell uploads, and response manipulation to exploit and gain control over servers.

- **Tools for Web Server Attacks and Analysis:** Tools like Nikto, Burp Suite, Nmap, Metasploit, and DirBuster help identify and exploit web server vulnerabilities.

- **Web Server Security Countermeasures:** Mitigate threats using patching, WAFs, secure configs, input validation, and strong access controls.

2. File and Directory Security: Restrict access and uploads, disable browsing, and monitor for unauthorized file changes to secure server files.

- **SSL/TLS and Protocol Hardening:** Use HTTPS with strong ciphers and certificates, and disable outdated protocols to secure communications.

- **Real-World Testing Techniques:** Regularly test web servers using black-box and white-box methods, IDS, and OWASP-based assessments.

3. Web Server Defense Tips

Break down defenses by category in your mind:

- **Ports:** Monitor all ports, restrict 80/443, block spoofed IPs

- **Certificates:** Know how to validate and verify authenticity

- **Machine.config:** Focus on disabling debugging and unused modules

- **File/System Security:** Remove ISAPI filters, restrict NTFS permissions

- **Code Access Security:** Secure coding, path traversal protection, ACLs

- **Deployment:** Never install IIS on a domain controller, use separate servers

- **Traffic & Monitoring:** Firewalls, IDPS, anti-bot tools, centralized logging

4. Monitoring and Incident Response

- Implement centralized log monitoring and regularly analyze for suspicious activity

- Set up alerts for critical security events

- Establish and maintain an incident response plan

Chapter 14: Hacking Web Applications

Introduction

In the realm of ethical hacking, penetration testers take proactive measures to safeguard systems and networks from cyberattacks. Merely understanding the vulnerabilities in web applications is insufficient; without implementing appropriate countermeasures, it is not possible to effectively defend against real-world threats. This chapter focuses on web application security and hacking methodologies, an essential area of ethical hacking. Web applications are a prime target for cyberattacks due to their exposure to the internet and the sensitive data they often process. Ethical hackers use similar techniques to attackers to assess and defend web applications against exploitation. The chapter covers the structure of web applications, common vulnerabilities, and the methodologies used by attackers, along with countermeasures to protect these systems from attack.

Web applications are software that is accessed and interacted with through web browsers over a network, typically the internet. Unlike traditional desktop applications, web applications rely on client-server architecture, where users interact with the frontend (client-side) and the backend handles the data processing and storage. Frontend technologies include HTML, CSS, and JavaScript, while backend technologies include Python, PHP, and Ruby, along with frameworks like Django and Node.js. These applications depend on web protocols such as HTTP, HTTPS, and REST for communication. However, due to the complexity of their design and the amount of user data they handle, web applications are vulnerable to a variety of cyber threats, such as SQL injection, Cross-Site Scripting (XSS), Cross-Site Request Forgery (CSRF), and file inclusion attacks. Ethical hackers use these vulnerabilities to strengthen defenses and ensure that sensitive data remains protected against malicious actors.

Web Application Attack

Web application attacks target web-based applications' logic, functionality, or vulnerabilities. Attackers exploit weaknesses in code, input validation, authentication mechanisms, or misconfigurations to gain unauthorized access, steal data, or disrupt operations. Common types of web application attacks include SQL injection, Cross-Site Scripting (XSS), Cross-Site Request Forgery (CSRF), file inclusion, authentication bypass, and session hijacking. These attacks can lead to data breaches, application downtime, reputation damage, and compliance violations.

Web Application Attack Countermeasures

Some countermeasures for preventing web application attacks are as follows.

- Use secure coding practices and perform regular code reviews to identify and fix vulnerabilities early in the development lifecycle

- Implement input validation and output encoding to prevent injection attacks such as SQL injection and cross-site scripting (XSS)

- Use parameterized queries and prepared statements when interacting with databases to block SQL injection attempts

- Enable Content Security Policy (CSP) headers to restrict the execution of unauthorized scripts and reduce the impact of XSS

- Validate and sanitize user inputs to prevent malicious commands or scripts from being processed by the application

- Use secure authentication mechanisms, including multi-factor authentication (MFA), and enforce strong password policies

- Apply session management best practices such as using secure cookies, implementing session timeouts, and regenerating session IDs upon login

- Protect against CSRF attacks by using anti-CSRF tokens and verifying the origin of each request

- Restrict file uploads by allowing only trusted file types, scanning uploads for malware, and storing them outside of the web root

- Use Web Application Firewalls (WAFs) to detect and block common web-based attack patterns targeting application vulnerabilities

- Conduct regular vulnerability scans and penetration tests to identify and fix flaws in the application and its supporting infrastructure

- Monitor application logs for signs of unusual or unauthorized behavior, such as repeated failed login attempts or abnormal traffic

- Keep all components of the web application stack updated, including the framework, libraries, and plugins, to patch known vulnerabilities

Web API and Webhooks

Web API and Webhooks are both integral to modern web development, enabling applications to communicate with each other and trigger specific actions. However, they differ in how they work and their use cases.

A Web API is a set of protocols and tools that allow one application to interact with another over the Internet. Web APIs enable communication between a client (like a web browser or mobile app) and a server, typically using HTTP methods like GET, POST, PUT, and DELETE to request or send data. APIs provide a standardized way for different systems to exchange information, and they can be used for tasks such as retrieving data from a database, sending messages, or integrating with third-party services. They typically return data in formats such as JSON or XML. A key feature of Web APIs is that the client must actively request information or services from the server, meaning the server responds to requests from clients when they are made.

Webhooks, on the other hand, are a way for an application to send real-time data to another application as soon as an event occurs. Unlike Web APIs, where the client initiates a request, Webhooks are event-driven and allow the server to push data to a client automatically. A Webhook works by setting up an endpoint on the receiving server (the client), where the server (the sender) can send HTTP POST requests containing data when a specific event happens, like a new order being placed or a user updating their profile. Webhooks are commonly used for tasks that require immediate action, such as sending notifications, updating databases, or triggering workflows. Since Webhooks are "push" based, they are often more efficient for real-time data delivery than polling an API repeatedly.

Web API and Webhooks Countermeasures

Some countermeasures for securing web APIs and webhooks are as follows.

- Use authentication and authorization mechanisms such as API keys, OAuth, or JWT to ensure only trusted parties can access APIs and webhooks

- Validate and sanitize all inputs received from API clients or webhook sources to prevent injection attacks or data corruption

- Enforce rate limiting and throttling to protect APIs against abuse or denial of service attacks from automated or excessive requests

- Use HTTPS to encrypt all communication to protect sensitive data in transit and prevent man-in-the-middle attacks

- Apply role-based access control (RBAC) to restrict API usage based on the user's permissions and context

- Verify the source of webhook requests using signed headers or HMAC-based tokens to confirm authenticity and prevent spoofing

- Log all API and webhook activity for auditing and forensic purposes, and monitor for unusual or unauthorized access patterns

- Keep API documentation up to date and limit public exposure of sensitive or admin-level endpoints

- Regularly rotate API keys, tokens, and credentials to limit the impact of potential leaks or unauthorized access

- Implement version control for APIs to manage changes securely and avoid exposing deprecated or vulnerable versions

- Use API gateways to centralize security features such as authentication, logging, rate limiting, and traffic monitoring

- Conduct regular security assessments and penetration testing of APIs and webhook endpoints to identify and address vulnerabilities

Injection Attacks

Injection attacks occur when an attacker sends malicious input into a program to alter its execution or access unauthorized data. These attacks exploit poor input validation and weak query construction in web applications and systems. Common types include SQL injection, command injection, LDAP injection, XML injection, and NoSQL injection. Successful injection attacks can result in data breaches, command execution, privilege escalation, or complete system compromise.

Defend Against Injection Attacks

Some countermeasures for preventing injection attacks are as follows

- Use parameterized queries and prepared statements to separate user input from executable code in database operations

- Validate and sanitize all user inputs to ensure only expected and safe data is processed by the application

- Avoid dynamically constructing commands or queries using user-supplied input whenever possible

- Use input whitelisting where appropriate to limit input to known good values rather than filtering known bad ones

- Employ Object-Relational Mapping(ORM) frameworks to interact with databases securely and reduce direct query manipulation

- Implement proper error handling to prevent detailed error messages from exposing backend logic or query structures

- Limit database permissions and privileges to restrict what actions can be performed in case of a successful injection

- Escape special characters in inputs where necessary, particularly when interacting with shell commands, HTML, or XML

- Use Web Application Firewalls (WAFs) to detect and block common injection patterns targeting web apps

- Regularly test applications for injection vulnerabilities using automated scanners and manual security assessments

- Keep all backend systems, libraries, and frameworks updated to patch known injection-related vulnerabilities

WebSocket Connections

WebSocket is a protocol that enables real-time, full-duplex communication between clients and servers over a single, long-lived connection. It is commonly used in chat applications, live updates, online gaming, and collaborative tools. However, insecure WebSocket implementations can expose applications to risks such as data interception, cross-site WebSocket hijacking, and unauthorized message injection. Since WebSocket connections bypass traditional HTTP protections, they require additional security considerations.

Securing WebSocket Connection

Some countermeasures for securing WebSocket connections are as follows.

- Use wss:// (WebSocket Secure) to encrypt traffic using TLS and protect data in transit from interception or tampering

- Implement authentication and authorization checks before upgrading the connection to WebSocket to prevent unauthorized access

- Validate and sanitize all incoming and outgoing WebSocket messages to prevent injection attacks and malformed data handling

- Use origin checks to ensure that only trusted domains can initiate WebSocket connections to the server

- Limit the lifetime of WebSocket sessions and implement automatic timeouts for idle or long-lived connections

- Monitor WebSocket traffic for unusual behavior such as message flooding or unexpected command patterns

- Apply rate limiting and connection throttling to prevent abuse from automated bots or denial-of-service attacks

- Restrict access to WebSocket endpoints using firewalls, reverse proxies, or API gateways to filter unauthorized or malformed requests

- Keep the server-side application and WebSocket libraries updated to patch known vulnerabilities

- Log and audit WebSocket activity to detect anomalies and support incident response

- Avoid sending sensitive information over WebSockets unless it is encrypted and properly secured within the application layer

- Conduct regular penetration testing to identify and fix WebSocket-specific vulnerabilities

💡 **Important Exam Tips for the Certified Ethical Hacker (CEH) Exam on Hacking Web Applications**

Understanding Hacking Web Applications is crucial for the CEH exam. Here are key exam tips to help you master this topic:

1. Web Server Concepts: Understand the basic components of a web server, including hardware, server software (e.g., Apache, Nginx), protocols (HTTP/HTTPS), DNS, domain names, ports, and configuration files (e.g., .htaccess, nginx.conf).

- **Web Server Attacks**: Familiarize yourself with common web server attacks such as Directory Traversal, SQL Injection, Cross-Site Scripting (XSS),

Cross-Site Request Forgery (CSRF), DoS/DDoS, and the impact of these attacks on availability and security.

- **Code Injection Attacks**: Know how SQL injection and command injection attacks work to manipulate databases or execute malicious commands, and the tools used to exploit these vulnerabilities.

- **Web Server Attack Methodology**: Understand the attack methodology involving reconnaissance, scanning for vulnerabilities (using tools like Nmap, Nikto), exploitation, and post-exploitation steps.

- **Web Server Attack Countermeasures**: Be aware of countermeasures such as configuring firewalls, deploying IDS/IPS, using secure coding practices, patching software, configuring WAFs, and securing sensitive data with HTTPS.

2. Authentication and Access Control: Learn about authentication bypass techniques and the importance of strong access controls to prevent unauthorized access to sensitive web server areas.

3. Tools for Web Server Attacks: Know commonly used tools like Nmap, Burp Suite, Nikto, and OWASP ZAP for scanning, exploiting, and defending web servers.

Chapter 15: SQL Injections

Introduction

SQL injection (SQLi) is a common and critical vulnerability in web applications that enables attackers to alter SQL queries executed by the underlying database. This attack targets the application's database layer, enabling unauthorized access, data manipulation, or even full system compromise. Understanding the fundamental concepts of SQL injection, along with strategies for defense and detection, is critical for securing web applications.

This chapter covers the key concepts of SQL injection (SQLi) attacks, including how they work and their potential impact on applications and organizations. It also discusses practical defenses against these attacks. Additionally, it will also discuss methods for detecting SQL injection attempts and explore evasion techniques used by attackers, along with corresponding countermeasures.

SQL Injection Concepts

Structured Query Language (SQL) is a text-based language used by database servers to perform operations such as INSERT, SELECT, UPDATE, and DELETE, which allow manipulation of data within the database. Developers typically write sequential SQL commands that include parameters provided by users. However, this approach can leave applications vulnerable to SQL injection if inputs are not properly sanitized.

SQL injection is an attack technique that exploits these input validation flaws, allowing an attacker to insert malicious SQL commands through a web application. These commands are then executed by the backend database, potentially leading to unauthorized access or data retrieval. This type of vulnerability stems from weaknesses in the web application's code, not from flaws in the database or web server itself.

Attackers can craft SQL queries to bypass authentication, escalate privileges, extract sensitive data, or modify database contents. Since applications often rely on SQL for user authentication, access control, and data retrieval, improper handling of user input can open the door to direct database manipulation through injected SQL code.

SQL Injection and Server-Side Technologies

Server-side technologies like ASP.NET, PHP, and Python enable the development of dynamic, data-driven web applications. These technologies communicate with databases like Microsoft SQL Server, Oracle, MySQL, and IBM DB2. However, if developers overlook secure coding practices, the applications can become susceptible to SQL injection attacks. SQL injection targets poorly coded web applications, not the underlying software, to access or manipulate data in relational databases.

HTTP POST Request

An HTTP POST request is used to send data to a web server by including it in the message body, unlike the HTTP GET method, which appends data to the URL. This makes POST generally more secure than GET, especially for sensitive information. POST requests can also handle larger amounts of data, making them suitable for interacting with XML web services. When a user enters information and clicks Submit, the browser sends the data, such as credentials, to the server in the body of the HTTP or HTTPS POST request, such as:

```
select * from Users where (username = 'smith' and password = 'simpson');
```

Figure 15-01: Example of HTTP POST Request

Normal SQL Query

A query is an SQL command used to interact with a database. Developers write and execute SQL queries to perform tasks such as selecting, retrieving, inserting, updating data, or creating database objects like tables. These queries typically start with keywords like SELECT, UPDATE, CREATE, or DELETE. In server-side technologies, queries serve as the bridge between the application and its database. User inputs are often used to fill placeholders within these queries. Once constructed with the provided values, the query is executed to retrieve data or carry out other operations.

Figure 15-02 illustrates a standard SQL query built using user-supplied input and returning results from the database.

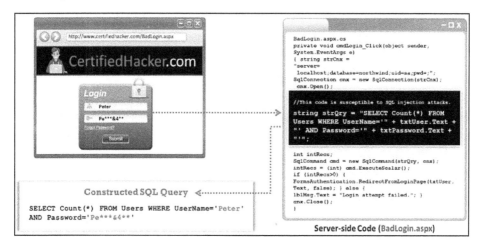

Figure 15-02: Example of Normal SQL Query

SQL Injection Query

An SQL injection query takes advantage of the standard execution of SQL commands. Attackers craft input values that appear normal but are designed to retrieve specific data from the database. This is possible when an application fails to properly filter or validate user input before processing it. Without proper input validation, the application becomes vulnerable to SQL injection attacks.

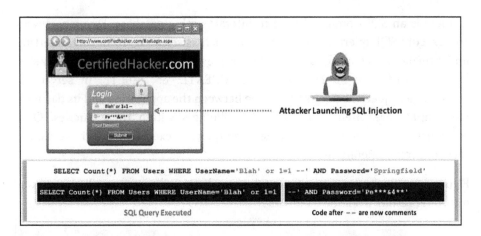

Figure 15-03: Example of SQL Injection Attack

SQL Injection Attack

SQL injection attacks are a form of web security vulnerability that allows an attacker to interfere with the queries an application makes to its database. These attacks occur when user-supplied input is not properly validated or sanitized and is directly included in SQL statements. As a result, an attacker can inject malicious SQL code into input fields such as login forms, search bars, or URL parameters to manipulate the underlying database.

The goal of an SQL injection attack can vary, it might involve bypassing authentication, retrieving sensitive information like usernames and passwords, modifying or deleting data, or even gaining administrative control over the database. For instance, by entering specially crafted input, an attacker can change the logic of a query so that it always returns true, effectively logging in without valid credentials.

Detecting SQL Injection Attacks

Security professionals need to create and implement detection rules within Intrusion Detection Systems (IDS) to identify regular expressions commonly used in SQL injection attacks targeting web servers. This involves using regex patterns to spot SQL injection meta-characters, such as the single quote (') and double dash (--). Below are some regular expressions designed to detect these SQL injection-specific characters, along with their meanings:

- ': Single-quote character

- |: Logical OR operator

- **%27**: Hex equivalent of single-quote character

- **--**: Double-dash

- **%2D**: Hex equivalent of double-dash

- **#**: Hash or pound character

- **%23**: Hex equivalent of hash character

- **I**: Case-insensitive flag in regex

- **X**: Ignores white spaces in the pattern

- **%3D**: Hex equivalent of = (equal) character

- **%3B**: Hex equivalent of ; (semi-colon) character

- **%6F**: Hex equivalent of o character

- **%4F**: Hex equivalent of O character

- **%72**: Hex equivalent of r character

- **%52**: Hex equivalent of R character

- **%3C**: Hex equivalent of < (opening angle bracket) character

- **%3E**: Hex equivalent of > (closing angle bracket) character

- **%2F**: Hex equivalent of / (forward slash for a closing tag) character

- **\s**: Whitespace equivalents

- **^\n**: Hex equivalent of a non-newline character

Security professionals can utilize regular expressions to identify SQL meta-characters.

Regular Expression for Detection of SQL Meta-Characters

- The following expression detects common SQL meta-characters used in injection attacks such as single-quote (') and its hex equivalent **%27**, double-dash (--) and hash (#) and its hex equivalent **%23**:

/(\')|(\%27)|(\-\-)|(#)|(\%23)/**ix**

- The double-dash (--) is not an HTML character and web request does not perform any encoding for it

- These characters can indicate attempts to terminate or manipulate SQL queries

- Security professionals must look for these regular expressions in logs of the security control devices such as WAF and IDS

- Helps identify SQL injection attempts embedded in user input

Modified Regular Expression for Detection of SQL Meta-Characters

- Security professionals must use the following regular expression to check for the '=' sign or its hex value (%3D) in user requests:

/((\%3D)|(=))[^\n]*((\%27)|(\')|(\-\-)|(\%3B)|(;))/ix

- The expression [^\n]* indicates the presence of zero or more non-newline characters

- It then checks for the presence of single-quote ('), double-dash (--), or semi-colon (;)

Regular Expression for Typical SQL Injection Attack

- Security professionals must use the following expression to detect zero or more alphanumeric and underscore characters involved in an attack:

/\w*((\%27)|(\'))((\%6F)|o|(\%4F))((\%72)|r|(\%52))/ix

- The single-quote (') character or its equivalent hex value is detected using the expression ((\%27)|(\'))

- The remaining expression detects the word "or" in any case variation ("or", "Or", "oR", or "OR") and its respective hex values

Regular Expression for Detecting SQL Injection with the UNION Keyword

- Some attackers use the UNION keyword in SQL injection queries to enhance attacks and enable further exploitation

- Security professionals must use the following expression to detect SQL queries containing the UNION keyword:

/((\%27)|(\'))union/ix

- This expression checks for a single quote (') or its equivalent hex value, followed by the union keyword in HTTP requests

- Security professionals must develop similar expressions for the keywords insert, update, select, delete, and drop to detect SQL injection attempts

Regular Expression for Detecting SQL Injection Attacks on an MS SQL Server

- If attackers discover that a web application is vulnerable to injection attacks and the backend database is MS SQL, they may use complex queries involving stored procedures (sp) and extended procedures (xp)

- Attackers may attempt to use extended procedures like xp_cmdshell, xp_regread, and xp_regwrite to execute shell commands and modify registry entries from the SQL Server

- The following regular expression can be used for detection:

/exec(\s|\+)+(s|x)p\w+/ix

- This expression checks for the exec keyword, whitespace characters or their hex equivalents, the letter combinations sp or xp, and an alphanumeric or underscore character

Defending against SQL Injection Attacks

To defend against SQL injection, developers must carefully configure and build secure applications by following established best practices and using effective countermeasures.

Some countermeasures to defend against SQL injection attacks are as follows:

- Check string variable content and accept only expected input

- Do not assume anything about the size, type, or content of input data

- Validate the size and type of inputs and enforce limits to prevent buffer overflows

- Reject input containing binary data, escape sequences, or comment characters

- Avoid constructing Transact-SQL statements directly from user input

- Use stored procedures to validate user input

- Apply multiple layers of input validation

- Never concatenate unvalidated user input

- Avoid building dynamic SQL queries using user-supplied data

- Ensure web configuration files do not store sensitive information

- Use the least privileged SQL accounts for application access

- Deploy network, host, and application intrusion detection systems

- Conduct automated black box testing, source code analysis, and manual penetration testing

- Separate untrusted input from commands and queries

- If parameterized APIs are unavailable, use escape syntax to remove special characters

- Store passwords using secure hashing algorithms like SHA256 instead of plain text

- Enforce secure data access through a data access abstraction layer

- Remove debug messages and code tracing before deploying applications

- Properly trap and handle exceptions in application code

- Run applications accessing the database using the least privilege principle

- Validate all user-supplied and untrusted data on the server side

- Avoid using quoted or delimited identifiers due to the complexity of validation

- Use prepared statements and parameterized queries to prevent SQL injection

- Sanitize all user inputs before including them in SQL queries

- Use regular expressions and stored procedures to detect malicious input

- Avoid using untested web applications

- Isolate the web server within separate domains for added security

- Keep all software components and patches up to date

- Monitor SQL queries from applications regularly for suspicious activity

- Use database views to restrict access and mask sensitive base table data

- Disable shell access for the database

- Do not reveal database error messages to end users
- Use safe APIs that support parameterized interfaces or bypass interpreters entirely
- Outsource authentication using solutions like OAUTH to centralize login handling
- Use ORM frameworks to safely handle database interactions
- Choose modern programming languages with built-in SQL injection protections
- Apply whitelist-based input validation instead of relying on blacklists
- Assign separate database accounts to different applications
- Disable unused or unnecessary database features
- Avoid using commands like xp_cmdshell to limit server-level interactions
- Deploy a web application firewall (WAF) to filter out malicious input
- Avoid extended or excessively long URLs that may cause buffer overflows
- Convert user inputs such as usernames and passwords into string format before validation
- Remove all default database accounts
- Allocate sufficient buffer size for command variables and dynamic SQL within EXECUTE statements
- Use ORM frameworks like Hibernate and Spring Data JPA for secure query handling and built-in injection protection

Evasion Techniques

Firewalls and Intrusion Detection Systems (IDS) often detect SQL injection attempts using predefined signatures. However, attackers can bypass these network security measures by employing various evasion techniques. These techniques include hex encoding, whitespace manipulation, in-line comments, advanced pattern variations, character encoding, and more.

Evading IDS

An Intrusion Detection System (IDS) is deployed on a network to identify malicious activity, typically using either signature-based or anomaly-based detection models. To detect SQL injection attacks, IDS sensors are strategically positioned near the database server to monitor SQL statements. However, attackers often use evasion techniques to disguise input strings and avoid detection by signature-based systems. A signature, in this context, refers to a regular expression that defines a known attack pattern.

In a signature-based IDS, the system must have prior knowledge of the attack to detect it. It relies on a database of attack signatures and compares incoming input strings against this database at runtime. When a match is found, the IDS triggers an alert. This issue is particularly common in Network-based IDS (NIDS) and signature-based NIDS.

To bypass such systems, attackers use various signature evasion techniques. These include alternate encoding methods, packet fragmentation, transforming expressions into equivalent forms, inserting white spaces, and other obfuscation strategies.

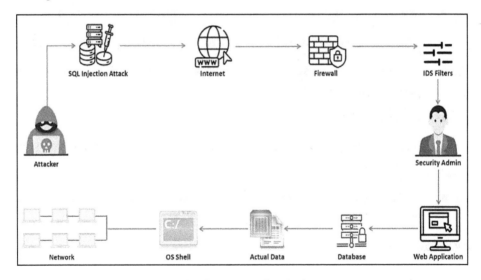

Figure 15-04: Evading IDS

Types of Signature Evasion Techniques

Different types of signature evasion techniques are listed below:

In-line Comment

An evasion technique is considered successful when a signature fails to properly handle white spaces in input strings. In this method, attackers obfuscate their

input by inserting in-line comments. These comments can make SQL statements appear syntactically unusual yet still valid, allowing them to bypass input filters. In-line comments enable attackers to construct SQL queries without relying on white spaces. For example, SQL uses /* ... */ to define multi-line comments, which can be exploited to hide parts of a malicious payload.

'/**/UNION/**/SELECT/**/password/**/FROM/**/Users/**/WHERE/**/user name/**/ LIKE/**/'admin'--

Char Encoding

Attackers can use the char() function to encode commonly used injection variables within input strings, helping them evade detection by signature-based network security mechanisms. This function translates hexadecimal or decimal values into characters, allowing the payload to slip through SQL engine parsing undetected. In MySQL, the char() function can facilitate SQL injection even without the use of double quotes.

For example:

- Inject without quotes (string = "%")

' or username like char(37);

- Inject without quotes (string = "root")

' union select * from users where login = char(114,111,111,116);

- Check for existing files (string = "n.ext")

' and 1=(if((load_file(char(110,46,101,120,116))<>char(39,39)),1,0));

String Concatenation

This evasion technique involves splitting a single string into multiple segments and concatenating them within the SQL query. The SQL engine reconstructs these segments into a complete string during execution. Attackers use this method to break up recognizable keywords, making it harder for intrusion detection systems to recognize malicious patterns. Since the syntax for string concatenation varies across databases, signature-based detection becomes ineffective, especially when it only checks complete strings on either side of the equals sign.

For instance, in SQL Server, strings can be concatenated using the + operator, while Oracle uses the || operator. A simple injection like **"OR 'Simple' = 'Sim'** +

'**ple'**" in SQL Server can evade detection. Attackers can also split commands to avoid signature matches using dynamic execution. Examples include:

- **Oracle:** '; EXECUTE IMMEDIATE 'SEL' || 'ECT US' || 'ER'

- **MSSQL:** '; EXEC ('DRO' + 'P T' + 'AB' + 'LE')

Obfuscated Code

There are two common techniques attackers use to obfuscate malicious SQL queries and evade detection by an IDS:

1. **Wrapping:** In this method, attackers use a wrapping utility to obfuscate the malicious SQL query before sending it to the database. Since the obfuscated query does not match any known IDS signatures, it can pass through undetected.

2. **SQL String Obfuscation:** This technique involves hiding SQL strings by splitting them into smaller parts and using string concatenation, or by encrypting or hashing the strings and decrypting them during execution. These obfuscated strings typically do not match predefined IDS signatures, allowing attackers to bypass detection mechanisms.

Manipulating White Spaces

Many modern signature-based SQL injection detection engines can identify attacks that involve variations in the amount or encoding of white spaces around malicious SQL code. However, these engines often fail to detect similar attacks when spaces are removed entirely. The white space manipulation technique obfuscates malicious input by adding or removing white spaces between SQL keywords, string literals, or number values, without changing the SQL statement's behavior.

Attackers may insert special white space characters such as tabs, carriage returns, or line feeds to alter the appearance of a query while keeping it functionally the same. For example, the signature for **"UNION SELECT"** differs from **"UNION\rSELECT"**, making detection more difficult. Similarly, removing all spaces from a query, such **as 'OR'1'='1'**, does not impact its execution in some SQL databases, but can help it evade signature-based detection.

Hex Encoding

Hex encoding is an evasion technique where strings are represented using their hexadecimal equivalents. Attackers use this method to conceal SQL queries in a way that bypasses detection by security systems, as many IDS solutions are not

designed to recognize hex-encoded inputs. By leveraging this gap, attackers can craft SQL injection payloads that slip past signature-based protections. Hex encoding offers numerous ways to disguise each part of a URL or query.

For example, the string **'SELECT'** can be encoded as **0x73656c656374**, which is unlikely to match any standard signature pattern, making it harder for detection systems to identify the threat.

```
; declare @x varchar(80);

set @x = X73656c656374

20404076657273696f6e;

EXEC (@x)
```

Null Byte

An attacker can use a null byte (**%00**) character at the beginning of a string to bypass detection mechanisms. This technique takes advantage of how different programming environments handle string termination. While web applications are typically built using high-level languages like PHP or ASP, they often rely on underlying C/C++ functions, where a null byte (\0) signifies the end of a string. This mismatch in handling allows for null byte injection attacks.

For example, an attacker might use the following SQL query to retrieve an admin's password from the database:

```
' UNION SELECT Password FROM Users WHERE UserName='admin'--
```

If the server is protected by a WAF or IDS, the attacker can prepend a null byte to evade detection:

```
%00' UNION SELECT Password FROM Users WHERE UserName='admin'--
```

By doing so, the injected query may bypass the filtering mechanism and allow the attacker to successfully extract sensitive data like the admin's password.

Case Variation

Most database servers treat SQL statements as case-insensitive by default. Because of this, attackers can exploit the case-insensitive nature of regular expression filters by mixing uppercase and lowercase letters in their attack vectors to evade detection.

For example, if a filter is configured to detect a specific query such as:

> union select user_id, password from admin where user_name='admin'--
>
> UNION SELECT USER_ID, PASSWORD FROM ADMIN WHERE USER_NAME='ADMIN'--

An attacker can bypass it by altering the case of the query like so:

> UnIoN sEleCt UsEr_iD, PaSSwOrd fROm aDmiN wHeRe UseR_NamE='AdMIn'--

This variation does not change the logic or outcome of the SQL statement but can successfully avoid detection by poorly designed case-sensitive filters.

Declare Variables

During a web session, an attacker may closely analyze the queries being executed to identify patterns or variables that can be exploited to extract sensitive data from the database. Once such a variable is found, the attacker can inject a series of carefully crafted SQL statements that are designed to bypass signature-based detection mechanisms.

For example, instead of using a straightforward SQL injection like:

> UNION SELECT Password

The attacker can redefine and execute the query using a variable, such as:

> ; declare @sqlvar nvarchar(70);
>
> set @sqlvar = (N'UNI' + N'ON' + N' SELECT' + N'Password');
>
> EXEC(@sqlvar)

This method builds the SQL statement dynamically at runtime, allowing the attacker to avoid detection by Intrusion Detection Systems (IDS) while still retrieving sensitive information like stored passwords from the database.

IP Fragmentation

Attackers often fragment IP packets into smaller pieces to distribute a malicious payload across multiple fragments. This tactic is designed to evade detection by IDS or WAF systems, which typically inspect packets individually. For these systems to identify an attack, they must correctly reassemble the fragmented packets, a task that becomes challenging when the attack payload is split across

fragments. If the fragments are modified or deliberately disordered, detecting the attack becomes even more difficult.

Several techniques used to bypass signature detection through IP fragmentation include:

- Introducing delays between sending fragments, hoping the IDS times out before the destination system reassembles the packet

- Sending packet fragments in reverse order

- Sending all fragments in order, except the first one, which is sent last

- Sending all fragments in order, except the last one, which is sent first

- Delivering fragments in a random or out-of-order sequence

Variation

Variation is an evasion technique that allows attackers to bypass comparison checks by altering the structure of basic SQL injection statements. This is typically done by inserting characters like "' or '1'='1'" into a query, transforming a numeric comparison such as or 1=1 into a string-based one. Since comparisons between two strings (e.g., '1'='1') or two numbers (e.g., 1=1) both evaluate to true, the outcome of the query remains unaffected. The SQL engine processes the statement as valid, allowing unauthorized access or data retrieval.

Attackers exploit this behavior by crafting numerous variations of injection payloads using different combinations of strings, numbers, and SQL comments, creating an almost infinite number of possibilities. The core objective is to ensure that the WHERE clause always evaluates to true, enabling the execution of the injected statement.

For instance, both of the following queries will produce the same result set:

```
SELECT * FROM accounts WHERE userName = 'Bob' OR 1=1 --

SELECT * FROM accounts WHERE userName = 'Bob' OR 2=2 --

SELECT * FROM accounts WHERE userName = 'Bob' OR 1+1=2 --

SELECT * FROM accounts WHERE userName = 'Bob' OR "evade"="ev"+"ade" -
-
```

Evasion Techniques Countermeasures

Countermeasures for different evasion techniques are as follows:

In-line Comment

- Normalize and remove SQL comments from inputs before signature inspection

- Use SQL parsers that handle irregular syntax to detect malicious intent

- Disallow comment markers (e.g., --, /* */) in user input fields

Char Encoding

- Decode input characters (e.g., char(), CHR(), hex, unicode) before inspection

- Use input filters to block the use of encoding functions in SQL queries

- Leverage context-aware detection engines that understand the encoded syntax

String Concatenation

- Flatten or normalize concatenated strings before performing signature checks

- Block use of concatenation operators (+, ||) where not necessary

- Apply deep SQL query inspection at the database layer

Obfuscated Code

- Use de-obfuscation engines to reconstruct and analyze actual intent

- Apply behavior-based detection rather than relying solely on syntax

- Limit execution privileges in the database to reduce risk from hidden code

Manipulating White Spaces

- Normalize all white spaces (spaces, tabs, carriage returns) before filtering

- Reject inputs with excessive or suspicious spacing

- Use regex patterns that detect white space variations

Hex Encoding

- Automatically decode hex-encoded input before it reaches the inspection engine

- Block hex representations of SQL keywords in input fields

- Apply input sanitization and use allowlists for valid inputs

Null Byte

- Sanitize and strip null bytes (%oo) from all inputs

- Ensure backend frameworks handle null byte injection properly

- Use secure coding practices in languages like PHP and C/C++ to avoid null termination vulnerabilities

Case Variation

- Convert input to lowercase or uppercase before comparing it against signatures

- Use case-insensitive matching in regex or detection logic

- Maintain normalized pattern libraries for the detection

Declare Variables

- Restrict dynamic SQL execution permissions (e.g., EXEC, sp_executesql)

- Use static queries instead of allowing the runtime variable declaration

- Detect and block the use of DECLARE, SET, and EXEC in user-controlled input

IP Fragmentation

- Enable packet reassembly at the IDS/IPS or WAF level

- Use advanced network monitoring tools that can track and correlate fragments

- Set rules to detect abnormal or deliberately fragmented packets

Variation

- Use fuzzy matching or pattern generalization in signature rules

- Combine static and dynamic analysis for robust detection

- Design flexible detection models to account for infinite variation possibilities

---

💡 **Important Exam Tips for the Certified Ethical Hacker (CEH) Exam on SQL Injections**

Understanding SQL injections is crucial for the CEH exam. Here are key exam tips to help you master this topic:

1. SQL Injection Concepts

- SQL injection (SQLi) is an input-based attack where malicious SQL code is injected into queries to manipulate database operations

- It targets vulnerable input fields like login forms, search boxes, and URL parameters

- **Countermeasures:** Use input validation, parameterized queries, and avoid constructing SQL queries with user input directly

2. SQL Injection Attack

- Common attack types include Union-based, Error-based, and Blind SQL injection (Boolean and Time-based)

- Attackers use SQLi to bypass authentication, extract sensitive data, or escalate privileges

- **Countermeasures:** Apply the principle of least privilege to database accounts, avoid displaying detailed error messages, and sanitize all inputs

3. Evasion Techniques

- Attackers use evasion methods to bypass security controls, including comment-based injections, string concatenation, and encoded inputs

- Techniques like altering case sensitivity, white space manipulation, and using alternate SQL syntax are also common

- **Countermeasures:** Normalize and sanitize inputs, use secure coding practices, and implement detection rules that account for evasion patterns

---

Chapter 16: Hacking Wireless Networks

Introduction

In today's hyper-connected world, wireless networks are everywhere, from homes and offices to airports and coffee shops. While they offer unparalleled convenience and mobility, wireless networks also introduce unique security vulnerabilities that can be exploited by malicious actors. This chapter delves into the various techniques used to compromise wireless networks and the corresponding defenses that can be implemented to mitigate these threats.

We will explore a range of wireless attacks, from common methods like cracking WPA/WPA2/WPA3 encryption to more advanced exploits such as KRACK and aLTEr attacks. Each section will provide a brief overview of the attack vector, followed by practical countermeasures and security best practices. You will also learn about the role of Wireless Intrusion Prevention Systems (WIPS) and how to detect and neutralize rogue access points.

By the end of this chapter, you will have a foundational understanding of how attackers target wireless networks, and more importantly, how to defend against them effectively.

Wireless Attack

Wireless attacks target Wi-Fi networks to eavesdrop, hijack sessions, or inject malicious data. These attacks often exploit weaknesses in wireless protocols or misconfigured access points. Common types include sniffing, Man-In-The-Middle (MITM), and DoS attacks.

Wireless Attack Countermeasures

Best Practices for Configuration

- Modify the default SSID once the WLAN setup is complete
- Turn off SSID broadcasting to keep the network hidden
- Disable remote access and wireless administration features on the router
- Use MAC address filtering on access points or routers for added control
- Activate encryption on access points and update passphrases regularly
- Block all unused ports to reduce the risk of attacks targeting access points
- Separate the network so guests cannot access the internal or private network

- Use closed networks by providing SSIDs to employees manually instead of broadcasting them
- Turn off DHCP and assign IP addresses manually to enhance security
- Disable SNMP, or if it is necessary, configure it with minimum required privileges
- Change the router's default console IP address to a non-standard one
- Opt for WPA3 encryption wherever possible; if not, use WPA2 with AES
- Deactivate WPS on the router to prevent unauthorized access
- Implement VLANs or different SSIDs to isolate various types of network traffic
- Reduce the router's signal strength to limit wireless coverage to the necessary area
- Disable services and close ports that are not essential for network function
- Utilize the router's built-in firewall to manage and filter both inbound and outbound traffic
- Create a separate, restricted guest network to isolate visitor access from core network systems

Best Practices for SSID Settings

- Enable SSID cloaking to prevent the SSID from being openly broadcasted in default wireless messages
- Install a firewall or packet filtering system between the access point and the corporate intranet
- Reduce wireless signal strength to ensure it does not extend beyond the organization's physical boundaries
- Routinely inspect wireless devices for any setup or configuration issues
- Apply an extra layer of encryption for data transmission, such as using IPsec over wireless connections
- Customize the SSID with unique characters or strings instead of retaining the default one provided by the manufacturer
- Set up a dedicated SSID for guest access to keep them separate from the internal network
- Divide the internal network into different segments with individual SSIDs to minimize potential impact during a security breach
- Keep the SSID broadcast turned off on all organizational wireless devices
- Make sure each SSID is secured with WPA3 encryption when available, or at least WPA2 using AES
- Update SSIDs and their associated passwords at regular intervals

Best Practices for Authentication

- Activate WPA3 to ensure the strongest available wireless security, offering advanced encryption and defense mechanisms
- If WPA3 is not supported by your device, opt for WPA2 with AES encryption and avoid older protocols like WPA or TKIP
- Use 802.1X authentication in conjunction with a RADIUS server for enterprise environments to assign unique credentials to each user
- In 802.1X setups, manage digital certificates properly by using strong encryption and keeping certificates up to date
- Turn off the wireless network when it is not in use to minimize exposure
- Secure wireless access points by placing them in physically protected areas
- Regularly update drivers on all wireless devices to maintain optimal performance and security
- Utilize a centralized authentication server to manage user access efficiently
- On client devices using 802.1X, enable server verification to guard against Man-In-The-Middle (MITM) attacks
- Add an extra security layer by enabling two-factor authentication
- Implement rogue access point detection or use wireless intrusion prevention/detection systems to defend against unauthorized wireless threats

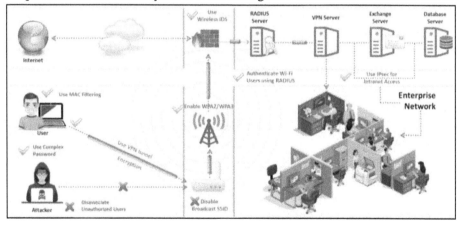

Figure 16-01: Defense Against Wireless Attacks

Wireless Security Layer

The wireless security layer refers to the mechanisms used to protect wireless communication, including encryption, authentication, and network access control. It ensures data confidentiality and integrity over wireless channels. Protocols like WPA2 and WPA3 operate in this layer.

Wireless Security Layer Countermeasures

- Enable WPA3 encryption for maximum wireless security; use WPA2 with AES if WPA3 is not supported
- Disable legacy protocols like WEP, WPA, and TKIP to avoid weak encryption vulnerabilities
- Use strong, complex passphrases for all wireless networks and update them regularly
- Disable SSID broadcasting to prevent unauthorized devices from easily discovering the network
- Implement MAC address filtering to control which devices can connect to the network
- Position Access Points (APs) centrally and reduce signal range to prevent leakage beyond secure areas
- Use VLANs or separate SSIDs to segment traffic by department, user role, or security level
- Disable Wi-Fi Protected Setup (WPS) to avoid vulnerabilities related to PIN-based access
- Set up a dedicated guest network isolated from internal systems and sensitive data
- Implement 802.1X authentication with a RADIUS server for enterprise-level access control
- Regularly audit wireless networks for misconfigurations, unauthorized devices, and outdated security settings
- Keep firmware and drivers for all wireless infrastructure and client devices up to date
- Use firewalls and packet filters between wireless access points and the internal network
- Disable wireless functionality on devices when not in use to minimize attack surfaces

WPA/WPA2/WPA3 Cracking

These attacks focus on breaking the encryption or authentication mechanisms of wireless protocols. WPA2 is vulnerable to dictionary attacks on the handshake, while WPA3 has improved protections but still faces downgrade or side-channel threats. Successful cracking allows unauthorized access to Wi-Fi networks.

Defense Against WPA/WPA2/WPA3 Cracking

- Set a strong and complex Wi-Fi password that is difficult to guess

- Use a password with 12–16 characters, including a mix of uppercase and lowercase letters, numbers, and special symbols
- Configure clients to use WPA2 with AES/CCMP encryption only
- Regenerate encryption keys with every new network connection for enhanced security
- Use VPN technologies such as remote access VPN, extranet VPN, or intranet VPN to protect data transmission
- Implement secure communication protocols like IPsec and SSL/TLS
- Deploy Network Access Control (NAC) or Network Access Protection (NAP) to manage and secure device connectivity
- Turn off TKIP in router settings and enforce the use of AES encryption only
- Restrict network access by allowing only specific MAC addresses to connect
- Upgrade to WPA3 wherever possible to prevent device exploitation and improve defense against brute-force attacks
- Disable remote management features on the router to block external access
- Turn off WPS to eliminate risks associated with WPS PIN brute-force vulnerabilities
- Regularly update router firmware to fix known security issues, check for updates on the manufacturer's website and install them promptly
- Reduce Wi-Fi signal strength by adjusting the router's transmission power and placing it centrally to limit range outside the intended area
- Continuously monitor the network for unusual activity or unauthorized devices using appropriate monitoring tools
- Use WPA3-SAE for enhanced protection against offline dictionary attacks and to ensure forward secrecy
- Disable WPA2/WPA3 mixed or transition mode if all devices support WPA3 to maintain the highest security level

KRACK Attacks

Key Reinstallation Attack (KRACK) exploits vulnerabilities in the WPA2 handshake process. It allows attackers to intercept and decrypt sensitive data by forcing the reuse of encryption keys. Devices that do not properly implement the protocol are most at risk.

Defense Against KRACK Attacks

- Ensure all routers and Wi-Fi devices are updated with the latest security patches
- Enable automatic updates for all wireless devices and keep device firmware up to date

- Avoid using public Wi-Fi networks whenever possible
- Only visit secure websites and avoid accessing sensitive information when connected to an unsecured network
- Audit IoT devices and avoid connecting them to insecure Wi-Fi routers
- Always use the HTTPS Everywhere browser extension for enhanced security
- Enable two-factor authentication to add an extra layer of protection
- Use a VPN to encrypt data and secure information while it is being transmitted
- Always opt for WPA3 security protocol for your wireless networks
- Disable fast roaming and repeater mode on wireless devices to better protect against KRACK attacks
- Use the EAPOL key replay counter to ensure that access points only recognize the most recent counter values
- Consider using third-party routers if the ISP-provided routers lack necessary security patches
- Implement network segmentation to separate critical systems from general user access, reducing the impact of potential KRACK attacks
- Temporarily disable the 802.11r protocol, which is vulnerable to KRACK attacks, if seamless roaming is not required
- Use 802.1X authentication with RADIUS server for added security, particularly in enterprise networks

aLTEr Attacks

aLTEr attacks manipulate unencrypted LTE traffic to redirect users or inject malicious content. They exploit vulnerabilities in the LTE data link layer, mainly affecting DNS and IP packet handling. Though limited, these attacks threaten mobile network integrity.

Defense Against aLTEr Attacks

The most effective method to safeguard a network against aLTEr attacks is by encrypting DNS queries with appropriate security measures. Cisco, in partnership with Apple, developed the "Cisco Security Connectors" app, which prevents clients from accessing unintended websites. This app encrypts DNS queries and sends them to Cisco Umbrella (intelligence block) for validation, offering protection at both the IP and DNS levels. The following countermeasures can be adopted to defend against aLTEr attacks:

- Encrypt DNS queries and rely only on trusted DNS resolvers
- Resolve DNS queries using HTTPS protocol
- Only access websites that use HTTPS connections

- Implement RFC 7858/RFC 8310 to prevent DNS spoofing attacks, enhance encryption, and improve intelligent name resolution policies
- Add a Message Authentication Code (MAC) to user plane packets
- Use the DNSCrypt protocol to authenticate the communication between DNS clients and resolvers
- Use mobile security tools like Zimperium to detect phishing and other malicious attacks from harmful websites
- Apply correct HTTPS parameters, such as HTTP Strict Transport Security (HSTS), to prevent redirection to malicious sites
- Implement a virtual network tunnel with integrity protection and endpoint authentication
- Upgrade to a 5G network connection for enhanced security
- Implement eSIM technology for better authentication and encryption
- Enable DNSSEC to secure the DNS lookup process, ensuring the authenticity of response data
- Ensure that all LTE network infrastructure, including base stations and core network equipment, is up-to-date with the latest firmware and software patches
- Regularly apply patches from network equipment vendors to address known vulnerabilities
- Employ robust encryption methods, such as AES-256, to protect data transmitted over LTE networks, ensuring end-to-end encryption
- Ensure mutual authentication between User Equipment (UE) and the network to prevent unauthorized access
- Use secure SIM cards with enhanced security features to prevent cloning and unauthorized access, including support for Over-The-Air (OTA) updates and secure storage
- Implement location-based access controls to restrict access to sensitive network services from unauthorized locations
- Protect physical network infrastructure with security measures like surveillance, access controls, and tamper-evident seals to prevent tampering

Rogue AP

A rogue access point is an unauthorized Wi-Fi AP set up to mimic a legitimate one. Attackers use it to trick users into connecting, enabling them to steal credentials or monitor traffic. Rogue APs pose serious security risks in enterprise environments.

Detection and Blocking of Rogue AP

Detection of Rogue APs

- RF sensors, which are repurposed APs that only capture and analyze packets, are placed throughout the wired network to detect and notify WLAN administrators of any wireless devices in the vicinity.
- APs with the ability to detect nearby APs will share this data through their MIBS and web interface.
- By maintaining a list of authorized APs and comparing it with detected devices, any unauthorized APs can be identified. Tools like AirMagnet WiFi Analyzer can assist in comparing detected devices against the authorized list.
- Analyzing the signal strength of detected APs helps identify devices that may be physically close but unauthorized. Tools such as Ekahau Survey for Wi-Fi Planning and Analysis can assist in detecting unexpected APs based on their signal strength.
- Monitoring the network for MAC addresses of known authorized APs helps flag any unfamiliar MAC addresses. Cisco Wireless LAN Controllers provide built-in rogue AP detection and MAC address filtering capabilities.

Blocking of Rogue APs

- Prevent new clients from connecting to the rogue AP by launching a Denial-of-Service (DoS) attack on it
- Block the switch port where the rogue AP is connected, or locate the AP manually and physically disconnect it from the LAN
- Utilize Wireless Intrusion Prevention Systems (WIPS) to monitor the wireless spectrum for unauthorized devices and automatically block rogue APs
- Implement Access Control Lists (ACLs) to restrict network access to only authorized MAC addresses
- Enforce 802.1X authentication to regulate network access and ensure that only authenticated users and devices can connect
- Isolate critical network resources from general wireless access by segmenting the network
- Disable the broadcast of open SSIDs to minimize the risk of unauthorized connections
- Keep a whitelist of authorized MAC addresses and configure the wireless controller to block any unlisted devices

Figure 16-02: Blocking of Rogue APs

Wireless Intrusion Prevention System

WIPS is a security solution designed to detect and prevent unauthorized wireless activity. It continuously monitors the radio spectrum for rogue APs, attacks, or suspicious behavior. WIPS is critical for securing enterprise wireless networks against evolving threats.

Wireless Intrusion Prevention System Countermeasures

- Continuously monitor the wireless spectrum for unauthorized devices and intrusions
- Detect and block rogue APs by identifying unauthorized access points in the network
- Monitor and alert for suspicious behavior such as unusual traffic patterns or device connections
- Use behavior-based analysis to detect anomalies that could indicate malicious activity or unauthorized devices
- Enforce policies to automatically block devices or connections that do not comply with security standards
- Configure WIPS to enforce network segmentation, ensuring critical resources are isolated from general wireless access
- Detect and mitigate Denial-of-Service (DoS) attacks targeting wireless networks
- Protect against Man-In-The-Middle (MITM) attacks by monitoring for devices impersonating legitimate APs
- Perform encryption checks to ensure that communications use secure protocols such as WPA3 or WPA2 with AES encryption
- Use geofencing to limit wireless access based on physical location, preventing unauthorized access from outside designated areas

- Set up automated responses to disconnect or quarantine devices that exhibit suspicious activity
- Integrate WIPS with existing network security tools, such as firewalls and Intrusion Detection System/ Intrusion Prevention System (IDS/IPS), to enhance overall protection
- Conduct regular security audits to ensure WIPS configurations are up to date and aligned with evolving threats
- Employ machine learning or AI-driven detection to adapt to new types of wireless attacks and vulnerabilities

---

💡 **Important Exam Tips for the Certified Ethical Hacker (CEH) Exam on Hacking Wireless Networks**

It is important to know how attackers target wireless networks and how to defend against them effectively. Here are key exam tips to help you master this topic:

1. **Wireless Attack**
- Exploits vulnerabilities in wireless networks to gain unauthorized access or disrupt services
- Common methods include eavesdropping, spoofing, and Denial-of-Service (DoS)
- **Countermeasures:** Set a strong router access password and activate firewall protection
- Avoid using the SSID, organization name, or simple, predictable strings in wireless passphrases
- Implement multifactor authentication wherever feasible to enhance overall network security

2. **Wireless Security Layer**
- Protects wireless networks using encryption (e.g., WEP, WPA, WPA2, WPA3) and authentication
- Ensures data confidentiality, integrity, and access control
- **Countermeasures:** Deploy Wireless Intrusion Detection System/ Wireless Intrusion Prevention System (WIDS/WIPS) to monitor and block rogue APs and unauthorized access attempts

3. **WPA/WPA2/WPA3 Cracking**
- Involves breaking encryption keys (e.g., via brute force or dictionary attacks) to access secured networks
- WPA3 improves security but may still face vulnerabilities in implementation

---

- **Countermeasures:** Ensure client devices validate the authentication server, specify the correct server address, and do not prompt for untrusted servers
4. **KRACK Attacks**
- Exploits weaknesses in WPA2's handshake process to intercept or manipulate data
- Affects all devices using WPA2, requiring patches to mitigate
- **Countermeasures:** Switch to a wired Ethernet connection or mobile data immediately if a KRACK vulnerability is detected
5. **aLTEr Attacks**
- Targets 4G/LTE networks by manipulating DNS responses to redirect traffic
- Exploits lack of encryption in certain LTE signaling protocols
- **Countermeasures:** Use DNS over Transport Layer Security (TLS) or DNS over Datagram TLS (DTLS) to encrypt DNS traffic and ensure integrity protection
6. **Rogue AP**
- An unauthorized access point set up to mimic a legitimate network, often for phishing or MITM attacks
- Can bypass security controls if users unknowingly connect to it
- **Countermeasures:** Network management software can detect rogue APs by monitoring devices connected to the LAN, utilizing protocols like Telnet, SNMP, and Cisco Discovery Protocol (CDP)
7. **Wireless Intrusion Prevention System (WIPS)**
- Monitors and blocks malicious activities like rogue APs or unauthorized connections
- Enhances security by enforcing policies and detecting anomalies in real-time
- **Countermeasures:** Implement device fingerprinting to identify and track devices based on unique characteristics

Chapter 17: Hacking Mobile Platforms

Introduction

Mobile platforms have become an integral part of modern life, serving as the gateway to personal, financial, and professional activities. However, their increasing role and connectivity have made them prime targets for cyberattacks. The mobile ecosystem is continually evolving, with attackers developing increasingly sophisticated techniques to exploit vulnerabilities within mobile devices, apps, and the networks they connect to.

This chapter explores key mobile platform attack vectors, highlighting various threats and the necessary countermeasures to mitigate them. It addresses the security challenges of Bring Your Own Device (BYOD) policies, offers solutions for preventing SMS phishing and OTP hijacking, and discusses how to protect against camera/microphone capture attacks. It also covers the secure storage of critical data on Android and iOS devices and highlights the risks posed by reverse engineering, along with strategies to mitigate these threats.

Mobile Platform Attack Vectors

Mobile security is facing growing challenges as complex attacks increasingly leverage multiple attack vectors to compromise mobile devices. These threats target sensitive data, financial information, and personal user details, and can also harm the reputation of mobile networks and organizations.

The increasing use of mobile devices has made them a major target for attackers. These devices often access the same resources as traditional computers, while also incorporating unique features that have introduced new attack vectors and protocols. As a result, mobile platforms are vulnerable to malicious attacks both over networks and through physical access.

Table 17-01 illustrates some of the key attack vectors that can be exploited to target vulnerabilities in mobile operating systems, device firmware, and mobile applications.

Malware	Data Exfiltration	Data Tampering	Data Loss
Virus and rootkit	Extracted from data streams and email	Modification by another application	Application vulnerabilities
Application modification	Print screen and screen scraping	Undetected tamper attempts	Unapproved physical access
OS modification	Copy to USB key and loss of backup	Jailbroken device	Loss of device

Table 17-01: List of Attack Vectors

The increasing adoption of smartphones, driven by rapid advancements in technology, has elevated mobile device security to a top priority for the IT sector. With continuous improvements in mobile operating systems and hardware, these devices have become high-value targets for attackers. Furthermore, the introduction of new smartphone features brings about additional security challenges. As smartphones continue to overtake PCs as the primary means of accessing the internet, managing communications, and performing daily tasks, attackers are increasingly focusing their efforts on mobile platforms, developing sophisticated attack strategies to compromise user privacy, steal sensitive data, or even take full control of the device.

Below are some vulnerabilities and risks associated with mobile platforms:

- Malicious apps in stores

- Mobile malware

- App sandboxing vulnerabilities

- Weak device and app encryption

- OS and app update issues

- Jailbreaking and rooting

- Mobile application vulnerabilities

- Privacy issues (Geolocation)

- Weak data security

- Excessive permissions

- Weak communication security

- Physical attacks

- Insufficient code obfuscation

- Insufficient transport layer security

- Insufficient session expiration

Mobile Platform Attack Vectors Countermeasures

Countermeasures for mobile attack vectors are as follows:

- Only download apps from official app stores such as Google Play or the Apple App Store.

- Ensure sensitive data is encrypted both at rest and in transit

- Use strong authentication mechanisms (MFA, biometrics)

- Regularly update OS and apps with the latest security patches

- Implement app code obfuscation to prevent reverse engineering

- Avoid storing sensitive information in plain text or unprotected storage

- Identify and block jailbroken or rooted devices from accessing organizational resources

- Educate users on recognizing phishing and SMiShing attempts

- Enable remote wipe and lock for lost or stolen devices

- Enforce app whitelisting and blacklisting policies

- Conduct regular security audits and vulnerability assessments

- Utilize secure APIs and vet third-party libraries before integration

- Monitor device activity using Mobile Device Management (MDM) or EMM solutions

- Apply the least privilege principle for app permissions and data access

Bring Your Own Device (BYOD)

Bring Your Own Device (BYOD) is a policy that allows employees to use their personal devices, like smartphones, laptops, and tablets, to access organizational resources in accordance with their designated access privileges. This approach enables employees to work on devices they are familiar with and that suit their

preferences and job functions. While BYOD supports a flexible "work anywhere, anytime" model, it also introduces significant challenges in securing corporate data and ensuring compliance with regulatory requirements.

Adopting BYOD is advantageous for the company as well as the employee. Some of the benefits of BYOD are discussed below:

- **Increased Productivity:** Employees are more efficient using familiar, up-to-date personal devices with the latest features.

- **Employee Satisfaction:** BYOD allows the use of preferred devices, combining personal and work data on one device, reducing the need for multiple gadgets.

- **Work Flexibility:** Employees can work from anywhere with access to corporate data, enjoying fewer restrictions than with company-issued devices.

- **Cost Savings:** Organizations save on device and data costs, as employees invest in and maintain their own devices.

When employees use their personal mobile devices to connect to the corporate network or access company data, they introduce potential security risks. Below are some common BYOD-related security threats:

- **Unsecured Networks:** Accessing corporate data on public Wi-Fi can lead to data leakage due to lack of encryption

- **Data Leakage:** Lost or stolen devices synced with corporate apps can expose sensitive information

- **Improper Disposal:** Devices discarded without wiping data may leak confidential info

- **Device Diversity:** Supporting various platforms increases IT complexity and costs

- **Personal-Corporate Data Mix:** Blending data complicates security; separation enables encryption and remote wiping

- **Loss or Theft:** Portable devices are easily lost, risking unauthorized access to corporate data

- **Lack of Awareness:** Untrained employees may unknowingly compromise security

- **Policy Bypass:** BYOD devices on wireless networks may bypass LAN-specific security policies

- **Infrastructure Challenges:** Supporting multiple devices and OS versions strains IT resources

- **Disgruntled Employees:** Former or unhappy staff may misuse or leak company data

- **Jailbreaking/Rooting:** Alters device security, increasing vulnerability

- **Poor Backup:** Lack of regular data backups can result in loss or corruption

- **Outdated Software:** Unpatched devices are more prone to exploits

- **Shadow IT:** Utilizing unauthorized cloud services can circumvent established IT controls

BYOD Security Guidelines

For the Administrator

Below are key security guidelines administrators should implement to protect the organization's network and data:

- Secure the organization's data centers using multi-layered protection systems

- Educate employees about the BYOD policy

- Clearly define ownership of apps and data

- Use encrypted channels for all data transfers

- Specify which apps are permitted or prohibited

- Enforce access control based on the need-to-know principle

- Prohibit the use of jailbroken or rooted devices

- Apply session authentication and timeout policies on access gateways

- Require connection to the company WLAN when on-site

- Enforce the use of strong, regularly updated passcodes

- Ensure mobile devices are registered and authenticated before granting network access

- Consider multi-factor authentication methods to enhance security when remotely accessing the organization's information systems

- Make users agree to and sign the BYOD policy before they can access the organization's information system

- Define whether a total device wipe or selective wipe of apps and data is necessary when an employee leaves, ensuring the organization's data is kept separate from personal data

- Use strong encryption algorithms to protect all organizational data stored on users' mobile devices and ensure data transfers are encrypted

- In the event of a lost or stolen device, remotely reset or wipe the device's passwords to prevent unauthorized access to sensitive data

- Deploy an SSL-based VPN to ensure secure remote access

- Ensure users' devices are regularly updated with the latest OS and software to address and fix security vulnerabilities

- Restrict offline access to sensitive organizational information, ensuring it is only available via the company's network

- Permit periodic re-authentication to ensure legitimate user access to devices

- Monitor devices in real-time using an Enterprise Mobility Management (EMM) system to ensure optimal security

- Create a blacklist of restricted applications for BYOD devices

- Backup device data to offsite servers or the cloud to enable quick data recovery

- Conduct regular security audits and vulnerability assessments to identify and mitigate risks in BYOD environments

- Implement containerization or sandboxing to separate corporate data from personal data on BYOD devices, improving security and control

- Enable remote wipe and lock capabilities to quickly remove corporate data from lost or stolen devices and prevent unauthorized access

- Use application whitelisting or blacklisting to control which apps can be installed or executed on BYOD devices

- Enforce device encryption to protect data at rest on BYOD devices using tools like BitLocker or FileVault

- Develop an offboarding strategy to ensure the elimination of sensitive data from the device and restrict former employees' access to corporate networks and data

For the Employee

Here are the guidelines employees should follow to secure sensitive personal or corporate information stored on a mobile device:

- Use encryption mechanisms to store data

- Maintain a distinct separation between personal and business data

- Register devices with remote locate and wipe capabilities if permitted by company policy

- Regularly update your device with the latest OS and patches

- Use anti-virus and Data Loss Prevention (DLP) solutions

- Set a strong passcode for the device and change it frequently

- Apply strong encryption algorithms to protect data

- Set passwords for apps to restrict unauthorized access

- Avoid downloading files from untrusted sources

- Be cautious when browsing websites and opening links or attachments in emails

- Erase all organizational data, access credentials, and applications from devices when leaving the organization (e.g., changing jobs or retirement)

- Always rely on authorized dealers and stores for device repairs or hardware changes

- Do not upload or backup company data to personal cloud storage unless specified by the company

- Report any theft or loss of a mobile device to the IT team and relevant authorities

- Utilize a secure VPN connection when connecting to public Wi-Fi networks

- Avoid synchronizing your mobile device with personal devices like TVs, desktops, and Bluetooth devices

- Do not jailbreak iOS or root Android devices as it compromises device security

- Review app permissions prior installing and only grant the necessary ones`

- Enable automatic device locking or biometric authentication to prevent unauthorized access in case of theft or loss

- Deploy device tracking software to remotely locate the device in case it is lost or stolen

SMS Phishing

Text messaging is the most widely used non-voice communication method on mobile phones, with billions of text messages sent and received globally every day. This large volume of messages increases the risk of spam and phishing attacks.

SMS phishing, or SMiShing, is a type of fraud where attackers send fraudulent text messages to steal personal and financial information. These deceptive messages typically contain malicious links, fake URLs, or phone numbers that trick victims into revealing sensitive details, such as Social Security numbers, credit card information, and online banking login credentials. Additionally, attackers use SMiShing to distribute malware to the victim's mobile device and associated networks.

The attacker typically purchases a prepaid SMS card under a false identity and then sends out an enticing or urgent message to the target. These messages may claim to offer a lottery prize, a gift voucher, an online purchase, or an account suspension notice, all while including a malicious link or phone number. When the user clicks the link, they are redirected to the attacker's phishing site and unknowingly provide sensitive information like their name, phone number, date of birth, credit card details, Social Security number, or email address. This stolen information can then be exploited for activities such as identity theft and unauthorized online purchases.

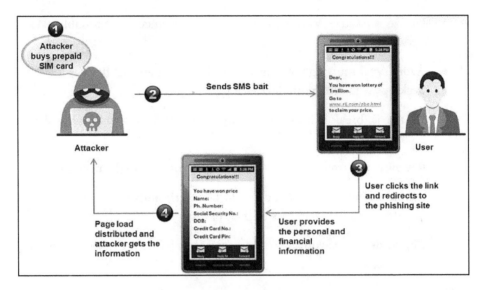

Figure 17-01: SMS Phishing Process

SMS Phishing Countermeasures

Some countermeasures for defending against SMS phishing attacks are listed below:

- Avoid replying to suspicious SMS messages without verifying the sender's identity

- Refrain from clicking on any links embedded in an unverified SMS

- Do not respond to text messages requesting personal or financial details

- Familiarize yourself with your bank's official SMS communication policy

- Activate your provider's option to block text messages sent via the internet

- Be cautious of messages that pressure you to respond urgently or immediately

- Never call phone numbers provided in unsolicited or suspicious SMS messages

- Stay alert for unexpected messages offering gifts, prizes, or unbelievable deals

- Be wary of messages sent from internet text relay services or nonstandard numbers

- Look out for spelling errors, poor grammar, or unusual language that may indicate a scam

- Opt out of unknown third-party subscriptions or sign-up offers to avoid spam

- Avoid storing confidential information such as passwords, PINs, or credit card data on your mobile device

- Report fraudulent or suspicious messages to reduce the likelihood of future smishing attacks

- Use anti-phishing or SMS filtering applications to detect and block malicious messages

- Ensure your device is protected with the latest anti-malware software

- Enable Multi-Factor Authentication (MFA) to enhance account security

- Organizations should utilize official short codes for SMS to help users identify legitimate communications

- Establish a structured response plan for smishing incidents and communicate it clearly to employees using BYOD devices

- Conduct simulated phishing exercises to assess user awareness and improve readiness against smishing attacks

- Use secure, authorized messaging apps like Signal or WhatsApp for internal communication

- Implement user training programs focused on identifying smishing and practicing safe digital communication habits

OTP Hijacking

One-Time Passwords (OTPs) are used to securely authenticate users and are typically sent via SMS, an authenticator app, or email. While this method appears secure, attackers can hijack OTPs and redirect them to their own devices using techniques like social engineering and SMS jacking. This attack can be hard to detect, as users may assume a network issue when they fail to receive an OTP, not realizing that it has been redirected to the attacker's device. Once the attacker has the stolen OTP, they can log into the victim's online accounts, reset passwords, and steal sensitive information.

The attacker often begins by acquiring the victim's Personally Identifiable Information (PII), either by bribing or tricking mobile store employees or exploiting the reuse of phone numbers across different customers. They may also use social engineering tactics on telecom providers, convincing them that the victim's device was lost and requesting a SIM swap. In some cases, attackers use SIM jacking attacks to infect the victim's SIM card with malware, enabling them to intercept and read OTPs.

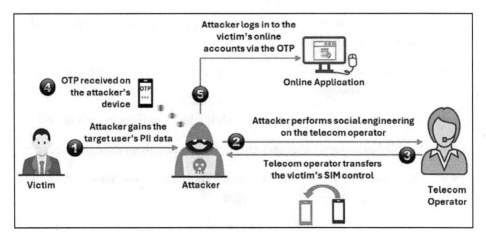

Figure 17-02: OTP Hijacking via SMS

OTP Hijacking Countermeasures

The following are various countermeasures for defending against OTP hijacking attacks:

For Users

- Follow a robust password policy that includes the creation of strong, unique passwords for each service

- Refrain from using the same password across multiple platforms

- Regularly change passwords to enhance account security

- Store passwords securely using an encrypted password manager

- Keep software and operating systems up to date by installing the latest versions regularly

- Remain cautious of suspicious emails and embedded links that may lead to malicious websites

- Access only websites that are SSL-certified to ensure secure communication

- Activate SIM lock with a PIN to prevent unauthorized access to the SIM card

- Turn off the display of sensitive information in lock screen notifications

- Avoid using applications that rely on SMS for authentication

- Limit the use of SMS or email-based recovery options whenever possible

- Never forward One-Time Passwords (OTPs) or share them with others

- Avoid entering OTPs into browsers while on phone calls

- Always manually enter OTPs into browsers rather than using autofill or pasting

For Developers

- Ensure that applications send OTPs through secure channels like encrypted SMS or secure push notifications

- Transmit OTPs with end-to-end encryption for added security

- Combine OTPs with additional authentication factors, such as biometrics or hardware-based methods

- Limit the number of OTP requests from a single user to prevent brute-force attacks

- Set short expiration times for OTPs to minimize the window of opportunity for attackers

- Use behavioral analytics to detect patterns of unusual activity, such as multiple OTP requests in a short time

- Educate users on phishing threats to avoid sharing OTPs with unauthorized individuals

- Consider utilizing hardware-based OTP generators or security keys to mitigate OTP hijacking

- Implement secure protocols for push notifications to protect the data in transit

- Use secure algorithms like HMAC-based OTP (HOTP) or Time-based OTP (TOTP) for generating OTPs

- Ensure OTPs are unique for each authentication attempt and are never reused

Camera/Microphone Capture Attacks

With the growing use of personal devices connected to the Internet, numerous security concerns have emerged alongside their benefits. Attackers are increasingly targeting digital users with sophisticated attacks to gain unauthorized access to their devices, steal sensitive data, or compromise the devices.

Below are two common attack methods that attackers use to exploit cameras and microphones on devices.

Camfecting Attack

A camfecting attack is a form of webcam hijacking where the attacker gains access to the camera on a target's computer or mobile device. The attacker typically infects the device with a Remote Access Trojan (RAT), allowing them to take control of the camera and microphone. In some cases, the attacker can disable the camera's indicator light to avoid detection. This enables them to capture sensitive data, including personal photos, recorded videos, and the user's location. The attacker can also control the camera remotely.

Steps involved in camfecting attack are as follows:

- To initiate the attack, the attacker often sends a phishing email containing a malicious link or tricks the victim into visiting a harmful website.

- When the victim clicks on the link or visits the malicious site, malware is downloaded and installed on their device, granting the attacker remote access.

- Once the malware is active, the attacker can capture personal data such as photos and videos.

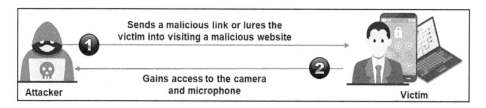

Figure 17-03: Camfecting Attack

Android Camera Hijack Attack

Attackers may attempt to exploit Google's default camera app, which is commonly used on Android devices. By taking advantage of multiple security vulnerabilities in Android, attackers can bypass the required permissions to gain unauthorized access to the victim's camera and microphone. This vulnerability can even be exploited when the mobile device is locked. Typically, Android camera apps require storage permissions to save photos and videos. These apps also require the victim to grant specific permissions, such as:

- android.permission.CAMERA

- android.permission.RECORD_AUDIO

- android.permission.ACCESS_COARSE_LOCATION

- android.permission.ACCESS_FINE_LOCATION

These storage permissions grant attackers unrestricted access to the device's internal storage, enabling them to perform actions such as capturing photos, recording videos and voice calls, and accessing stored content like photos, videos, GPS locations, and other sensitive information.

Attackers take advantage of bypass vulnerabilities on target Android devices by deceiving users into downloading malicious applications. These apps covertly install a Trojan on the victim's device. Once the infected app is launched, a persistent connection is established between the attacker and the victim. This connection remains active even after the app is closed, enabling the attacker to secretly capture photos and record videos without the user's awareness.

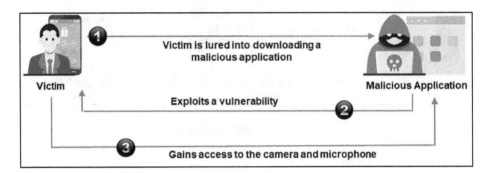

Figure 17-04: Android Camera Hijack Attack

Camera/Microphone Capture Attacks Countermeasures

Some countermeasures for camera/microphone capture attacks are:

- Install antivirus and anti-malware software to detect and block malicious apps that may attempt to access the camera or microphone

- Review app permissions regularly to ensure that apps only have the necessary access to the camera and microphone

- Disable camera/microphone when not in use or use physical covers for the camera when not in use

- Limit app permissions to access the camera and microphone, granting access only to trusted and necessary apps

- Regularly update software and operating systems to patch vulnerabilities that could be exploited by attackers

- Use Mobile Device Management (MDM) solutions to control and monitor device access, particularly for corporate devices

- Enable strong authentication mechanisms to ensure only authorized users can install or grant permissions to apps

- Monitor app behavior using security tools that can detect unusual activity related to camera or microphone access

- Install a firewall or network security tool to block unauthorized network access or data transmissions

- Educate users on safe app download practices and how to recognize malicious apps and phishing attempts

- Consider using security apps or features that notify the user when the camera or microphone is being accessed

- Use secure communication channels for sensitive voice or video calls, ensuring encryption of data in transit

- Avoid granting unnecessary permissions such as location, camera, or microphone access to apps that do not need them for functionality

Critical Data Storage in Android and iOS

Critical Data Storage in Android and iOS involves securely managing sensitive user and application data such as login credentials, access tokens, personal identifiers, and financial information. Both platforms offer distinct mechanisms and security models to ensure data confidentiality, integrity, and availability while preventing unauthorized access.

Android

In Android, sensitive data can be stored using internal storage, shared preferences, and the Android Keystore system. Internal storage is private to each application and is a safer choice compared to external storage, which is accessible by other apps and should never be used for storing sensitive information. Shared preferences are commonly used for storing small data items like settings and tokens. To enhance security, Android provides **EncryptedSharedPreferences**, which encrypts data at rest. The Android Keystore System is designed for securely storing cryptographic keys and ensuring that private keys never leave the secure hardware (Trusted Execution Environment or StrongBox on supported devices). This system enables secure operations like encryption, decryption, and digital signing without exposing the keys to the app or user.

iOS

In iOS, critical data is primarily stored using the Keychain and the file system with data protection classes. The Keychain is a secure storage container that allows apps to store small pieces of sensitive data such as passwords and certificates, encrypted using keys tied to the device's passcode and hardware. iOS also provides data protection classes that assign different levels of access to stored files based on the device's lock state, ensuring data remains protected even when the device is lost or stolen. For added security, iOS uses a Secure Enclave, a dedicated chip that handles cryptographic operations and key management in isolation from the main processor, preventing even privileged code from accessing stored keys.

Critical Data Storage in Android and iOS Countermeasures

Android

- Use authentication techniques like patterns PINs passwords and fingerprints to protect keys in the Android KeyStore

- Utilize a hardware-backed Android KeyStore to enhance the security of stored data

- Apply encryption techniques to store data in an unreadable format

- Implement proper authorization mechanisms for key creation and import

- Restrict server-stored key access to authenticated users only

- Store the master key and other keys in separate secure locations

- Generate keys using user-provided passphrases

- Store the master key within the software-based Android KeyStore if needed

- Keep encryption keys in a secure and private directory

- Encrypt data stored in SharedPreferences for added protection

- Apply the principle of least privilege by allowing access to sensitive data only to necessary app components

- Avoid embedding sensitive data like API keys tokens or credentials directly in the source code

- Obfuscate application code and data to make reverse engineering more difficult

- Use secure communication protocols such as TLS for data transmission over the network

- Ensure content providers that share data across apps have proper permissions and secure communication mechanisms in place

iOS

- Use authentication options such as Touch ID Face ID passcodes or passwords to protect the keychain

- Apply hardware-backed 256-bit AES encryption for storing critical data

- Use access-control lists to define which applications can access keychain data

- Store only minimal essential data directly in the keychain

- Set AccessControlFlags to require authentication for key access

- Implement a method to erase keychain data to prevent unauthorized access after app uninstallation

- When using app extensions ensure that shared data between the main app and extensions are encrypted and secured

- Follow secure coding practices to avoid vulnerabilities like buffer overflows and SQL injection

- Use secure interprocess communication methods when sharing data between apps or extensions

- Verify that any cloud storage service used offers encryption and secure data management policies

Reverse Engineering

Reverse engineering refers to the process of analyzing and extracting the source code of software or an application, and if necessary, modifying and regenerating it. This method is often employed to disassemble software or mobile applications to examine design flaws and fix any existing bugs. It also helps uncover hidden vulnerabilities and enhance security measures to defend against potential attacks. In mobile platforms, reverse engineering can be used to recreate or clone apps.

Its primary purposes include:

- Interpreting and understanding the source code

- Identifying and exposing hidden vulnerabilities

- Locating sensitive information embedded within the code

- Analyzing malware within applications

- Rebuilding the application with specific changes

- Ensuring mobile apps comply with legal and security regulations such as GDPR or HIPAA

- Assessing app compatibility across various platforms and devices

- Diagnosing and resolving application issues to improve functionality and performance

- Checking for possible patent or copyright violations by mobile applications

Reverse Engineering Countermeasures

Some countermeasures for reverse engineering are:

- Use code obfuscation to make the source code more difficult to understand and reverse-engineer

- Encrypt sensitive data within the app to prevent it from being easily accessed during reverse engineering

- Implement anti-debugging techniques to detect when the app is being analyzed in a debugger and prevent it from functioning properly

- Use code signing to ensure the integrity of the application and detect any unauthorized modifications

- Utilize hardware-based security mechanisms such as Trusted Execution Environments (TEEs) to protect critical code and data

- Minimize the amount of sensitive data stored in the app to reduce the value of reverse engineering attempts

- Monitor app behavior to detect unusual or suspicious actions indicative of reverse engineering efforts

- Implement runtime protections such as integrity checks to ensure the app hasn't been tampered with while running

- Use secure communication protocols to encrypt data in transit and prevent attackers from gaining valuable information through network interception

- Obfuscate API calls and external libraries to prevent attackers from easily understanding the app's functionality

- Regularly update and patch apps to close any security vulnerabilities that could be exploited by reverse engineers

- Educate developers about secure coding practices and the risks of reverse engineering to improve app security from the start

- Avoid storing sensitive keys or passwords within the app code to prevent extraction by reverse engineers

- Leverage Runtime Application Self-Protection (RASP) to provide real-time detection and prevention of reverse engineering and tampering attempts

---

Important Exam Tips for the Certified Ethical Hacker (CEH) Exam on Mobile Hacking Platforms

Understanding session hijacking is crucial for the CEH exam. Here are key exam tips to help you master this topic:

1. Mobile Platform Attack Vectors

- Mobile platforms are targeted through app repackaging, malicious links, insecure Wi-Fi, and OS vulnerabilities

- Attackers exploit weaknesses in mobile app permissions, outdated OS versions, and unsecured communication

- **Countermeasures:** Keep OS and apps updated, restrict app permissions, use Mobile Threat Defense (MTD) solutions

2. Bring Your Own Device (BYOD)

- BYOD introduces risks such as data leakage, unauthorized access, and weak device security policies

- Devices may lack proper encryption, security updates, or enterprise-grade protection

- **Countermeasures:** Enforce Mobile Device Management (MDM), implement access control policies, and separate work/personal data

3. SMS Phishing (Smishing)

- Attackers send fraudulent SMS messages to trick users into revealing sensitive information or installing malware

- Smishing is used to harvest credentials, deliver malicious links, or initiate social engineering attacks

---

- **Countermeasures:** Educate users, block suspicious numbers, use anti-phishing tools, and filter mobile messages

4. OTP Hijacking

- OTP hijacking involves intercepting or stealing one-time passwords sent via SMS or push notifications

- Common methods include malware, SIM swapping, and phishing for OTPs

- **Countermeasures:** Use app-based authenticators, enable multi-factor authentication, detect SIM change events

5. Camera/Microphone Capture Attacks

- Attackers use malware or rogue apps to silently activate and capture data from mobile cameras or microphones

- Examples include camfecting and remote audio recording to spy on users

- **Countermeasures:** Restrict camera/mic access in app settings, monitor permissions, use mobile antivirus tools

6. Critical Data Storage in Android and iOS

- Storing sensitive data insecurely can expose users to data theft or modification

- Android risks include storing data on external storage or unprotected shared preferences

- iOS risks include weak keychain protection or improper data handling by apps

- **Countermeasures:** Use encrypted storage APIs, secure key management, and sandboxing techniques

7. Reverse Engineering

- Attackers decompile mobile apps to analyze code, extract sensitive data, or bypass protections

- Tools like JADX and APKTool are used to reverse engineer Android apps

- **Countermeasures:** Use code obfuscation, encrypt sensitive strings, and implement runtime detection of tampering

Chapter 18: IoT and OT Hacking

Introduction

As the world increasingly relies on interconnected devices and automated systems, the lines between the digital and physical realms continue to blur. Internet of Things (IoT) and Operational Technology (OT) are at the heart of this transformation, powering everything from smart homes and wearable tech to industrial control systems and critical infrastructure. However, this rapid digital expansion introduces new vulnerabilities that cybercriminals are quick to exploit. This chapter explores the threats and attack techniques targeting IoT and OT environments, highlighting the unique risks they pose and the importance of securing these systems.

IoT Hacking

IoT hacking involves compromising internet-connected devices such as smart cameras, thermostats, medical wearables, or even connected cars. These devices often have limited processing power and run outdated software, making them attractive targets for attackers. Common attacks include unauthorized access, data interception, botnet creation (e.g., Mirai), and remote control of devices. The decentralized and diverse nature of IoT ecosystems further complicates detection and response efforts.

IoT Attack Countermeasures

This section explores IoT security strategies, device management practices, and security tools to safeguard IoT devices and networks. These measures aim to prevent, detect, and mitigate different attacks while enabling recovery from potential breaches. Organizations can establish robust security protocols by adopting these countermeasures to protect sensitive data exchanged between IoT devices and the corporate network.

How to Defend Against IoT Hacking

1. **Account Management**:

    - Disable unused accounts like "guest" and "demo"
    - Use lockout features to prevent brute-force attacks after repeated failed login attempts
    - Enforce strong authentication mechanisms

2. **Network and Access Controls**:

   - Place IoT systems behind firewalls and isolate them from business networks
   - Deploy Intrusion Detection System/Intrusion Prevention System (IDS/IPS)
   - Restrict access to trusted IPs only
   - Disable telnet (port 23) and UPnP on routers

3. **Encryption and Secure Communication**:

   - Use end-to-end encryption and Public Key Infrastructure (PKI)
   - Employ secure communication via VPNs

4. **Device Hardening**:

   - Protect devices from physical tampering
   - Regularly patch vulnerabilities and update firmware
   - Enable secure boot to ensure only OEM-authorized code is executed

5. **Authentication and Password Policies**:

   - Require strong passwords (8–10 characters with letters, numbers, and symbols)
   - Use CAPTCHA and account lockout policies to prevent brute-force attacks

6. **Data Security**:

   - Protect data confidentiality with symmetric encryption
   - Ensure data authentication to verify the source
   - Implement privacy measures to hide user identities

7. **Traffic and Port Monitoring**:

   - Monitor port 48101 for malicious activity
   - Use DNS filtering tools like dnswall to prevent DNS rebinding attacks

8. **Configuration Management**:

   - Change router default settings (e.g., name and password)
   - Disable unnecessary features on IoT devices

9. **Advanced Security Measures**:

   - Secure keys and credentials using trusted modules like SAM, TPM, or HSM
   - Validate code to prevent TOCTOU attacks

- Use trusted execution environments (e.g., ARM TrustZone)

10. **Web and Cloud Security**:

- Prevent IP address disclosure by disabling WebRTC in browsers
- Use ad-blockers and non-trackable extensions for web safety
- Leverage cloud-based anti-DDoS solutions and CDNs for added protection

11. **Device Management**:

- Use centralized systems for monitoring, updating, and configuring IoT devices
- Regularly scan and address vulnerabilities

12. **Vendor and Policy Compliance**:

- Work with vendors adhering to security standards
- Maintain a vulnerability disclosure policy with periodic assessments

13. **Access Control and Isolation**:

- Limit privileged access to hardware and firmware
- Run applications in containers or sandboxes for isolation

14. **Deception and Monitoring**:

- Deploy honeypots to detect malicious activity
- Use Runtime Application Self-Protection (RASP) to monitor IoT applications

15. **Zero-Trust Model**:

- Assume no device or user is trustworthy by default; continuously verify identity and permissions

16. **Blockchain and Emerging Technologies**:

- Consider blockchain for secure, tamper-proof IoT data management

How to Prevent SDR-Based Attacks

IoT devices face threats from determined attackers equipped with specialized tools. To stay ahead, proactive measures are essential to safeguard these devices before they are compromised. Below are key methods to mitigate SDR-based threats:

1. **Secure Signal Transmission**

- Encrypt signals with robust and standardized encryption techniques to safeguard communication from unauthorized access

2. **Prevent Replay Attacks with Rolling Commands**

   - Avoid repeated use of identical commands by implementing a rolling window scheme. This ensures each command is unique, reducing the risk of replay and brute-force attacks

3. **Incorporate Synchronization and Preamble Nibbles**

   - Enhance protocol security by segregating command sequences with preamble and synchronization nibbles. This prevents brute-force attacks that exploit overlaps in command sequences, such as using a de Bruijn sequence to reduce necessary bits

4. **Implement Anti-Jamming Measures**

   - Deploy anti-jamming technologies to detect and counteract unauthorized or disruptive signal interference

5. **Utilize Frequency Hopping**

   - Adopt Frequency-Hopping Spread Spectrum (FHSS) techniques to frequently change radio frequencies, making it challenging for attackers to intercept or disrupt signals.

6. **Strengthen Key Management**

   - Employ secure key management systems, such as Hardware Security Modules (HSMs), to protect cryptographic keys and ensure secure operations in SDR-based communications

7. **Secure OTA Updates**

   - Ensure firmware updates and configuration changes are delivered over secure, cryptographically signed channels to guarantee authenticity and integrity

General Guidelines for IoT Device Manufacturers

IoT device manufacturers must take necessary measures to implement the following
fundamental security practices:

- Conduct mutual verification of SSL certificates and maintain a certificate revocation list

- Enforce the use of strong, secure passwords
- Store credentials in secure, trusted storage instead of hardcoding them
- Ensure a simple and secure update process with a chain of trust
- Implement account lockout mechanisms to prevent brute force attacks after repeated failed login attempts
- Harden devices against attacks by restricting unnecessary features and configurations
- Regularly remove unused tools and use whitelisting to permit only trusted applications
- Employ secure boot chains to validate all executed software
- Test new product features for potential security vulnerabilities before release
- Avoid risky functions like gets() using secure alternatives to prevent buffer overflow vulnerabilities
- Integrate security measures into the IoT software development lifecycle
- Protect users' data with clear data-sharing and transfer policies
- Provide consumers with guidelines for secure device configuration
- Equip devices with external hardware tamper alerts to ensure physical security
- Incorporate network security tools such as firewalls, intrusion detection systems, and network segmentation
- Maintain transparency about security features and risks while offering clear channels for reporting vulnerabilities
- Use secure, industry-standard communication protocols like MQTT, CoAP, or HTTPS for data transmission
- Add hardware-based security components, such as Trusted Platform Modules (TPM) or secure elements, for cryptographic key protection, secure boot, and tamper-resistant data storage

OWASP Top 10 IoT Vulnerabilities Solutions

The rapid advancement of IoT technology has often overlooked critical security aspects, leaving devices vulnerable to exploitation. Weak security measures in IoT systems have led to escalating risks, including cyberattacks, data breaches, and privacy violations. To mitigate these threats, developers and security experts must rigorously assess IoT devices for vulnerabilities before deployment.

Below are the OWASP Top 10 IoT Security Vulnerabilities, along with their respective countermeasures:

1. Weak, Guessable, or Hardcoded Passwords

Security Measures:

- Implement Automated Password Management (APM) tools
- Enforce strong, complex passwords (minimum length, special characters)

2. Insecure Network Services

Security Measures:

- Disable unused ports and services
- Turn off Universal Plug and Play (UPnP) to prevent unauthorized access
- Implement TLS encryption for all network communications

3. Insecure Ecosystem Interfaces

Security Measures:

- Enable account lockout after multiple failed attempts
- Conduct regular security audits of all interfaces
- Implement input validation and output filtering
- Require Multi-Factor Authentication (MFA) for critical systems

4. Lack of Secure Update Mechanism

Security Measures:

- Authenticate update sources and verify digital signatures
- Implement end-to-end encryption for update distribution
- Establish clear update notification protocols for users

5. Use of Insecure or Outdated Components

Security Measures:

- Conduct regular component vulnerability scans
- Eliminate redundant libraries and features
- Vet third-party components through secure supply chain practices

6. Insufficient Privacy Protection

Security Measures:

- Adopt data minimization principles
- Implement robust data anonymization techniques
- Provide user-configurable data collection preferences

7. Insecure Data Transfer and Storage

Security Measures:

- Enforce strong encryption for all data transmissions
- Maintain updated TLS configurations
- Use standardized, peer-reviewed encryption methods

8. Lack of Device Management

Security Measures:

- Implement device reputation systems
- Verify device metadata and configurations
- Establish secure device retirement procedures

9. Insecure Default Settings

Security Measures:

- Mandate credential changes during initial setup
- Configure optimal security settings by default
- Disable unnecessary remote access features

10. Lack of Physical Hardening

Security Measures:

- Secure low-level access with firmware passwords
- Configure secure boot sequences
- Reduce physical attack surfaces by removing unused ports

IoT Framework Security Considerations

To ensure the security of IoT devices, a well-designed framework must integrate robust protections from the ground up. A secure IoT framework should enforce security by default, minimizing the need for developers to implement additional safeguards later.

The security evaluation criteria for IoT frameworks can be divided into four key components, each with distinct security requirements:

1. Edge Security

The edge consists of physical IoT devices (sensors, actuators, etc.) that interact with the environment. These devices vary in hardware, OS, and connectivity, making security challenging.

Framework Requirements:

- Cross-platform compatibility to function in diverse environments
- Secure communication and storage encryption (e.g., TLS, AES)
- Elimination of default credentials with enforced strong passwords

2. Gateway Security

The gateway bridges edge devices and the cloud, serving as a critical security checkpoint.

Framework Requirements:

- End-to-end encryption for secure data transmission
- Strong authentication mechanisms (e.g., mutual TLS, certificate-based auth)
- Multi-directional authentication to verify both edge and cloud endpoints
- Automatic updates to patch vulnerabilities without manual intervention

3. Cloud Platform Security

The cloud acts as the central hub for data aggregation and Command and Control (C2), making it a high-risk target.

Framework Requirements:

- Strict access controls (RBAC, MFA)
- Encrypted communications and storage (e.g., TLS, data-at-rest encryption)
- Secure APIs and web interfaces (e.g., OAuth 2.0, rate limiting)
- Automated patch management for C2 systems and backend services

4. Mobile Interface Security

Mobile apps enable remote IoT device management, often with elevated privileges, increasing attack risks.

Framework Requirements:

- Strong user authentication (biometrics, OTP)
- Account lockout mechanisms after repeated failed attempts
- Secure local storage (e.g., encrypted keychains)
- Encrypted data transmission (HTTPS, certificate pinning)

IoT Hardware Security Best Practices

Hardware-Level Security Countermeasures

To defend against persistent cyber threats targeting IoT devices, organizations should implement the following hardware-level security measures:

1. **Minimize Attack Surface by Restricting Entry Points**

- Disable unnecessary physical ports (e.g., USB, serial) to prevent unauthorized access
- Lock or deactivate unused interfaces to block direct hardware exploitation

2. **Deploy Hardware Tamper Detection and Protection**

- Integrate tamper-evident mechanisms (e.g., seals, sensors) to detect physical breaches like board tampering or enclosure removal
- Use GPS tracking for stolen/lost devices to enable recovery and remote deactivation

3. **Enforce Secure Boot and Trusted Storage**

- Validate boot integrity to prevent malicious firmware injection or bootloader attacks
- Leverage hardware-backed security (e.g., TPM, Secure Element) for cryptographic key storage and device authentication

4. **Firmware and Patch Management**

- Deploy timely firmware updates to address vulnerabilities during pre-patch and post-patch phases
- Use secure Over-the-Air (OTA) mechanisms to prevent exploitation during updates

5. **Secure Interface Integration**

- Implement hardened APIs and libraries during development to prevent data leaks or unauthorized access
- Monitor interface activity to detect and block suspicious behavior

6. **Physical Security Hardening**

- Seal unused ports (e.g., USB, Ethernet) to deter tampering in public deployments
- Use ruggedized enclosures for devices in harsh environments

7. Authentication and Key Security

- Store cryptographic keys securely (e.g., TPM, HSM) and tie them to unique device IDs
- Enforce Multi-Factor Authentication (MFA) for device access

8. Logging and Threat Monitoring

- Maintain detailed audit logs for security events to enable rapid incident response
- Deploy Security Information and Event Management (SIEM) for real-time anomaly detection

9. Malware Protection

- Install endpoint protection to scan for malware at device entry points
- Restrict executable permissions to prevent unauthorized code execution

10. Credential and Access Control

- Encrypt credentials and implement dynamic magic-number authentication
- Isolate administrative access to authorized personnel only

11. Power Supply Protection

- Use surge protectors and voltage regulators to prevent Rowhammer-style electrical attacks
- Implement fail-safe power cutoffs for critical components

12. Root-Level Security

- Adopt a root-of-trust model (e.g., TEEs) to restrict privileged access
- Disable default root accounts and enforce Role-Based Access Control (RBAC)

13. Legacy Device Security

- Deploy secure gateways to add encryption and access controls for older devices
- Segment legacy devices to limit exposure to modern threats

14. Wireless Security

- Enable WPA3, AES encryption, and MAC filtering for Wi-Fi/Bluetooth/Zigbee
- Rotate keys periodically and disable unused wireless protocols

15. Debug Interface Lockdown

- Disable JTAG/UART interfaces post-development or protect them with authentication
- Monitor debug port activity for unauthorized access attempts

16. Hardware-Based Security

- Leverage TEEs/secure enclaves for tamper-proof cryptographic operations
- Embed intrusion detection sensors to alert on physical breaches

17. Sensor Data Protection

- Validate and encrypt sensor data end-to-end
- Anonymize sensitive data to comply with privacy regulations (e.g., GDPR)

Countermeasures For Securing Communication Data

Here are the countermeasures for securing communication data and TPMs in IoT hardware units:

- **Use Third-Party Authentication Software**

Incorporate third-party authentication tools, such as Bitlocker drive encryption, to authenticate data imported from external storage locations beyond the TPM perimeter.

- **Apply Software Tools for TPM Communication**

Software solutions like Nuvoton for IoT devices manage communication via interfaces like I2C and SPI in TPM-equipped hardware.

- **Bind Data Using TPM Keys**

Secure data by binding it with a TPM-specific encryption key based on the RSA encryption standard before transferring it.

- **Implement Sealing and Unsealing during Updates**

Apply the sealing and unsealing concept of hardware authentication during critical computational updates, such as firmware updates or security patch installations.

- **Use HMAC-based Secure Communication**

Implement HMAC-key-based secure communication between the TPM-based IoT device and the end user to protect data during transmission.

- **Use Symmetric-Key Encryption for Low-Data Applications**

Employ symmetric-key encryption for applications involving minimal data transmission outside the TPM perimeter to maintain data authenticity and integrity.

- **Verify Sender Authentication Before Decryption**

Ensure sender authenticity before decrypting data by utilizing HMAC verification with TPM devices and applying block-mode encryption algorithms like CBC or CFB.

- **Use RSA-based Encryption for Data Integrity**

Guarantee data integrity by applying RSA-based encryption and digital signatures to verify the data.

- **Store Keys in Non-Volatile Memory**

Leverage TPMs to store encryption keys in Non-Volatile Random-Access Memory (NVRAM), ensuring read/write capabilities during incidents like data loss caused by environmental stress or attacks.

- **Use Canonical Data Transfer Mode**

Optimize data transfer using the canonical mode, which removes unnecessary bytes from extended data-stream communications in TPM-enabled IoT devices.

- **Implement Root-of-Trust Models**

Use root-of-trust models like RT for Measurement (RTM) and RT for Verification (RTV) from TPM devices to ensure secure booting and data transmission in IoT units.

- **Ensure Perfect Forward Secrecy**

Enable perfect forward secrecy by ensuring each communication session uses a unique session key independent of long-term keys.

- **Use Certificate-Based Authentication**

Authenticate IoT devices and backend servers using certificate-based mechanisms before establishing secure connections.

- **Apply Remote Attestation via TPM**

Utilize remote attestation features from TPMs to verify the integrity of IoT devices and evaluate their security posture against remote servers or services.

- **Use Authenticated Encryption with Associated Data (AEAD)**

Implement AEAD algorithms, such as AES-GCM or AES-CCM, to provide confidentiality and integrity for communication data.

- **Leverage Hardware-Based Random Number Generators**

Use hardware-based Random Number Generators (RNGs) to generate cryptographic keys and Initialization Vectors (IVs) for encryption processes.

- **Use Cryptographic Hardware Acceleration**

Offload encryption and decryption operations from the CPU using cryptographic hardware acceleration features in modern processors or dedicated cryptographic coprocessors.

- **Implement Key Rotation Policies**

Establish key rotation policies to periodically change the encryption keys used for communication between IoT devices and backend servers.

Secure Development Practices for IoT Applications

Here are some secure development practices to safeguard IoT applications:

- **Ensure Secure Boot**

Verify that devices only run authenticated and validated code during the boot process to prevent unauthorized firmware updates or modifications.

- **Secure API Endpoints**

Protect APIs with proper authentication and ensure thorough data validation to avoid vulnerabilities like SQL injection, Cross-Site Scripting (XSS), and Cross-Site Request Forgery (CSRF).

- **Implement Threat Modeling**

Assess potential security risks and threats specific to the IoT application and its ecosystem, considering factors like data privacy, device authentication, and communication protocols.

- **Follow Secure Coding Practices**

Adhere to secure coding guidelines to avoid common issues such as buffer overflows, injection attacks, and XSS vulnerabilities within the IoT application code.

- **Perform Security Testing**

Throughout the development process, carry out extensive security testing, penetration testing, vulnerability scanning, and code reviews to identify and address security weaknesses.

- **Secure Firmware or Software Updates**

Implement secure Over-The-Air (OTA) mechanisms to safely deliver patches and firmware updates to IoT devices, preventing unauthorized alterations and reducing the risk of exploitation.

- **Ensure Device Identity Management**

Use unique identifiers and digital certificates for IoT devices to enable secure authentication and establish trust within the IoT ecosystem.

- **Implement Hardware Security**

Leverage hardware-based security features such as Trusted Platform Modules (TPM), secure elements, or Hardware Security Modules (HSM) to store cryptographic keys, perform secure operations, and protect sensitive data.

- **Allow Code Signing**

Digitally sign firmware, software updates, and application codes to verify their authenticity and integrity before installation, reducing the risk of unauthorized changes or malware insertion.

- **Implement Runtime Protection**

Adopt runtime protection strategies like monitoring code execution, preventing stack overflows, and ensuring memory safety to detect and block software vulnerabilities at runtime.

- **Ensure Secure Cloud Integration**

Implement appropriate authentication, access control, and data encryption measures to protect sensitive data stored or processed in the cloud and ensure secure connectivity with cloud services.

- **Utilize Secure Communication Protocols**

Use secure communication protocols, such as MQTT with TLS/SSL, for device-to-cloud communication, ensuring data confidentiality, integrity, and secure exchange between IoT devices and backend servers.

IoT Device Management

IoT device management plays a crucial role in mitigating cyber threats by offering:

- Ensures only verified and secure devices with valid credentials are registered, reducing unauthorized access
- Manages device settings to maintain optimal performance and correct operation, including restoring factory defaults when decommissioning
- Identifies vulnerabilities, operational errors, and software bugs by analyzing system logs for timely resolution
- Keeps devices secure by performing remote upkeep and deploying the latest security patches regularly

IoT Security Tools

The Internet of Things (IoT) is not just a network of internet-connected devices, it is a highly complex and rapidly evolving technology. To effectively assess and mitigate risks, robust security measures must be implemented to safeguard IoT ecosystems. IoT security tools play a vital role in reducing vulnerabilities and defending devices and networks against cyber threats.

Key IoT Security Solutions:

SeaCat.io

- A security-first SaaS platform designed for reliable, scalable, and secure IoT operations
- Protects end-users, businesses, and sensitive data through centralized device management
- Enables remote access, real-time monitoring, and automated updates to patch vulnerabilities
- Implements strong cryptographic authentication to prevent unauthorized access
- Ensures compliance with regulations and prevents devices from being hijacked for botnet attacks

Armis Centrix

- Provides complete visibility, protection, and management of all IoT assets and processes
- Identifies vulnerabilities and enforces customized security policies to meet compliance standards
- Detects outdated OS versions and ensures timely updates
- Proactively identifies signature-based attacks and Indicators of Compromise (IOCs)
- Collects and analyzes forensic data before, during, and after incidents, enabling data-driven threat response

Listed below are some of the additional IoT security tools and solutions:

- FortiNAC
- Microsoft Defender for IoT
- Symantec Critical System Protection
- Cisco Industrial Threat Defense
- AWS IoT Device Defender
- Forescout
- NSFOCUS Anti-DDoS System
- Azure Sphere
- Overwatch
- Barbara
- Sternum
- Asimily
- ByteSweep
- Entrust IoT Security
- IOT ASSET DISCOVERY

OT Hacking

Operational Technology (OT) hacking targets industrial systems that manage physical processes, such as SCADA systems, PLCs, and HMIs used in manufacturing, utilities, and critical infrastructure. Unlike traditional IT attacks, OT attacks can have real-world consequences, ranging from production halts to safety hazards. Threat actors may exploit insecure network configurations, legacy systems, or unsegmented networks to disrupt or manipulate operations. The infamous Stuxnet worm is a notable example of an OT-targeted cyberattack.

OT Attack Countermeasures

This section covers a range of OT security strategies, OT vulnerabilities and their corresponding solutions, security measures aligned with the Purdue model, global OT security organizations, and OT security solutions and tools. Organizations can implement effective mechanisms to safeguard critical industrial infrastructure and related IT systems against cyber threats by adopting these security measures.

How to Defend Against OT Hacking

To mitigate OT hacking risks, the following countermeasures are recommended:

- Regularly perform risk assessments to minimize exposure to potential threats
- Deploy specialized sensors designed to identify vulnerabilities within the network passively
- Consistently update OT hardware and software tools to maintain security
- Disable unused ports and services to reduce attack surfaces
- Apply secure configurations and follow secure coding practices for OT applications
- Ensure systems are upgraded to the latest technologies and patched frequently
- Maintain a comprehensive asset inventory to monitor outdated or unsupported systems
- Continuously analyze log data from OT systems for real-time attack detection
- Provide employees with training on updated security policies and enhance their awareness of emerging threats
- Enforce strong, hashed passwords and replace default factory-set passwords
- Protect remote access by implementing multi-layered security measures such as two-factor authentication, VPNs, encryption, and firewalls
- Develop and implement incident response and business continuity plans
- Strengthen the network perimeter to block and filter unauthorized inbound traffic
- Conduct regular scans of systems and networks using anti-malware tools
- Limit network traffic using techniques such as rate-limiting and whitelisting to mitigate DDoS and brute-force attacks
- Enhance system security by disabling unnecessary services and functions
- Apply patches for vulnerabilities promptly, as released by manufacturers
- Monitor DNS logs frequently to identify unauthorized access attempts
- Update and secure systems interacting with ICS/SCADA devices to prevent exploitation that could bypass security gateways
- Engage professional red teams to identify vulnerabilities in critical industrial infrastructure

- Deploy Intrusion Detection Systems (IDS) and flow-monitoring tools to detect potential attacks early
- Validate and sanitize all input data to prevent attacks like buffer overflow, command injection, and Cross-Site Scripting (XSS)
- Use library functions instead of external processes to achieve desired functionality securely
- Process SQL queries using prepared statements, parameterized queries, or stored procedures in ICS systems
- Host ICS web applications only on tested and trusted third-party web servers
- Design ICS systems to restrict unauthorized access and enforce the principle of least privilege
- Verify the integrity of transmitted messages by appending checksums to each message
- Ensure ICS vendors incorporate cryptographic signatures into application updates
- Conduct periodic audits of industrial systems to validate security controls, production, and management practices
- Use Demilitarized Zone (DMZ) connections between ICS and corporate networks to enable secure communication
- Validate the bounds and integrity of network data on server applications processing ICS protocol traffic
- Review source code for ICS applications handling network traffic to identify potential vulnerabilities
- Implement network traffic monitoring tools with Deep Packet Inspection (DPI) capabilities to detect malicious activities in OT networks
- Deploy Next-Generation Firewalls (NGFWs) with DPI features to monitor and filter traffic at network perimeters
- Utilize OT-specific Intrusion Detection and Prevention Systems (IDPS) designed to detect and block cyber threats targeting industrial control systems
- Integrate encryption, authentication, and integrity verification mechanisms to protect industrial protocols like Modbus, DNP3, and OPC
- Equip OT devices with endpoint protection solutions to guard against malware, ransomware, and other cyberattacks
- Establish secure remote access in OT environments through solutions like Virtual Private Networks (VPNs) with Multi-Factor Authentication (MFA) and encrypted sessions
- Implement Public Key Infrastructure (PKI) to authenticate and encrypt communications between servers, PLCs, engineering workstations, and clients

OT Vulnerabilities and Solutions

Industrial systems like ICS/SCADA, PLCs, and RTUs are vulnerable to cyber threats, posing substantial risks to critical infrastructure. To safeguard these systems, organizations must implement effective security measures and controls. The following are some of the most prevalent OT vulnerabilities along with their corresponding solutions:

1. **Publicly Accessible OT Systems**

- Enable multi-factor authentication for enhanced security
- Utilize enterprise-level firewalls and secure remote access solutions
- Create and routinely test incident response plans to ensure preparedness

2. **Insecure Remote Connections**

- Employ a secure multi-factor authentication system and enforce stringent password policies
- Adopt effective security patch management practices
- Utilize Role-Based Access Control (RBAC) to regulate remote access permissions

3. **Missing Security Updates**

- Conduct application testing in a sandbox environment before deploying them live
- Use firewalls and apply device hardening measures

4. **Weak Passwords**

- Establish distinct username conventions for corporate IT and OT networks
- Replace default credentials during installation
- Conduct security audits to ensure compliance with secure password policies across both IT and OT networks

5. **Insecure Firewall Configuration**

- Set up a secure firewall configuration
- Define and manage Access Control Lists (ACLs) on the firewall

6. **OT Systems Placed within the Corporate IT Network**

- Separate corporate IT and OT devices
- Create a Demilitarized Zone (DMZ) for all IT and OT systems connections
- Continuously monitor the DMZ

7. **Insufficient Security for Corporate IT Networks from OT Systems**

- Limit access to the IT/OT network according to business requirements
- Set up a secure gateway between the OT and IT networks
- Conduct regular risk assessments

8. **Lack of Segmentation within OT Networks**

- Differentiate between critical and non-critical systems
- Implement a zoning model that applies a defense-in-depth strategy
- Adopt a zero-trust security model, assuming no trust by default

9. **Lack of Encryption and Authentication for Wireless OT Networks**

- Implement robust wireless encryption protocols
- Utilize industry-standard cryptographic algorithms
- Perform regular security audits

10. **Unrestricted Outbound Internet Access from OT Networks**

- Perform a formal risk assessment
- Carefully monitor and isolate OT systems from external access
- Store security updates in a separate repository outside the OT network

How to Secure an IT/OT Environment

The convergence of IT and OT is increasingly embraced by industries such as traffic control systems, power plants, and manufacturing companies. These IT/OT systems are frequently targeted by attackers seeking to exploit vulnerabilities and launch cyberattacks. According to the Purdue model, the IT/OT environment is structured into multiple levels, with each level requiring appropriate security measures.

Let's look at the various types of attacks on an IT/OT environment and the security controls needed to strengthen the network against cyber threats:

1. **Spear phishing, Ransomware**

- Firewalls, IPS, Anti-bot, URL filtering, SSL inspection, Antivirus, DLP

2. **DoS attacks**

- Anti-DoS solutions, IPS, Antibot, Application control, ALF

3. **Ransomware, Bot infection, Unsecured USB ports**

Anti-bot, IPS, Sandboxing, Application Control, Traffic encryption, Port protection

4. **DDoS exploitation, Unencrypted protocols, Default credentials, Application and OS vulnerabilities**

- IPS, Firewall, Communication encryption using IPsec, Security gateways, Use of authorized RTU and PLC commands

5. **Physical security breach**

- Point-to-point communication, MAC authentication, Additional security gateways at levels 1 and 0

Implementing a Zero-Trust Model for ICS/SCADA

To defend against increasingly sophisticated attacks targeting Industrial Control Systems (ICS) and Operational Technology (OT) networks, organizations must adopt proactive security measures. Below are key countermeasures to strengthen ICS/OT security:

1. Implement a Zero-Trust Security Model

- **Define the Network Attack Surface**

  o Identify critical assets, sensitive data, and key applications within control centers and factory floors

- **Map and Monitor Network Traffic**

  o Document traffic flows to gain full visibility into device interactions and data movement

- **Design a Zero-Trust Architecture (ZTA)**

  o Deploy Next-Generation Firewalls (NGFW) for segmentation and access control
  o Restrict lateral movement by isolating critical zones

- **Establish a Zero-Trust Policy**

  o Enforce strict whitelisting for users, devices, and applications
  o Define access rules based on need-to-know and least-privilege principles

- **Continuous Monitoring and Maintenance**

- o Use real-time traffic analysis to detect anomalies
- o Regularly update and patch network devices

2. Strengthen Legacy System Security

- **Enforce Strict Access Controls**

  - o Replace default credentials with strong, unique passwords
  - o Implement Multi-Factor Authentication (MFA) for all users

- **Segment Networks to Limit Exposure**

  - o Separate IT and OT networks using DMZs
  - o Apply micro-segmentation to restrict unauthorized lateral movement

- **Monitor and Patch Outdated Systems**

  - o Deploy virtual patching where traditional updates are unavailable
  - o Use Intrusion Detection Systems (IDS) to detect exploitation attempts

3. Enhance Threat Detection and Response

- **Deploy Anomaly Detection Systems**

  - o Use AI/ML-based monitoring to identify unusual behavior

- **Develop an Incident Response Plan**

  - o Conduct regular drills to test response effectiveness
  - o Establish automated alerting for critical threats

- **Secure Remote Access**

  - o Replace VPNs with Zero-Trust Network Access (ZTNA) solutions
  - o Log and audit all remote sessions

4. Secure Wireless and External Communications

- **Encrypt All Data Transmissions**

  - o Use TLS 1.2+ for network communications
  - o Avoid proprietary encryption in favor of AES-256 or similar standards

- **Restrict Outbound Internet Access**

  - o Block unnecessary external connections from OT networks
  - o Use offline update repositories for patches

5. Physical and Operational Hardening

- **Disable Unused Ports and Services**

  o Remove or lock USB, serial, and debug ports where possible

- **Implement Tamper-Evident Measures**

  o Use Hardware Security Modules (HSM) for cryptographic key protection
  o Deploy environmental sensors to detect physical breaches

- **Conduct Regular Security Audits**

  o Perform penetration testing and red team exercises
  o Validate compliance with NIST, IEC 62443, or ISO 27001 standards

International OT Security Organizations

As OT systems become more widespread and integrated with IT, security experts must exercise heightened caution and implement robust security policies to safeguard OT networks. Several global cybersecurity organizations are dedicated to providing security frameworks and insights to enhance the resilience of critical infrastructure.

Below are a few international organizations that notify companies about potential threats and offer IT/OT solutions to defend OT industries against cyberattacks:

Operational Technology Cybersecurity Coalition (OTCC)

- Encourage industry-wide collaboration to address OT cybersecurity challenges
- Promote sharing of threat intelligence and best practices among stakeholders
- Advocate for government and private sector policies that support OT security
- Support the development of cybersecurity tools tailored for OT environments
- Facilitate joint efforts in threat detection and response across critical infrastructure sectors

Operational Technology Information Sharing and Analysis Center (OT-ISAC)

- Provide a secure platform for real-time threat intelligence sharing among OT sectors
- Disseminate alerts, advisories, and analysis related to current and emerging threats

- Conduct cybersecurity exercises and simulations to test OT network resilience
- Encourage peer-to-peer collaboration through trusted communities of interest
- Offer tools and methods to bridge IT-OT security gap through unified threat detection

North American Electric Reliability Corporation (NERC)

- Enforce mandatory security standards such as NERC Critical Infrastructure Protection (CIP)
- Conduct risk assessments and reliability studies for electric utility operators
- Monitor bulk power system operations to identify vulnerabilities and anomalies
- Offer certification and training programs to improve cybersecurity workforce competence
- Mandate incident reporting and response planning to enhance resilience

Industrial Internet Security Framework (IISF)

- Identify and categorize risks across IT and OT integrated systems
- Recommend layered security approaches to reduce system vulnerabilities
- Support real-time monitoring and anomaly detection for industrial systems
- Promote secure interoperability between legacy OT and modern IT systems
- Encourage stakeholder alignment on risk mitigation strategies and policies

ISA/IEC-62443 Standard

- Define security levels and corresponding technical requirements for OT components
- Implement a defense-in-depth approach across Industrial Automation and Control Systems (IACS)
- Ensure component-level security (embedded devices, host systems, network elements)
- Enable secure product development lifecycle for industrial automation vendors
- Support segmentation and zoning to limit lateral movement during attacks

OT Security Solutions

The industrial and corporate sectors are increasingly digitizing their operational processes, expanding access to OT devices across a wider range of the internet. However, the costs associated with managing security in heavy industries are often

underestimated, resulting in various security challenges. To mitigate these risks, industries should invest in cybersecurity programs and solutions.

Cybersecurity professionals should carefully assess the current challenges and requirements, adapting security measures to meet these evolving needs while implementing necessary operational changes. Consequently, many established OEM providers and start-ups have introduced new strategies and technologies to safeguard the OT environment.

Given the decentralized nature of heavy industries, security solutions can be integrated into all technology-related decisions within both IT and OT. Information Risk Management (IRM) can also serve as a second line of defense, with some industries even implementing internal audits as a third line of defense.

Some of the emerging technology solutions organizations are using to safeguard the OT environment include:

Firewalls

- Deploy industrial-grade firewalls between IT and OT networks to inspect and control traffic
- Use firewalls to detect and block threats trying to move laterally between systems
- Place critical systems (e.g., SCADA) in a DMZ to isolate them from external threats
- Utilize ruggedized, next-generation firewall solutions tailored for OT environments like:

    o FortiGate Rugged Next-Generation Firewalls

    o OTIFYD Next-Gen OT Firewalls

Unified Identity and OT Access Management

- Centralize user access control to streamline authentication and authorization
- Integrate OT access with corporate identity management systems for unified oversight
- Apply least privilege principles, limiting superuser privileges
- Monitor and log access to critical assets to identify and trace unauthorized actions
- Implement tools like:

    o Claroty

    o MetaDefender IT-OT Access

Asset Inventory and Device Authorization

- Maintain a real-time inventory of all devices connected to the OT network
- Allow only authorized devices to connect, blocking unapproved hardware
- Assess device vulnerabilities based on model, version, and manufacturer
- Detect malfunctioning devices and optimize operational efficiency
- Use tools such as:

  o SCADAfence

  o OTbase

  o Guardian

  o Dragos

OT Network Monitoring and Anomaly Detection

- Monitor OT traffic continuously and non-invasively to ensure smooth operations
- Use AI/ML algorithms to detect anomalies or signs of malicious behavior
- Enable early detection and response to security breaches
- Employ tools like:

  o iSID

  o Rhebo OT Security

Decoys to Mislead Attackers (Deception Technology)

- Deploy honeypots to trap and monitor attacker behavior within the OT network
- Use deception to reveal attacker intentions and movements early in the breach
- Add a proactive defense layer by confusing and misleading potential intruders
- Leverage deception tools like:

  o Attivo Networks ThreatDefend

  o Conpot

  o GasPot

OT Security Tools

Here are some tools available for securing OT systems and networks:

Flowmon

- Provides continuous monitoring of industrial network performance and security
- Detects anomalies such as malfunctioning devices or unauthorized access attempts
- Helps mitigate advanced threats like cyber espionage and zero-day vulnerabilities
- Prevents network downtime and ensures the availability of industrial services
- Enables quick response to malware or suspicious behavior in real-time

Here are some other tools for securing an OT environment:

- Tenable OT Security
- Nozomi Networks
- Forescout
- FortiGuard
- RAM2)

Important Exam Tips for the Certified Ethical Hacker (CEH) Exam on IoT and OT Hacking

It is important to understand the threats and attack techniques targeting IoT and OT environments, highlighting the unique risks they pose and the importance of securing these systems. Here are some key exam tips to help you excel in this area:

1. **IoT Hacking**

- Exploiting vulnerabilities in internet-connected smart devices (like cameras, thermostats, or wearables) to gain unauthorized access or control

Countermeasures:

- Implement two-way authentication with cryptographic algorithms (e.g., SHA-HMAC, ECDSA)
- Utilize SSL/TLS protocols for secure communication
- Eliminate hardcoded credentials in firmware/software
- Use of up-to-date components to mitigate known vulnerabilities

2. **OT Hacking**

- Targeting industrial control systems (like SCADA or PLCs) used in manufacturing or critical infrastructure to disrupt physical operations

Countermeasures:

- Utilize threat intelligence to detect potential risks and prioritize OT patching to protect critical assets

- Employ a secure multi-factor authentication system and enforce stringent password policies
- Deploy industrial-grade firewalls between IT and OT networks to inspect and control traffic

Chapter 19: Cloud Computing

Introduction

In today's digital landscape, cloud computing has revolutionized the way organizations store, manage, and process data. With the scalability, flexibility, and cost-effectiveness it offers, cloud platforms have become essential to modern IT infrastructure. However, with great innovation comes great responsibility, and risk. As businesses increasingly rely on cloud environments such as Amazon Web Services (AWS), Microsoft Azure, Google Cloud Platform (GCP), and containerized solutions like Docker and Kubernetes, the attack surface has expanded significantly. Threat actors are constantly evolving their techniques to exploit misconfigurations, vulnerabilities, and weak security practices in the cloud.

This chapter explores the most common hacking techniques targeting cloud platforms and services, followed by practical and strategic countermeasures to defend against them. We begin with an overview of cloud computing and delve into specific threats and countermeasures for leading cloud service providers. From AWS, Azure, and GCP hacking to the intricacies of container and Kubernetes vulnerabilities, we examine how attackers gain unauthorized access, escalate privileges, and compromise cloud resources. In parallel, we introduce actionable countermeasures that can help mitigate these risks, such as identity and access management best practices, logging and monitoring, encryption, network security, and container hardening.

Moreover, as serverless computing becomes more prevalent, this chapter highlights the unique security risks it introduces, along with tailored strategies to safeguard serverless functions and event-driven architectures.

By the end of this chapter, readers will gain a comprehensive understanding of the threat landscape in cloud computing and be equipped with a solid foundation of countermeasures to secure their cloud environments effectively.

Cloud Computing

Cloud computing is the delivery of computing services, including servers, storage, databases, networking, software, and moreover the internet. It allows organizations to scale resources dynamically and pay only for what they use. However, with increased accessibility comes increased exposure to cyber threats. Misconfigurations, lack of visibility, and shared responsibility models often lead to vulnerabilities that attackers can exploit.

Cloud Computing Countermeasures

- Implement mechanisms to protect, back up, and retain data securely
- Set and enforce Service Level Agreements (SLAs) for timely patching and fixing vulnerabilities
- Ensure vendors undergo regular AICPA SSAE 18 Type II compliance audits
- Regularly check if your cloud services appear on public domain blacklists
- Include legal agreements as part of your employee conduct policies
- Ban the sharing of login credentials across users, apps, and services
- Apply robust controls for authentication, access permissions, and audit tracking
- Ensure data protection measures are in place during design and operational phases
- Continuously inspect client network traffic for signs of malicious behavior
- Restrict unauthorized access to servers by implementing security checkpoints
- Provide customers with access to relevant logs and data when applicable
- Review and evaluate the cloud provider's security practices and service commitments
- Evaluate the security of cloud APIs and log client network activity for monitoring
- Conduct routine security reviews and implement updates to maintain cloud safety
- Maintain round-the-clock physical security all year long
- Apply strict security protocols during system installation and configuration
- Guarantee isolation of memory, storage, and network access for enhanced protection
- Use robust two-factor authentication methods wherever feasible
- Implement a standardized process for notifying security breaches
- Review dependencies within API-related software modules for potential risks
- Require rigorous registration and validation procedures
- Conduct regular assessments for vulnerabilities and misconfigurations
- Share relevant infrastructure details, security patch schedules, and firewall settings with customers
- Enforce comprehensive cloud security policies, software configuration controls, and transparent management practices
- Utilize security tools like Intrusion Detection Systems (IDS), Intrusion Prevention Systems (IPS), and firewalls to block unauthorized access to cloud data
- Apply strict supply chain controls and perform thorough evaluations of suppliers

- Implement strong security frameworks and policies including access control, information security governance, and contractual obligations
- Safeguard infrastructure through effective oversight, availability measures, virtual machine separation, and service reliability assurances
- Use Virtual Private Networks (VPNs) to secure user data and ensure complete data deletion, including replicas, when requested
- Use SSL encryption to protect the transmission of confidential and sensitive information
- Review the security framework of the cloud provider's user interfaces
- Carefully understand SLA terms, including uptime guarantees and penalties for service failures
- Apply essential information security measures like strong passwords, device protection, encryption, and network safeguards
- Maintain uniformity in resource configurations and enforce standard onboarding and disaster recovery practices
- Assess the organization's risk tolerance to shape minimally disruptive security policies
- Share infrastructure, patch management schedules, and firewall configurations with clients
- Use a unified identity management system across all cloud platforms
- Integrate automation and AI/ML tools to detect, evaluate, and neutralize threats swiftly
- Utilize behavioral analytics to monitor user activity and reduce the risk of internal and external data breaches
- Apply application whitelisting and memory protection methods for dedicated-use workloads
- Use advanced endpoint protection and anti-malware solutions for IaaS and PaaS environments
- Conduct regular penetration testing to verify the effectiveness of cloud security measures
- Deploy a Cloud Access Security Broker (CASB) to ensure strong security governance in the cloud
- Establish a data deletion policy that ensures secure and compliant removal of sensitive data from the cloud

AWS Hacking

Amazon Web Services (AWS) is one of the most widely used cloud platforms, offering a broad range of services. Due to its popularity, it is also a prime target for attackers. Common attack vectors include exposed access keys, misconfigured S3

buckets, and insecure IAM policies. Understanding how these attacks work is essential to building a strong security posture in AWS environments.

Aws Hacking Countermeasures

Basic AWS Security Practices

- Organize user identities by grouping them into accounts, roles, and groups to manage permissions effectively
- Use temporary security credentials to minimize risks associated with long-term access keys
- Set policies for routine credential updates, including access keys, passwords, and other authentication methods
- Apply the least privilege principle to ensure users only have access to what they need on AWS
- Develop clear and accessible AWS security policies for organizational use
- Separate AWS components like resources and user data based on their security requirements
- Use AWS Service Quotas to control and limit resource usage, preventing resource abuse and overuse
- Enable and integrate security tools that align with your organization's operational security standards
- Permanently remove unused data and inactive groups to maintain a clean and secure AWS environment
- Use IAM Access Analyzer to inspect user permissions and evaluate access policies
- Leverage AWS Git-based tools, such as git-secrets, Step Functions, and Lambda, to help secure code and restrict unauthorized access
- Activate Multi-Factor Authentication (MFA) for all AWS accounts to enhance login security
- Regularly update all systems and applications to ensure the latest security patches are applied

AWS Infrastructure Security Practices

- Utilize Information Security Management Systems (ISMS) to routinely evaluate and update security controls and policies
- Segment networks and define security zones to simplify control and monitoring of network traffic
- Deploy tools like load balancers, CDNs, and WAFs to protect against Denial-of-Service/Distributed Denial-of-Service (DoS/DDoS), Cross-Site Scripting (XSS), and SQL injection (SQLi) attacks

- Tailor AWS Security Hub insights to effectively monitor and address security issues across AWS resources
- Establish a unified policy framework for data loss prevention to safeguard sensitive information
- Conduct automated vulnerability scans on AWS infrastructure using Amazon Inspector to proactively detect security flaws

AWS Financial Services Security Practices

- Use end-to-end and Transport Data Encryption (TDE) to secure data transmission when interacting with external parties
- Conduct penetration tests on AWS services like EC2, NAT gateways, load balancers, RDS, and Aurora to uncover security weaknesses
- Utilize AWS CloudTrail and CloudWatch to track, log, and monitor activities across AWS resources for auditing purposes
- Manage multiple AWS accounts centrally with AWS Organizations and enforce governance using Service Control Policies (SCPs)

AWS Security Hub Practices

- Use AWS Labs scripts to activate Security Hub across all AWS accounts efficiently
- Implement threat detection tools like GuardDuty and Amazon Inspector to identify and respond to risks
- Enable AWS Config and CIS Foundations benchmarks across every AWS account and region for consistent security compliance
- Tag Security Hub resources to manage permissions and access more effectively
- Apply specific IAM policies for different user types and centralize identity management using Cloud Infrastructure Entitlement Management (CIEM) for streamlined control over accounts, groups, and roles
- Create custom actions to collect and review Security Hub findings for both internal and external assets to support remediation
- Prefer IAM roles over IAM users for granting application and service access to AWS resources
- Use IAM Access Analyzer to detect externally shared resources and confirm that proper security measures are in place

AWS Security Groups Practices

- Assign policies to user groups instead of individuals to simplify the management of access to AWS resources

- Enable VPC Flow Logs to monitor IP traffic and detect potential threats or suspicious behavior within the VPC
- Use Amazon VPCs to separate resources, and apply security groups and network ACLs to manage incoming and outgoing network traffic
- Set strict rules for security groups and network ACLs to tightly control data flow in and out of your instances
- Configure automated email alerts to promptly notify on critical security events

AWS Backup Data Practices

- Ensure regular and automated backups to maintain data availability and protection
- Protect backups with immutable storage to prevent unauthorized changes or deletions
- Integrate backup strategies into disaster recovery, business continuity, and incident response planning
- Set up configuration audits, monitoring, and alerting systems to track backup processes and identify issues
- Enable and monitor logs from AWS services like VPC Flow Logs, S3 access logs, and CloudFront logs for visibility and security
- Assess data recovery capabilities to ensure backups can be restored effectively when needed

Microsoft Azure Hacking

Microsoft Azure provides a comprehensive cloud platform with services spanning virtual machines, databases, identity management, and more. Threat actors may exploit weak authentication, overly permissive roles, or misconfigured services to gain unauthorized access. The complexity of Azure's role-based access and integration with on-premises systems introduces unique security challenges.

Microsoft Azure Hacking Countermeasures

- Treat identity as the foundational security boundary within Azure environments
- Monitor users who access the network through Azure ExpressRoute or site-to-site VPN connections
- Use Azure Network Watcher to diagnose frequent VPN and gateway-related issues
- Configure and enforce a Single Sign-On (SSO) policy to streamline secure access
- Make automated access control decisions using conditional access policies

- Apply Azure RBAC and Privileged Identity Management (PIM) to manage and oversee resource access
- Structure management groups with no more than three levels to minimize confusion between operational and security responsibilities
- Set up at least two emergency access accounts to ensure backup access to critical resources
- Use Microsoft security solutions like Defender for Cloud, Defender for Cloud Apps, and Microsoft Sentinel for identifying and stopping cyber threats
- Deploy Azure Security Center for proactive threat detection, vulnerability assessments (CVE scans), and integration with Defender for Endpoint
- Activate threat detection capabilities for Azure SQL databases
- Utilize cloud-native SIEM systems and integrate alerts from Defender for Cloud
- Manage client data access using Shared Access Signatures (SAS) to limit and control permissions
- Deny unnecessary access to administrative ports such as SSH, RDP, and WinRM
- Use Just-In-Time (JIT) access for virtual machines to allow temporary elevated privileges only when needed, reducing exposure
- Enforce robust operational security measures across your cloud infrastructure
- Automate deployment and configuration processes for apps and services to ensure consistency and efficiency
- Test applications and services thoroughly for performance before releasing them to production
- Enable password hash synchronization to support secure identity management
- Deactivate outdated authentication protocols to reduce security risks
- Consistently review and assess any changes made to enhance the security posture
- Perform routine audits of IAM policies to ensure they adhere to the principle of least privilege and eliminate any excess access rights
- Utilize Azure encryption tools like Azure Disk Encryption and Azure Key Vault to secure data both at rest and in transit
- Implement Azure Firewall to strengthen network security and to centrally manage and log both application and network traffic policies
- Secure and monitor access to APIs by using Azure API Management along with OAuth 2.0 authentication
- Activate Azure DDoS Protection to defend applications against Distributed Denial-of-Service attacks

- Use Azure Bastion to securely manage virtual machines through RDP and SSH without exposing them to the public internet

Google Cloud Hacking

Google Cloud Platform (GCP) offers powerful tools for data analytics, machine learning, and compute services. However, improper IAM configurations, exposed APIs, and weak network security can make GCP environments vulnerable. Attackers often focus on service account abuse and privilege escalation within the cloud environment.

Google Cloud Hacking Countermeasures

- Apply the Spoofing, Tampering, Repudiation, Information Disclosure, Denial-of-Service, and Privilege Escalation (STRIDE) threat modeling framework to identify and mitigate potential threats in Google Cloud
- Apply encryption at the application layer for services running on Google Kubernetes Engine (GKE)
- Secure GKE cluster nodes by enabling encryption with customer-managed keys and restrict access to them via HTTPS and specified IP addresses
- Mandate SSL encryption for securing data in Cloud SQL databases
- Disable interactive serial console access on Google VMs to prevent unauthorized control
- Use Terraform modules hosted in private Git repositories to automatically provision and manage infrastructure resources
- Deploy Shielded VMs to defend against rootkits, remote exploits, and unauthorized privilege escalation
- Utilize a sandboxed environment to test and analyze potential security threats
- Perform vulnerability scans on container images stored in the container registry to identify and fix known issues
- Enable Single Sign-On (SSO) for streamlined and secure user authentication
- Set up clearly defined user groups and assign roles based on specific naming standards rather than giving permissions directly to individual users
- Establish a dedicated and secure connection channel between on-premises infrastructure and Google Cloud
- Apply tag-based firewall policies to control and observe network traffic effectively
- Leverage the Cloud Logging API to collect, combine, and process logging data from various sources

- Use Google Security Command Center Enterprise to consolidate and manage security insights, helping identify misconfigurations, weaknesses, and active threats
- Keep oversight of storage volumes and resource usage across different Google Cloud projects
- Implement strong password requirements and enable Multi-Factor Authentication (MFA) across both cloud and corporate systems
- Actively monitor Admin Activity Logs to oversee access and changes to GCP resources
- Utilize IAM frameworks to control and govern access to Google Cloud assets
- Prevent cloud storage buckets from being publicly accessible within your organization's GCP environment
- Apply strict data retention policies for managing stored data in Google Cloud
- Turn on Private Google Access to allow virtual machines in VPCs to reach Google APIs and services without relying on public IPs

Container Hacking

Containers, especially those managed with Docker, have become a standard for deploying applications consistently across environments. Yet, containers can be compromised through untrusted images, exposed Docker daemons, and insecure inter-container communications. Since containers share the host OS kernel, a breach in one can potentially lead to wider system compromise if not properly isolated.

Container Security Countermeasures

- Enable full logging and auditing to track who accesses containers and what changes are made to them
- Set applications to run with non-root privileges to avoid potential privilege escalation risks
- Make the root file system of the host read-only to block write access and defend against malware attacks
- Refrain from using untrusted third-party tools, and use security scanning tools to detect harmful software in containers
- Scan container images in the repository on a routine basis to uncover security flaws or incorrect configurations
- Install application firewalls to strengthen container protection and block incoming threats
- Require authentication for access to container registries, especially when dealing with sensitive images and content

- Opt for lightweight base images to minimize potential vulnerabilities and reduce exposure
- Assign a dedicated database to each application to improve monitoring and better manage application-specific data
- Consistently apply the latest security updates to the host OS and its kernel
- Set up orchestrators to deploy workloads across separate hosts depending on their sensitivity classification
- Automate enforcement of compliance with container runtime configuration standards
- Continuously scan container images to detect any embedded malware
- Keep sensitive information in external storage and provide access to it dynamically during runtime
- Maintain an approved list of trusted registries and container images, and restrict usage to only those
- Utilize access control mechanisms like SELinux and AppArmor to defend applications and system services from threats
- Use real-time threat detection systems and have an incident response plan ready for security breaches
- Deploy immutable containers that cannot be altered once they are running
- Change user roles from default root access to non-root, and manage permissions through RBAC
- Refrain from embedding sensitive data into source code or configuration files
- Strengthen the host system by disabling unnecessary native services, and apply security hardening across the entire stack
- Minimize container size by eliminating unneeded components
- Use Infrastructure-as-Code (IaC) practices to provision cloud resources, and verify all configurations before deploying

Docker Security Countermeasures

- Avoid making the Docker daemon socket publicly accessible, as it is a primary entry point for the Docker API
- Only use Docker images from trusted sources, as images from malicious users could contain backdoors
- Regularly update the host OS and Docker software with the latest security patches
- Restrict container capabilities by granting only the necessary permissions; use the --cap-drop all command to remove all capabilities and then add back only what is required
- Always run Docker containers with the --security-opt=no-new-privileges flag to protect against privilege escalation using setuid or setgid binaries

- Disable inter-container communication when starting the Docker daemon by using --icc=false, and use the --link=CONTAINER_NAME_or_ID:ALIAS option for specific container-to-container communication
- Utilize Linux security modules, like seccomp, AppArmor, and SELinux, to have fine-grained control over processes
- Set limits on resources such as memory, CPU, file descriptors, process numbers, and container restarts to help mitigate DoS attacks
- Enable read-only mode for filesystems and volumes by using the --read-only flag
- Set the Docker daemon log level to 'info' and avoid using the 'debug' log level to reduce exposure of detailed logs
- The default user in Docker images is root; configure the container to run as a non-privileged user to mitigate the risk of privilege escalation
- Install only the essential packages needed to minimize the potential attack surface
- Verify that Docker images pulled from remote registries are digitally signed using Docker Content Trust
- Refrain from using environment variables to store sensitive information; instead, use Docker secrets management to securely encrypt secrets in transit
- Secure API endpoints by enabling HTTPS when exposing the RESTful API to prevent interception
- Avoid using the default bridge network for single-host applications with networking to enhance security
- Store sensitive data in Docker volumes to ensure better data security, persistence, and encryption
- Enable TLS to implement basic authentication for secure communication between the Docker client and the daemon over HTTPS
- Utilize tools like InSpec and Dive to identify vulnerabilities in Docker containers
- Restrict SSH login access to the admin when processing container log files and performing administrative tasks like testing and troubleshooting
- Implement an automated labeling system for containers to maintain consistency and avoid discrepancies during access
- Add the HEALTHCHECK command to Dockerfiles whenever possible to improve health monitoring and ensure secure container operations
- Leverage Docker's namespace features, such as PID, IPC, network, and user namespaces, to enhance container isolation
- Enable user namespaces to provide an extra layer of isolation between the host system and containers
- Use Docker's resource limits, such as --memory and --cpus, to control CPU and memory usage of containers

- Activate Docker Content Trust (DCT) to verify the authenticity and integrity of Docker images
- Use the Docker USER directive to specify a non-root user, preventing containers from running with root privileges

Cloud Security

Cloud security encompasses the strategies and technologies used to protect cloud-based systems, data, and infrastructure. The shared responsibility model means cloud providers secure the infrastructure, but users are responsible for securing their own data and applications. Risks include data breaches, account hijacking, and insecure APIs, all of which demand a proactive security approach.

Cloud Security Countermeasures

- Cloud computing services should be customized by the vendor according to the specific security needs of the clients
- Cloud services must have a disaster recovery plan to ensure data can be recovered in case of unexpected events
- Continuous monitoring of Quality of Service (QoS) is essential to uphold service level agreements between consumers and providers
- Data stored in cloud services should be securely managed to maintain data integrity
- Cloud services should be fast, reliable, and able to deliver quick responses to new requests
- Both symmetric and asymmetric cryptographic algorithms should be implemented for enhanced data security in the cloud
- The operational processes of cloud services must be securely engineered, managed, and integrated with organizational security practices
- Load balancing should be integrated into cloud services to optimize network performance and improve response times while maximizing throughput
- CSPs should provide strong resilience and better protection against physical threats
- Public cloud services should adopt advanced networking options like carrier-grade networks and dedicated VPNs for enhanced security
- Cloud Service Providers (CSPs) must implement effective incident response and handling plans
- CSPs should utilize services that enforce role-based protections, such as role assignments, authorization, and transaction approval
- Cloud services should integrate a global threat intelligence database containing extensive security data

- Cloud providers should incorporate Cloud Access Security Broker (CASB) solutions to offer secure web gateways with Data Loss Prevention (DLP) features
- Apply zero-trust principles to segment business applications for improved security
- CSPs must implement stringent Identity and Access Management (IAM) policies to control access to cloud resources
- Cloud services should enforce the least privileged principle using Role-Based Access Control (RBAC) and related policies
- Cloud services must comply with relevant laws, regulations, and industry standards
- CSPs should regularly test backup and recovery processes to ensure their effectiveness

Kubernetes Vulnerabilities

Kubernetes, the leading container orchestration platform, introduces its own set of security risks. These include misconfigured RBAC, insecure API server access, and lack of network segmentation. Since Kubernetes manages containerized applications at scale, any vulnerability can impact multiple services simultaneously, making its security crucial for cloud-native deployments.

Kubernetes Vulnerabilities Countermeasures

- Validate file contents and paths at every stage of processing to ensure correctness
- Use configuration methods for credential paths instead of relying on hardcoded paths
- Explicitly raise errors after each step in a compound operation to ensure proper error handling
- Employ the copy-then-rename method for log rotation to avoid losing logs when restarting the kubelet
- Avoid using compound shell commands without proper validation, as they can alter the system state
- Explicitly check the returned error value of **os.Readlink /proc/<pid>/exe** to verify if the PID corresponds to a kernel process
- Use centralized libraries and common parsing functions (e.g., **ParsePort**) across the codebase to improve code readability and consistency
- Replace log rotation with persistent logs to maintain a continuous log flow and create new logs when rotation is necessary

- Use a single encoding format for all configuration tasks to facilitate centralized validation
- Limit the size of manifest files to prevent memory overflow errors in the kubelet
- Use **kube-apiserver** instances that support Certificate Revocation Lists (CRLs) to verify the validity of presented certificates
- Rely on key management services for encrypting sensitive data, and avoid using insecure algorithms like AES-GCM or cipher block chaining
- Ensure all HTTPS connections are authenticated by default to confirm certificate authenticity and defend against Man-In-The-Middle (MITM) attacks
- Refrain from using outdated SSH tunnels as they lack proper validation of server IPs
- Implement Online Certificate Status Protocol (OCSP) stapling to verify certificate revocation statuses
- Default to secure TLS configurations for both development and production to avoid risks from misconfiguration
- Utilize Access Control Lists (ACLs) to control file access and prevent unauthorized usage
- Apply log filtering to exclude sensitive credentials like bearer tokens and basic authentication details from logs
- Activate robust logging and monitoring solutions for Kubernetes clusters using tools like Prometheus, Grafana, or the ELK Stack
- Deploy policy enforcement tools such as Open Policy Agent (OPA) or Kyverno to maintain security policy consistency across clusters
- Keep Kubernetes and its dependencies up to date by applying patches and updates regularly
- Set resource quotas and limits to guard against resource depletion and ensure cluster stability
- Use network policies and service meshes to regulate and secure communication between pods
- Periodically audit and rotate Kubernetes secrets to reduce the chances of credential leaks

Serverless Security Risks

Serverless computing allows developers to run code without managing servers, but it also introduces new attack surfaces. Common risks include insecure function permissions, event injection, and inadequate monitoring. Since serverless functions are often short-lived and triggered by events, traditional security tools may not be sufficient to detect and respond to threats.

Serverless Security Countermeasures

- Continuously monitor function layers to detect attempts of code injection and other server-related attacks
- Utilize external security tools to gain enhanced visibility and control over the serverless environment
- Keep serverless functions and their dependencies consistently updated with the latest patches
- Use scanning tools like Snyk to identify and fix known vulnerabilities in serverless applications
- Keep functions isolated and avoid depending on their access patterns or execution order for security
- Ensure all event inputs are properly sanitized to prevent injection-based attacks
- Use security-focused libraries that enforce resource restrictions and support runtime least-privilege execution
- Break functions down into smaller, focused units to avoid granting broad or implicit global roles
- Validate data using defined schemas and data transfer objects rather than relying on (de)serialization methods
- Utilize API gateways to filter input data, control traffic rates, apply throttling, and defend against DDoS attacks
- Conduct audits and enforce detailed, safe logging of function activities to enhance visibility and monitoring
- Follow secure coding standards, review code regularly to fix vulnerabilities, and use shared security libraries
- Ensure secure data transmission by using TLS/HTTPS and encrypt credentials using robust cryptographic methods
- Confirm SSL certificates to verify remote identities and halt communication if verification fails
- Use signed request mechanisms from cloud providers to secure data in transit and avoid replay attacks
- Store sensitive data in secure secret management systems that support access controls and key rotation
- Set execution time limits for serverless functions to prevent them from running indefinitely
- Apply network security measures like Virtual Private Cloud (VPC) setups to restrict access to functions
- Securely configure all event triggers (e.g., API Gateway, S3, DynamoDB) to ensure only authorized access

 Important Exam Tips for the Certified Ethical Hacker (CEH) Exam on Cloud Computing

Understanding the threat landscape in cloud computing is crucial, along with having a strong foundation in countermeasures to effectively secure cloud environments. Here are some key exam tips to help you excel in this area:

1. **Cloud Computing**

- Cloud computing delivers computing services, like servers, storage, and databases, over the internet, enabling flexibility, scalability, and cost-efficiency, but also introduces new security challenges
- **Countermeasure:** Use strong practices for key creation, secure storage, proper management, and safe disposal

2. **AWS Hacking**

- AWS environments can be targeted through misconfigurations, exposed credentials, or overly permissive roles, making it essential to understand specific attack vectors within this platform
- **Countermeasure:** Utilize AWS Trusted Advisor to identify and correct potential security misconfigurations

3. **Microsoft Azure Hacking**

- Azure can be vulnerable to attacks due to insecure identity configurations, mismanaged access controls, and improper resource permissions
- **Countermeasure:** Enable Multi-Factor Authentication (MFA) combined with conditional access settings

4. **Google Cloud Hacking**

- Google Cloud Platform (GCP) faces threats such as weak IAM policies, misconfigured APIs, and insufficient logging, which attackers can exploit
- **Countermeasure:** Use Key Management Services (KMS) and Customer-Supplied Encryption Keys (CSEKs) to securely encrypt and manage your data

5. **Container Hacking**

- Containers can be compromised through vulnerable images, insecure configurations, or escalated privileges, affecting the entire application stack

---

- **Countermeasure:** Continuously monitor known vulnerabilities (CVEs) in the container runtime and apply fixes when issues are found

6. **Cloud Security**

- Cloud security involves safeguarding data, applications, and infrastructure in the cloud from unauthorized access, data breaches, and other cyber threats
- **Countermeasure:** Cloud Service Providers (CSPs) should offer robust multi-tenancy capabilities to maximize resource utilization while ensuring the security of data and applications

7. **Kubernetes Vulnerabilities**

- Kubernetes, while powerful for orchestration, can be exploited via misconfigured components, exposed dashboards, or insecure secrets management
- **Countermeasure:** Ensure secure and reliable handling of JSON data by using trusted JSON libraries and proper type structures for interactions with Kubernetes APIs

8. **Serverless Security Risks**

- Serverless applications reduce infrastructure management but are still susceptible to risks like insecure function permissions, event injection, and third-party dependencies
- **Countermeasure:** Limit permissions during the development of serverless applications to minimize exposure to threats

Chapter 20: Cryptography

Introduction

Cryptography is a critical component of cybersecurity used to protect sensitive data through encryption and ensure secure communication across systems. It helps maintain confidentiality, integrity, authenticity, and non-repudiation of information. However, weak cryptographic practices, outdated algorithms, or implementation flaws can be exploited through attacks aimed at breaking encryption or bypassing authentication mechanisms. Understanding cryptographic principles and attack vectors is essential for ethical hackers to assess and strengthen system defenses.

Cryptography Attack

Cryptography attacks target the methods and algorithms used to secure information through encryption. These attacks attempt to break or bypass encryption to gain unauthorized access to data. Cryptographic weaknesses can arise from poor algorithm choices, weak key management, flawed implementations, or human error. Common types of cryptography attacks include brute-force attacks, dictionary attacks, Man-in-the-Middle (MitM), side-channel attacks, replay attacks, and cryptanalysis techniques. If successful, such attacks can lead to the exposure of confidential information, data tampering, or impersonation of users or services.

Proper implementation of cryptography and adherence to security best practices are essential to protecting data integrity, confidentiality, and authenticity.

Cryptographic Attacks Countermeasures

The following countermeasures can be adopted to prevent cryptographic attacks:

- Direct access to cryptographic keys should be granted only to the application or user

- An Intrusion Detection System (IDS) should be set up to monitor key exchange and access

- Passphrases or passwords must be used to encrypt keys when they are stored on a disk

- Keys should never be included in source code or binaries

- Private key transfers for certificate signing should be prohibited

- For symmetric algorithms, use a 256-bit key size to ensure system security, particularly in large transactions

- Implement message authentication for symmetric-key encryption protocols

- For asymmetric algorithms, use a key size of at least 2048 bits for secure applications

- Hash algorithms should employ a hash length of 256 bits or more for secure applications

- Use only recommended tools and products, avoiding self-developed cryptographic algorithms or functions

- Limit the number of operations per key to reduce the risk of exposure

- Increase the bit length of hash function outputs to make them more difficult to decrypt

- Design applications and protocols to prevent simple key relationships; each encrypted key should be derived from a Key Derivation Function (KDF)

- Regularly update to the latest security standards

- Utilize strong key schedules to mitigate risks from related key attacks

- Implement hardware-backed security, like Hardware Security Modules (HSMs), to enhance key security

- Avoid using a single cryptographic key for multiple functions

- Use redundant cryptosystems to encrypt data multiple times for additional protection

- Regularly rotate keys to limit their exposure to potential attacks

- Employ digital signatures to sign critical messages or documents and verify them before processing to ensure data integrity

- Use hardware-based Random Number Generators (RNGs) or collect entropy from diverse sources to generate keys, nonces, and initialization vectors

- Prepare for quantum computing threats by adopting quantum-resistant algorithms such as lattice-based cryptography or hash-based signatures

- Utilize Zero-Knowledge Proof protocols like zk-SNARKs for secure authentication and data verification without disclosing sensitive information

- Plan for the shift to post-quantum cryptography by evaluating candidate algorithms recommended by bodies like NIST

- Use Advanced Encryption Standard (AES) algorithms for reliable encryption that resists cryptanalysis

- Incorporate techniques like key stretching and salting to make brute-force attacks more computationally expensive

- Add unique, random values (salts) to each password before hashing to prevent the use of precomputed hash dictionaries

- Employ protocols such as TLS to encrypt communications and verify the identity of both parties, preventing interception and tampering

- Use encryption schemes that do not produce predictable outputs for chosen inputs, like probabilistic encryption methods

- Apply encryption schemes that combine confidentiality and integrity, such as Galois/Counter Mode (GCM) or Encrypt-then-MAC, to prevent ciphertext manipulation

- Periodically change encryption keys and derive keys from passwords using functions like PBKDF2, bcrypt, or Argon2 to strengthen key generation

- Use collision-resistant hash functions like SHA-256 or SHA-3 instead of weaker algorithms such as MD5 or SHA-1

- Adopt quantum-resistant algorithms to protect against quantum attacks, including lattice-based, hash-based, or code-based cryptography

Brute-Force Attack

A brute-force attack is a trial-and-error method used by attackers to gain access to systems, accounts, or encrypted data by systematically trying every possible combination of passwords, encryption keys, or credentials until the correct one is found. This attack does not rely on vulnerabilities in software but exploits weak or

predictable authentication mechanisms. Brute-force attacks can be time-consuming but are effective against accounts with weak passwords, poorly secured systems, or encryption that uses short or outdated keys. Variants include dictionary attacks, credential stuffing, and hybrid attacks that combine brute-force techniques with known patterns.

Brute-Force Attack Countermeasures

Some countermeasures for preventing brute-force attacks are as follows:

- Enforce strong password policies that require complexity, length, and the use of special characters

- Implement account lockout policies after a limited number of failed login attempts to prevent unlimited guessing

- Use multi-factor authentication to add an extra layer of security even if a password is compromised

- Apply CAPTCHA mechanisms to login forms to block automated bots from executing brute-force attempts

- Limit login attempts through rate limiting or IP-based throttling to reduce the effectiveness of rapid-fire attacks

- Monitor authentication logs for repeated failed login attempts from the same IP or user account

- Use account-specific login delays or progressive delays to slow down brute-force attempts

- Employ Intrusion Detection and Prevention Systems (IDS/IPS) to identify and block brute-force attack patterns

- Educate users on the risks of using weak or reused passwords across multiple systems

- Avoid using default credentials and ensure all accounts, including admin or service accounts, have unique and strong passwords

- Encrypt sensitive login data using secure protocols such as HTTPS to prevent interception during brute-force attacks

- Use biometric authentication or token-based systems where possible to reduce reliance on passwords alone

Blockchain Attacks

Blockchain attacks target vulnerabilities within blockchain protocols, smart contracts, consensus mechanisms, or network infrastructure. While blockchain is designed to be secure and decentralized, attackers can exploit flaws in implementation, design, or usage. Common blockchain attacks include 51% attacks, where an attacker controls the majority of network hashing power; smart contract vulnerabilities, like reentrancy attacks; Sybil attacks, where an attacker floods the network with fake nodes; and double-spending, which involves spending the same digital token more than once. These attacks can lead to financial loss, network instability, and compromised trust in decentralized systems.

Defend Against Blockchain Attacks

The following countermeasures can help protect blockchain systems from various types of attacks:

- Implement Decentralized Identifiers (DIDs) to enhance identity verification security and privacy

- Use zero-knowledge proofs to verify transactions and identities without revealing sensitive information

- Store cryptographic keys in HSMs to protect against unauthorized access and tampering

- Use multi-signature wallets that require multiple keys to authorize a transaction

- Implement real-time monitoring systems or use machine learning algorithms to detect abnormal transaction patterns that may indicate double-spending activities

- Combine Proof-of-Work (PoW) with Proof-of-Stake (PoS) to mitigate the risks associated with high energy consumption in blockchain networks

- Implement advanced DDoS protection mechanisms, such as decentralized DDoS mitigation networks, to defend against attacks that overwhelm network nodes

- Employ formal verification methods to mathematically prove the correctness and security of smart contracts

- Conduct regular and thorough code audits of blockchain and smart contract code

- Implement secure interoperability protocols to protect against attacks that exploit cross-chain transactions

- Use atomic swaps for cross-chain trading to reduce the risk of incomplete transactions

- Boost mining pool surveillance

- Avoid storing blockchain keys in unsecured computer files, such as Word documents, notepad files, or sticky notes

- Make sure to use a trusted encryption program to store keys on a device

- Implement randomized peer selection algorithms to prevent attackers from predicting the peers to which a node will connect

- Implement timeouts for peer connections to force periodic reconnections

- Maintain secondary trusted communication channels on which nodes can fall if they detect unusual network behaviors

- Use out-of-band verification methods to check the validity of the blockchain data from trusted sources

- Implement reputation systems that score peers based on their behavior and reliability, and prefer connecting to high-reputation peers

- Use a set of trusted bootstrapping nodes to help new nodes securely connect to the network

- Wait for multiple confirmations to accept transactions

- Increase the speed at which transactions propagate across the network to minimize attack windows

- Hide the details of pending transactions to prevent front-running attacks

- Use batch processing and fair sequencing to prevent transaction reordering and manipulation

- Develop secure consensus and order-matching algorithms to resist double spending and transaction manipulation

- Use mechanisms that randomize the submission times of transactions to make it more difficult for attackers to predict and manipulate order executions

Quantum Computing Attacks

Quantum computing attacks exploit the computational power of quantum computers to break traditional cryptographic algorithms. Classical encryption methods such as RSA, ECC, and DSA rely on the complexity of mathematical problems like integer factorization and discrete logarithms, which quantum computers can solve efficiently using algorithms like Shor's algorithm. These attacks pose a serious threat to data security, digital signatures, and secure communications, especially for systems relying on public-key cryptography. Although large-scale quantum computers are not yet widely available, the potential future impact has led to the development of post-quantum cryptography to protect against such threats.

Defend Against Quantum Computing Attacks

The following countermeasures can help secure systems against the threat of quantum-enabled adversaries:

- Implement quantum-resistant cryptographic algorithms such as lattice-based, hash-based, or code-based cryptography

- Utilize the principles of quantum mechanics to securely distribute cryptographic keys

- Combine classical cryptographic methods with quantum-resistant algorithms to ensure security during transitional phases

- Opt for larger keys in symmetric cryptography to mitigate the impact of quantum attacks on security

- Regularly rotate cryptographic keys to minimize their exposure to potential vulnerabilities

- Protect against side-channel attacks, such as power analysis and electromagnetic emissions

- Build VPNs using quantum-resistant encryption methods.

- Design and deploy authentication protocols that remain secure against quantum computing threats

- Use digital certificates based on quantum-resistant cryptographic algorithms.

- Enhance multi-factor authentication with quantum-resistant methods to maintain security even if one factor is compromised

- Design cryptographic systems in a modular way, allowing for quick updates and algorithm replacements

- Use software frameworks that support multiple cryptographic algorithms and enable easy algorithm switching without significant disruption

- Integrate quantum-resistant digital signatures into blockchain protocols to ensure transaction integrity and authenticity

- Encrypt stored data with quantum-resistant algorithms to keep it secure even as quantum computing advances

- Break data into fragments and distribute them across various locations, ensuring that even if some fragments are compromised, the original data cannot be reconstructed

- Isolate critical systems from less-secure networks and apply multiple security layers to reduce the impact of potential quantum threats

- Use cloud-based key management services that utilize quantum-resistant algorithms

- Implement secure Multi-Party Computation (MPC) protocols in cloud environments

- Develop quantum-specific firewalls to filter and protect quantum communication channels

- Utilize quantum-resistant zero-knowledge proofs for secure user authentication without exposing sensitive information

- Adopt quantum-resistant Distributed Ledger Technology (DLT) to secure decentralized transaction records

- Apply quantum-resistant threshold cryptography to require multiple parties for transaction approval

- Ensure the random number generation used in cryptographic systems is resistant to quantum attacks

- Use Trusted Platform Modules (TPMs) that support quantum-resistant cryptographic algorithms to secure the boot process

- Implement Role-Based Access Control (RBAC) and Attribute-Based Access Control (ABAC) with quantum-safe cryptographic protection

- Incorporate quantum-resistance checks into the Software Development Life Cycle (SDLC) and code review processes

- Integrate quantum-safe security measures into Continuous Integration/Continuous Deployment (CI/CD) pipelines

- Utilize Hardware Security Modules (HSMs) for securely storing quantum-resistant cryptographic keys and ensuring they are regularly updated with quantum-safe firmware

---

💡 **Important Exam Tips for the Certified Ethical Hacker (CEH) Exam on Cryptography**

Understanding cryptography is crucial for the CEH exam. Here are key exam tips to help you master this topic:

1. Cryptographic Basics: Understand the core principles of cryptography, Confidentiality, Integrity, Authentication, and Non-repudiation. Be familiar with symmetric encryption (e.g., AES, DES) vs. asymmetric encryption (e.g., RSA, ECC), and hashing algorithms (e.g., SHA-2, SHA-3).

- **Cryptography Attacks**: Know the various types of cryptographic attacks such as brute-force, dictionary attacks, cryptanalysis, replay attacks, man-in-the-middle (MitM), and side-channel attacks.

- **Brute-Force and Dictionary Attacks**: Understand how attackers try every possible key or use common wordlists to break encryption or passwords. Know how to defend using strong passwords, account lockout policies, and MFA.

2. Key Management: Be aware of best practices in key generation, key rotation, secure key storage, and disposal. Poor key management is a major vulnerability in cryptographic systems.

3. Digital Signatures and Certificates: Know how digital signatures work and the role of Certificate Authorities (CAs). Understand public key infrastructure

---

(PKI) and how certificates are used in authentication and secure communication.

- **TLS/SSL and Secure Communication**: Understand how TLS secures data in transit and why older versions like SSLv2, SSLv3, and TLS 1.0/1.1 should be avoided. Be familiar with concepts like Perfect Forward Secrecy (PFS) and certificate validation.

4. Blockchain Attacks: Learn common blockchain threats such as 51% attacks, double-spending, smart contract vulnerabilities, and Sybil attacks. Understand the importance of smart contract auditing and network monitoring.

5. Post-Quantum Cryptography: Recognize the threat posed by quantum computing to classical encryption methods like RSA and ECC. Be aware of post-quantum cryptographic algorithms and NIST's efforts in standardizing them.

- **Quantum Computing Attacks:** Understand how Shor's algorithm and Grover's algorithm threaten current cryptographic techniques and what future-ready strategies (e.g., quantum-safe encryption, QKD) can be used to defend against them.

6. Tools and Techniques: Be familiar with tools like OpenSSL, GnuPG, and Hashcat for encryption, key generation, and password cracking.

7. Best Practices and Standards: Know how to apply cryptographic countermeasures such as using secure libraries, enforcing strong encryption standards (e.g., AES-256, RSA-2048), and staying updated on cryptographic policies and compliance.

About Our Products

Other products from IPSpecialist LTD regarding CSP technology are:

- AWS Certified Cloud Practitioner Study guide
- AWS Certified SysOps Admin - Associate Study guide
- AWS Certified Solution Architect - Associate Study guide
- AWS Certified Developer Associate Study guide
- AWS Certified Advanced Networking – Specialty Study guide
- AWS Certified Security – Specialty Study guide
- AWS Certified Big Data – Specialty Study guide
- Microsoft Certified: Azure Fundamentals
- Microsoft Certified: Azure Administrator
- Microsoft Certified: Azure Solution Architect
- Microsoft Certified: Azure DevOps Engineer
- Microsoft Certified: Azure Developer Associate
- Microsoft Certified: Azure Security Engineer
- Microsoft Certified: Azure Data Engineer Associate
- Microsoft Certified: Azure Data Scientist
- Microsoft Certified: Azure Network Engineer
- Oracle Certified: Foundations Associate
- Microsoft Certified: Security, Compliance, and Identity Fundamentals
- Terraform Associate Certification Study Guide
- Docker Certified Associate Study Guide
- Certified Kubernetes Administrator Study Guide

Other Network & Security related products from IPSpecialist LTD are:

- CCNA
- CCDA Study Guide
- CCDP Study Guide
- CCNP Security SCOR Study Guide
- CCNP Enterprise ENCOR Study Guide
- CCNP Service Provider SPCOR Study Guide
- CompTIA Network+ Study Guide
- CompTIA Security+ Study Guide
- Ethical Hacking Certification v 12 First Edition Study Guide
- Ethical Hacking Exam – AI Edition
- Certified Blockchain Expert v2 Study Guide

- Fortinet Professional Certification Study Guide
- Palo Alto Certified Network Security Administrator
- Palo Alto Certified Network Security Engineer

www.ingramcontent.com/pod-product-compliance
Lightning Source LLC
Chambersburg PA
CBHW080355060326
40689CB00019B/4023